SCOTLAND:
1001 Things to See

Published by the Scottish Tourist Board
23 Ravelston Terrace Edinburgh EH4 3EU
Telephone: 031-332 2433

Cover
St Andrews: the Castle, and ruined Cathedral seen
from St Rule's Tower

How to use this book

Entries in this book are listed alphabetically by name ie Dunnottar Castle, and not by the nearest town, except for the entries for the cities of Aberdeen, Dundee, Edinburgh and Glasgow, where, for simplicity, they are listed alphabetically under the name of the city.

There is a series of maps covering the whole of Scotland between pages 4 and 23, with the entries marked for your convenience and for cross-referencing. The numbers on the map are the same as the numbers of the entries in the text. Also, each entry in the text has a reference to help you find it on the correct map.

In these entries, the first section (in italics) gives details of the location, opening hours, ownership and admission charge. 'Child' means under 14 and 'closing time' means the latest time that visitors are admitted. The second section tells you what you can see. The abbreviations used in the entries are listed below, together with the head offices of the organisations concerned.

Abbreviations

AM Ancient Monuments in the care of the Secretary of State for Scotland and maintained on his behalf by the Scottish Development Department, 17 Atholl Crescent, Edinburgh EH3 8JN, Tel: 031-229 9321.

FC Forestry Commission (Scotland), 231 Corstorphine Road, Edinburgh EH12 7AT. Tel: 031-334 0303.

NCC The Nature Conservancy Council, 12 Hope Terrace, Edinburgh EH9 2AS. Tel: 031-447 4784.

NTS The National Trust for Scotland, 5 Charlotte Square, Edinburgh EH2 4DU. Tel: 031-226 5922.

RSPB The Royal Society for the Protection of Birds, 17 Regent Terrace, Edinburgh EH7 5BN. Tel: 031-556 5624.

SWT The Scottish Wildlife Trust, 8 Dublin Street, Edinburgh EH1 3PP. Tel: 031-557 1525.

Opening Standard The hours during which Historic Monuments are open to the public. April to September: Weekdays 0930-1900; Sundays 1400-1900. October to March: Weekdays 0930-1600; Sundays 1400-1600.

Distances

The distances indicated in the location of entries are approximate, and are normally the shortest by road, except in a few remote places where they are 'as the crow flies'.

Index

There is an index (pages 199-207) broken down into different interests: Gardens, Folk and Clan Museums, Castles etc.

1001 Things to See

There are thousands of things to see and places to visit in Scotland. Here are 1001 of the most important and most interesting.

Scotland of Old

You will find details of castles, abbeys and other historic buildings like brochs (Pictish fortified towers) to remind you of Scotland's colourful and romantic past. Reminders too of the life and work of the people of Scotland can be found in the folk and clan museums, the visitor centres and in the industrial and military relics preserved to bring the past to life for you.

Scotland of Today

Modern Scotland is well represented too. There are gardens for you to visit, especially in spring; wildlife reserves and country parks; theatres, art galleries, distilleries—and so much more: Other gardens are open for only a few days each year under Scotland's Gardens Scheme. Look for their yellow posters or contact Scotland's Gardens Scheme, 26 Castle Terrace, Edinburgh EH1 2EL. Tel: 031-229 1870.

Scottish Tourist Board Companion Publications

Touring Map of Scotland

This gazetteer is produced as a companion to the Scottish Tourist Board's Touring Map of Scotland, which shows the places listed here and also the places in Scotland where you can enjoy beaches and outdoor sports like golf, sailing and pony trekking.

Walks and Trails in Scotland

Another useful Scottish Tourist Board publication lists over 240 easy walks throughout Scotland which are suitable for families without specialist equipment. Many have signposts and guide books for sale.

Acknowledgments

The Scottish Tourist Board would like to thank everyone who has helped in the provision of information for this publication, and especially: The National Trust for Scotland, The Council for Museums and Galleries in Scotland, and the various government bodies concerned with the Ancient Monuments of Scotland.

The information quoted in this book is as supplied to the Board and to the best of our knowledge was correct at the time of going to press. There may have been amendments subsequently, particularly to admission charges, and the Scottish Tourist Board can accept no responsibility for any errors.

March 1979.

Map 1

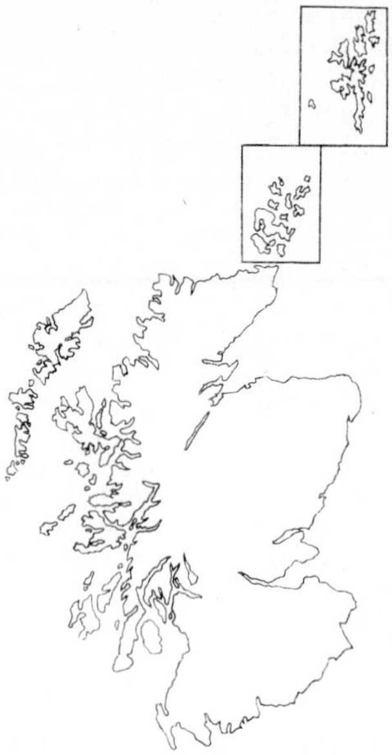

92 Blackhammer Cairn
113 Brough of Birsay
200 Click Mill
201 Clickhimin
204 Cobbie Row's Castle
235 Croft House, Dunrossness
248 Cuween Hill Cairn
327 Dwarfie Stane
330 Earl Patrick's Palace and Bishop's Palace
331 Earl's Palace, Birsay
421 Eynhallow Church
422 Fair Isle
443 Fort Charlotte
526 Grain Earth House
534 Gurness Broch
589 Italian Chapel
590 Jarlshof
631 Kitchener Memorial
632 Knap of Howar

691 Maes Howe
700 Martello Tower
715 Midhowe Broch and Tombs
724 Mousa Broch
730 Muness Castle
746 Ness of Burgi
751 Noltland Castle
758 Noss Nature Reserve
764 Old Man of Hoy
767 Orkney Chairs
769 Orphir Church
781 Pierowall Church
801 Quoyness Chambered Tomb
810 Rennibister Earth House
816 Ring of Brodgar
847 St Magnus Cathedral
848 St Magnus Church
858 St Ninian's Isle
866 Scalloway Castle
876 Scapa Distillery
868 Scapa Flow
883 Shetland Museum
884 Shetland Workshop Gallery
888 Skara Brae
905 Standing Stones of Stenness
906 Staneydale Temple
922 Stromness Museum
933 Tankerness House
945 Tingwall Valley Agricultural Museum
973 Unstan Chambered Tomb
987 Westside Church
993 Wideford Hill Cairn

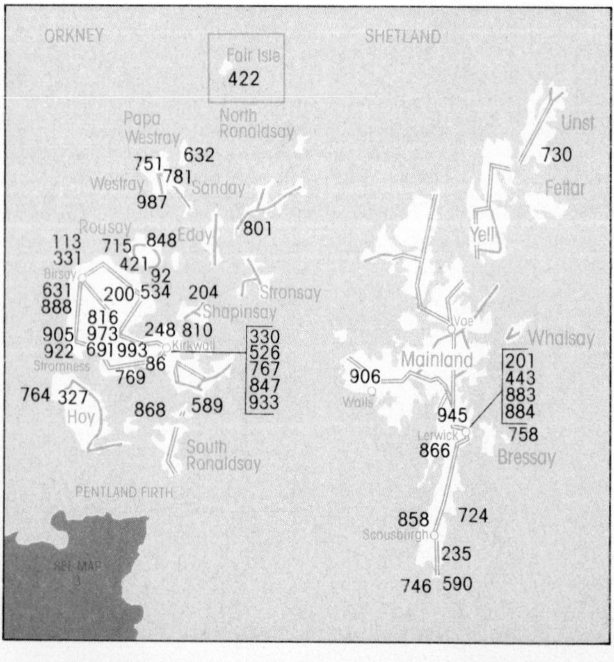

Map 2

78 Barra Airport
188 Church of
   St Moluag
190 Cille Barra
288 Dun Carloway
   Broch
419 Eriskay
610 Kilpheder Wheel-
   house
630 Kisimul Castle
649 Lewis Black House
650 Lewis Castle
   Grounds
660 Loch Druidibeg
   National Nature
   Reserve
681 Flora Macdonald's
   Birthplace
770 Our Lady of the
   Isles
771 Our Lady of
   Sorrows
840 St Clement's
   Church

846 St Kilda
882 Shawbost Folk
   Museum
901 South Uist Folk
   Museum
903 Standing Stones
   of Callanish
907 Steinacleit Cairn
   and Stone Circle
962 Trinity Temple
963 The Trushel Stone
969 Ui Church

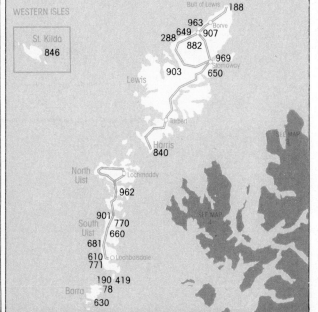

More touring details are to be found on the Scottish Tourist Board's Touring Map of Scotland.

Map 3

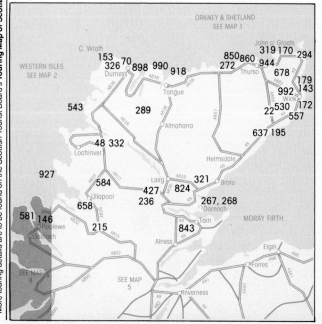

Map 4

435 Fingal's Cave
506 Glen Coe and Dalness
507 Glencoe and North Lorn Folk Museum
509 Glenelg Brochs
513 Glenfinnan Monument
571 Inchkenneth Chapel
607 Kilmuir Croft Museum
611 Kilt Rock
617 Kinloch Castle
623 Kintail
633 Knock Castle
664 Loch Morar
665 Loch Nan Uamh Cairn
667 Lochalsh Woodland Garden
718 Mingary Castle
726 Muck, Isle of
728 Mull and Iona Folklore Museum
729 Mull Little Theatre
745 Neptune's Staircase
762 Old Byre Folk Museum
763 Old Inverlochy Castle
800 Quiraing
815 Rhum, Isle of
891 Skye Water Mill and Black House
908 James Stewart Tablet
913 Storr
921 Strome Castle
953 Torosay Castle
956 Torridon
977 Victoria Falls
986 West Highland Museum

42 Ardchattan Priory
64 Bachuil
75 Barcaldine Castle
84 Beinn Eighe National Nature Reserve
88 Ben Nevis
89 Bernera Barracks
99 Bonawe Iron Furnace
152 Canna, Isle of
171 Castle Moil
175 Castle Stalker
177 Castle Tioram
193 Clan Donald Centre
282 Duart Castle
322 Dunsgiath Castle
324 Dunstaffnage Castle
325 Dunvegan Castle
412 Eigg, Isle of
413 Eilean Donan Castle
426 Falls of Glomach

CONT'D MAP 3

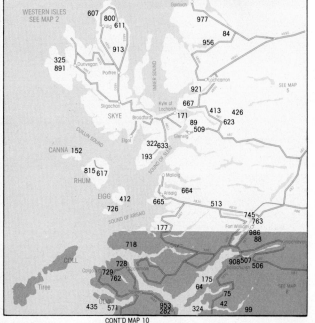

CONT'D MAP 10

583 Inverness Museum and Art Gallery
612 Kiltmaking Display
613 Kincorth
640 Landmark Visitor Centre, Carrbridge
661 Loch Garten Nature Reserve
666 Loch Ness
668 Loch-an-Eilean Visitor Centre
669 Lochindorb
682 Flora Macdonald Monument
683 MacDonald Tower
685 Roderick Mackenzie Memorial
689 Macpherson Monument
716 Hugh Miller's Cottage
741 Nairn Fishertown Museum
742 Nairn Literary Institute Museum
744 Nelson Tower
788 Pluscarden Abbey
797 Queen's Own Highlanders Museum
805 Randolph's Leap
809 Reindeer on the Range
828 Ruthven Barracks
865 Santa Claus Land
919 Strathspey Railway
926 Sueno's Stone
931 Tamdhu Distillery
948 Tomatin Distillery
949 Tomatin Museum
974 Urquhart Castle
985 Well of Seven Heads

43 Ardclach Bell Tower
61 Aviemore Centre
62 Aviemore Highland Craft Village
82 Beauly Priory
90 Birnie Church
97 Boar Stone
98 Boath Doocot
111 Bridge of Carr
124 Cairngorm Chairlift
144 Caledonian Canal
180 Cawdor Castle
196 Clan Macpherson Museum
197 Clan Tartan Centre
199 Clava Cairns
203 Cobb Memorial
213 Constabulary Garden
216 Corrimony Cairn
234 Culloden Moor
263 Dingwall Town House

285 Duffus Castle
329 Eagle Stone
335 Eden Court Theatre
423 Falconer Museum
428 Farigaig Forest Centre
442 Fort Augustus Abbey
444 Fort George
448 Fortrose Cathedral
455 Garvamore Bridge
511 Glenfarclas Distillery
518 Glenlivet Distillery Visitor Centre
520 Glenmore Forest Park
527 Great Glen Exhibition
552 Highland Folk Museum
555 Highland Wildlife Park
573 The 'Indian Temple'

More touring details are to be found on the Scottish Tourist Board's **Touring Map of Scotland.**

CONT'D MAP 4

CONT'D MAP 6

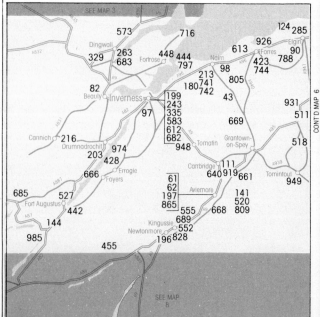

Map 6

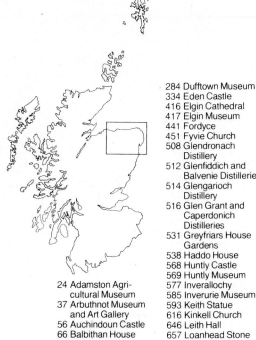

Map 7

Aberdeen
4 Art Gallery and Museum
5 Brig o'Dee
6 James Dun's House
7 Fishmarket
8 Gordon Highlanders Regimental Museum
9 His Majesty's Theatre
10 Marischal College
11 Mercat Cross
12 Provost Ross's House
13 Provost Skene's House

Old Aberdeen
14 Brig o'Balgownie
15 King's College
16 St Machar's Cathedral

19 Aberlemno Sculptured Stones
27 Alford Valley Railway
38 Arbuthnott Church
39 Arbuthnott House and Gardens
69 Balmoral Castle
72 Banchory Museum
79 Barrie's Birthplace
105 Braeloine Visitor Centre
109 Brechin Museum
110 Brechin Round Tower
127 Burns Family Tombstones and Cairn
150 Camphill Village Trust
166 Castle Fraser
181 The Caterthuns
214 Corgarff Castle
224 Craigievar Castle

230 Crathes Castle and Gardens
231 Crathie Church
242 Cullerlie Stone Circle
245 Culsh Earth House
274 Drum Castle
286 Dumbarton Castle
320 Dunnottar Castle
328 Dyce Symbol Stones
410 Edzell Castle and Gardens
429 Fasque
431 Fettercairn Arch
433 Finavon Castle
434 Finavon Doocot
504 Glenbuchat Castle
510 Glenesk Folk Museum
574 Ingasetter
602 Kildrummy Castle
603 Kildrummy Castle Gardens
619 Kinneff Church
638 William Lamb Studio
642 Lapidary Workshops
644 Lecht Ski Tow
684 McEwan Gallery
695 Maison Dieu
706 Meffan Institute
725 Muchalls Castle
777 Peel Ring of Lumphanan
807 Red Castle
814 Restenneth Priory
818 Rob Roy's Statue
873 Captain Scott and Dr Wilson Fountain
912 Stonehaven Tolbooth Museum
950 Tomnaverie Stone Circle

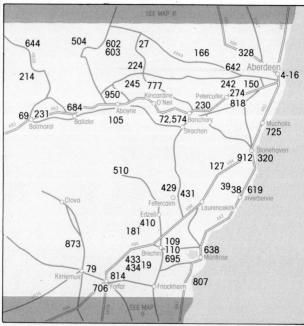

Map 8

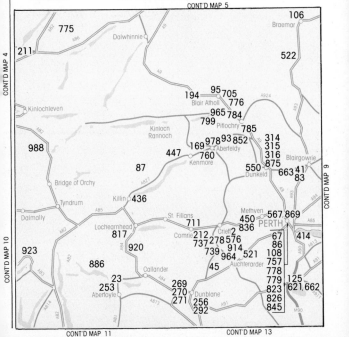

Map 9

306 Unicorn
307 Wishart Arch

333 Eassie Sculptured Stones
425 Falkland Palace
432 Fife Folk Museum
459 Glamis Castle
558 Hill of Tarvit
588 Isle of May
595 Kellie Castle, Arbroath
596 Kellie Castle and Gardens, Pittenweem
648 Leuchars Norman Church
653 Lindores Abbey
672 Lochty Private Railway
707 Megginch Castle Grounds
708 Meigle Museum
755 North Carr Lightship
790 Powrie Castle
808 Reedie Hill Farm
832 St Andrews Castle
833 St Andrews Cathedral
834 St Andrews Preservation Trust
835 St Andrews University
844 St Fillan's Cave
859 St Orland's Stone
861 St Vigean's Museum
872 Scotstarvit Tower
874 Scottish Fisheries Museum
885 Signal Tower
936 Tay Bridges
937 Tealing Earth House and Dovecot
939 Tentsmuir Point National Nature Reserve

20 Abernethy Round Tower
30 Alyth Folk Museum
32 Angus Folk Museum
35 Arbroath Abbey
36 Arbroath Art Gallery
44 Ardestie and Carlungie Earth Houses
59 Auchterlonie's Golf Museum
65 Balbirnie Craft Centre
68 Balmerino Abbey
118 Michael Bruce's Cottage
120 Buckie House
138 The Byre Theatre
189 Church of St Monan
220 Coupar Angus Museum
227 Crail Museum
228 Crail Tolbooth

232 Crawford Centre for the Arts
241 Robinson Crusoe Statue
249 Dalgairn House Gardens

Dundee
295 Barrack Street Museum
296 Bonar Hall
297 Broughty Castle Museum
298 Camperdown
299 Central Museum and Art Gallery
300 Claypotts Castle
301 Mills Observatory
302 Old Steeple
303 Orchar Gallery
304 Dundee Repertory Theatre
305 Spalding Golf Museum

CONT'D MAP 7

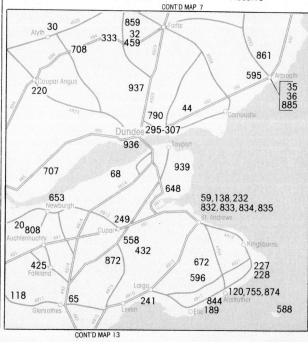

CONT'D MAP 13

CONT'D MAP 8

Map 10

239 Cruachan Hydro-Electric Power Station
290 Dunadd Fort
291 Dunaverty Rock
457 Gigha, Isle of
524 Goatfell
535 Gylen Castle
575 Inishail Chapel
578 Inveraray Bell Tower
579 Inveraray Castle
586 Iona
599 Kilberry Sculptured Stones
600 Kilchurn Castle
601 Kildalton Crosses
604 Kilmartin Sculptured Stones
605 Kilmory Knap Chapel
606 Kilmory Cairns
609 Kiloran Gardens
615 King's Cave
671 Lochranza Castle
679 McCaig's Tower
680 McDonald's Mill
717 Minard Castle
719 Monument Hill
721 Moss Farm Road Stone Circle
735 Museum of Islay Life
747 Nether Largie Cairns
821 Rothesay Castle
830 Saddell Abbey
837 St Blane's Chapel
841 St Columba's Cave
842 St Cormac's Chapel
849 St Mary's Chapel, Bute
878 Scottish White Heather Farm
890 Skipness Castle and Chapel
904 Standing Stones of Machrie Moor
1001 Younger Botanic Garden

21 Achamore House Gardens
31 An Cala
40 Ardanaiseig Gardens
47 Arduaine Gardens
53 Arran Nature Centre
57 Auchindrain Museum
76 Barguillean Garden
104 Bowmore Round Church
112 Brodick Castle and Gardens
123 The Burg
137 Bute Museum

149 Campbeltown Library and Museum
158 Carnasserie Castle
160 Carradale House Gardens
162 Carsaig Arches
176 Castle Sween
182 Celtic Cross
191 Clachan Bridge
208 Columba's Footsteps
217 Corryvreckan Whirlpool
229 Crarae Woodland Garden
234 Crinan Canal

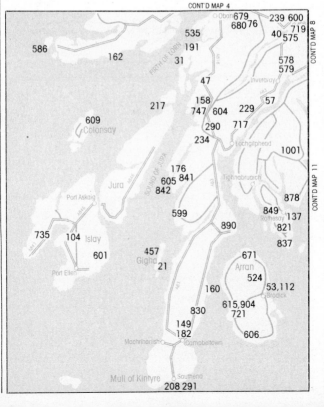

Map 11

Glasgow

460 Glasgow Art Gallery and Museum
461 Botanic Gardens
462 Calderpark Zoo
463 Ca d'Oro Building
464 Cathcart Castle
465 Glasgow Cathedral
466 Citizens' Theatre
467 City Chambers
468 Collins Exhibition Hall
469 Crookston Castle
470 Custom House Quay
471 Egyptian Halls
472 Gardner's Warehouse
473 George Square
474 Greenbank
475 Haggs Castle
476 Hunterian Museum
477 King's Theatre
478 Langside Memorial
479 Charles Rennie Mackintosh Society
480 Merchants' House
481 Mitchell Library
482 Museum of Transport
483 Necropolis
484 People's Palace
485 Pollok House
486 Provan Hall
487 Provand's Lordship
488 Regimental Headquarters of the Royal Highland Fusiliers
489 Rouken Glen

50 Argyll Forest Park
55 Auchentoshan Distillery
77 Barochan Cross
85 Bell Obelisk
96 Blantyre Obelisk
102 Bothwell Castle
119 George Buchan Obelisk
147 Cameron Loch Lomond
148 Cameronian (Scottish Rifles) Regimental Museum
161 Carrick Castle
174 Castle Semple Collegiate Church
185 Chapel of St Mahew
202 Cloch Lighthouse
286 Dumbarton Castle
420 Erskine Bridge
437 Finlaystone
454 Gargunnock Garden

CONT'D MAP 8

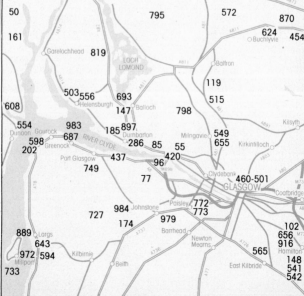

CONT'D MAP 10

CONT'D MAP 12

CONT'D MAP 15

Map 11

490 St Andrew's
491 St David's
   'Ramshorn' Church
492 St Vincent Street
   Church
493 Glasgow School
   of Art
494 Scottish Design
   Centre
495 Stirling's Library
496 The Stock
   Exchange–Scottish
497 Strathclyde Police
   Headquarters
   Museum
498 Templeton's Carpet
   Factory
499 Theatre Royal
500 Third Eye Centre
501 Victoria Park and
   Fossil Grove
503 Glenarn Gardens
515 Glengoyne
   Distillery
541 Hamilton District
   Museum
542 Hamilton
   Mausoleum
549 Heatherbank
   Museum and Library
   of Social Work
554 Highland Mary's
   Statue
556 The Hill House
565 Hunter Monument
572 Inchmahome Priory
594 Kelburn Country
   Centre
598 Kempock Stone
608 Kilmun Arboretum
624 Kippen Church
643 Largs Museum
655 Lillie Art Gallery
656 Livingstone
   National Memorial
687 McLean Museum
   and Art Gallery
693 Maid of the Loch
727 Muirshiel Country
   Park
733 Museum of the
   Cumbraes
749 Newark Castle,
   Port Glasgow
772 Paisley Abbey
773 Paisley Art Gallery
   and Museum
795 Queen Elizabeth
   Forest Park
798 Queen's View,
   Loch Lomond
819 Rossdhu
870 Scotland's Safari
   Park
889 Skelmorlie Aisle
897 Smollett Monument
916 Strathclyde Country
   Park
972 University Marine
   Biological Station
979 Wallace Memorial
983 P S 'Waverley'
984 Weaver's Cottage

Map 12

33 Antonine Wall
51 Argyll's Lodging
52 Argyll and Suther-
land Highlanders'
Museum
74 Bannockburn
100 Bo'ness Museum
142 Cairnpapple Hill
145 Cambuskenneth
Abbey
151 Canal Museum
155 Carfin Grotto
165 Castle Campbell
187 Church of the Holy
Rude
192 Clackmannan
Tower
210 Colzium House and
Park
244 Culross Palace
261 Devil's Mill and
Caldron Linn
266 Dollar Glen

313 Dunimarle Castle
318 Dunmore
Pineapple
424 Falkirk Museum
446 Forth/Clyde Canal
525 Grangemouth
Museum
533 Guild Hall
592 Keir Gardens
620 Kinneil House
641 Landmark Visitor
Centre, Stirling
654 Linlithgow Palace
690 MacRobert Arts
Centre
699 Mar's Wark
713 Menstrie Castle
774 Palacerigg Country
Park
822 Rough Castle
855 St Michael's Parish
Church
877 Scottish Railway
Preservation
Society
895 Smith Art Gallery
and Museum
910 Stirling Bridge
911 Stirling Castle
924 The Study
954 Torphichen Church
955 Torphichen
Preceptory
958 Town House
976 'Victoria'
980 Wallace Monument
1000 'Paraffin' Young
Heritage Trail

CONT'D MAP 8

592 · A84 · Bridge of Allan · A91 · Alva · Tillicoultry · 165 Dollar · 261
266
980 713
Stirling 145
51,52 · 74 · 192 · Alloa · Clackmannan
187,533
641,699 318 · Kincardine 958 924
690,895 313 244 Culross
910,911 525 Grangemouth
Denny · Larbert · 1000 620 100
210 · 33,822 · Falkirk · Polmont · Linlithgow
446 424,877 · 151,654
Cumbernauld 855,976
774 954 142
955
Armadale · Bathgate
Airdrie · Whitburn · West Calder
155
Hamilton · Motherwell · Wishaw

SEE MAP 13
SEE MAP 11
CONT'D MAP 16

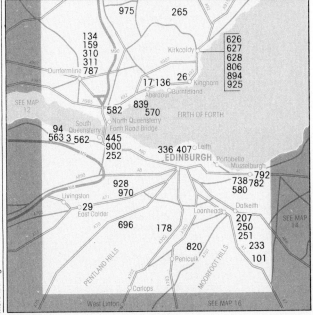

CONT'D MAP 8   CONT'D MAP 9

Map 13

Edinburgh cont'd

367 Museum of Childhood
368 Museum of Lighting
369 National Gallery of Scotland
370 National Library of Scotland
371 National Museum of Antiquities
372 Netherbow Arts Centre
373 New 57 Gallery
374 New Fountain Brewery
375 New Town Conservation Centre
376 Outlook Tower and Camera Obscura
377 Palace of Holyroodhouse
378 Parliament House
379 Philatelic Bureau
380 Printmakers' Workshop Gallery
381 Register House
382 Royal Botanic Garden
383 Royal Lyceum Theatre
384 Royal Observatory
385 Royal Scottish Academy
386 Royal Scottish Museum
387 Royal Scots Dragoon Guards Museum
388 St Cecilia's Hall
389 St Cuthbert's Church
390 St Cuthbert's Co-operative Association Transport Collection
391 St John's Church
392 St Mary's Cathedral
393 Scott Monument
394 Scottish Arts Council Gallery
395 Scottish Genealogy Society
396 Scottish National Gallery of Modern Art
397 Scottish National Portrait Gallery
398 Scottish National Zoological Park
399 Scottish Record Office
400 Lady Stair's House
401 Swanston Cottage
402 Talbot Rice Art Centre
403 Transport Museum
404 Traverse Theatre Club
405 Wax Museum
406 West Register House
407 White Horse Close
445 Forth Bridges
562 Hopetoun House
563 The House of the Binns
570 Inchcolm Abbey
580 Inveresk Lodge Garden
582 Inverkeithing Museum
626 Kirkcaldy Burgh School Plaques
627 Kirkcaldy Industrial Museum
628 Kirkcaldy Museum and Art Gallery
696 Malleny Gardens
738 Musselburgh Bridge
782 Pinkie House
787 Pittencrieff House Museum
792 Prestongrange Mining Museum and Historic Site
806 Ravenscraig Castle
820 Rosslyn Chapel
839 St Bridget's Church
894 Adam Smith Centre
900 South Queensferry Museum
925 John McDouall Stuart Museum
928 Suntrap
970 Union Canal
975 Vane Farm Nature Reserve

Map 14

18 Aberlady Church
54 Athelstaneford Church
81 Bass Rock
186 The Chesters Fort
198 Jim Clark Memorial Trophy Room
205 Coldingham Priory
264 Dirleton Castle
312 Dunglass Collegiate Church
408 Edinshall Broch
409 Edrom Norman Arch
430 Fast Castle
449 Foulden Tithe Barn
456 Gifford Church
536 Haddington
537 Haddington Museum
539 Hailes Castle
635 Lady Kirk
647 Lennoxlove House
676 Luffness Castle

697 Manderston
734 Museum of Flight
740 Myreton Motor Museum
753 North Berwick Law
754 North Berwick Museum
768 Ormiston Market Cross
791 Preston Mill
793 Prestonpans Battle Cairn
812 Rennie Memorial
831 St Abbs Head
854 St Mary's Pleasance
880 Duns Scotus Statue
881 Seton Collegiate Church
934 Tantallon Castle
960 Traprain Law
968 Tyninghame House Gardens
971 Union Suspension Bridge
989 Whitekirk
995 Winton House
997 Wool Stone

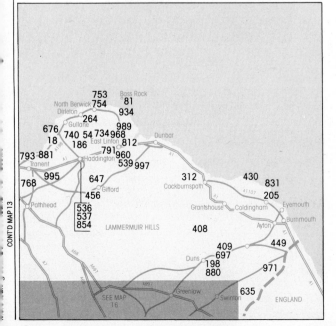

Map 15

SEE MAP 17

566 West Kilbride
Dunlop
547 915 959 Strathaven
A71

46 Ardrossan
862 752 Saltcoats
411 587 692 Irvine
317 Kilmarnock
825 Stewarton
133 255 262
Newmilns
Darvel
A71

308
FIRTH OF CLYDE
Troon
Symington
930
63
129,131,789 Mauchline
A70

60 675 686 932 981 Prestwick Ayr
645
553
58 Cumnock
545
A76 New Cumnock

28 126 132 639
415
246 247
238 704
966 899
Alloway

Kirkconnel
Sanquhar
863 864

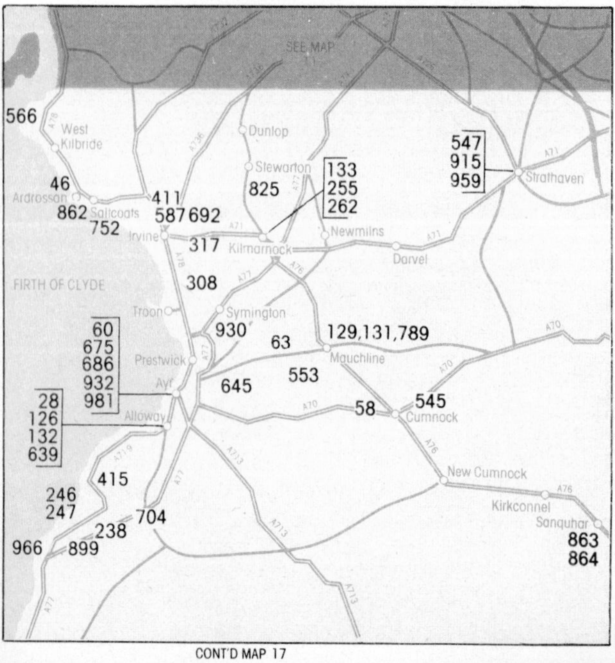

CONT'D MAP 16

CONT'D MAP 17

Map 16

532 Grey Mare's Tail
540 Halliwell's House
546 Harestanes
548 Hawick Museum and Art Gallery
559 The Hirsel
560 James Hogg Monument
564 Hume Castle
591 Jedburgh Abbey
597 Kelso Abbey
625 Kirk Yetholm
634 Lady Gifford's Well
651 Leyden Obelisk and Tablet
677 Lyte Plaque
698 Majoribanks Monument
702 Mary Queen of Scots House
709 Meilerstain House
710 Melrose Abbey
736 Museum of the Scottish Lead Mining Industry
743 Neidpath Castle
748 New Lanark
750 Newark Castle, near Selkirk
794 Priorwood Gardens
804 Allan Ramsay Library
811 Rennie's Bridge
827 Roxburghe Castle
838 St Bride's Church
853 St Mary's Loch
876 Scottish Museum of Wool Textiles
879 Scott's View
887 Sir Walter Scott's Courtroom
893 Smailholm Tower
940 James Thomson Obelisk
946 Tinnis Castle
961 Traquair House
967 Tweed Bridge
982 Waterloo Monument
999 Yarrow Kirk

1 Abbotsford House
103 Bowhill
164 Cartland Bridge
167 Castle Jail Museum
183 Chambers Institution Museum
206 Coldstream Museum
219 Coulter Motte
225 Craignethan Castle
237 Cross Kirk
254 Dawyck House Gardens
260 Devil's Beef Tub
273 Drochil Castle
280 Dryburgh Abbey
281 Dryhope Tower
438 Flodden Monument
439 Floors Castle
440 Fogo Church
458 Gladstone Court Street Museum
528 Greenknowe Tower
529 Greenlaw Church

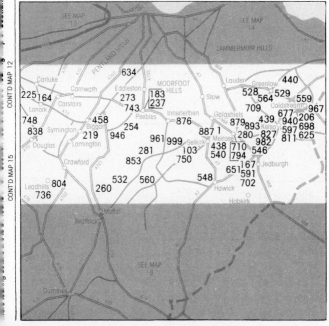

Map 17

452 Galloway Deer
    Museum
453 Galloway Forest
    Park
502 Glenapp Castle
    Gardens
519 Glenluce Abbey
544 Harbour Cottage
    Gallery
629 Kirkmadrine Stones
636 Laggangairn
    Standing Stones
659 Loch Doon Castle
673 Logan Botanic
    Garden
674 Logan Fish Pond
688 MacLellan's Castle
701 Martyrs' Monument
731 Murray Forest
    Centre
732 Murray's
    Monument
765 Old Place of
    Mochrum
802 Raiders' Road
856 St Ninian's Cave
857 St Ninian's Chapel
909 Stewartry Museum
942 Threave Castle
943 Threave House and
    Gardens and
    Wildfowl Refuge
951 Tongland Power
    Station
952 Torhouse Stone
    Circle
991 Whithorn Priory
    and Museum
994 Wigtown District
    Museum
998 Wren's Egg Stone
    Circle

 25 Ailsa Craig
 49 Ardwell House
    Gardens
 80 Barsalloch Fort
114 Broughton House
116 Bruce's Stone
117 Bruce's Stone
154 Cardoness Castle
156 Carleton Castle
163 Carsluith Castle
168 Castle Kennedy
    Gardens and
    Lochinch Castle
173 Castle of Park
184 Chapel Finian
218 Corsock House
    Gardens
222 Craigcaffie Castle
240 Cruggleton Church
    and Castle
279 Drumtrodden
309 Dundrennan Castle
323 Dunskey Castle

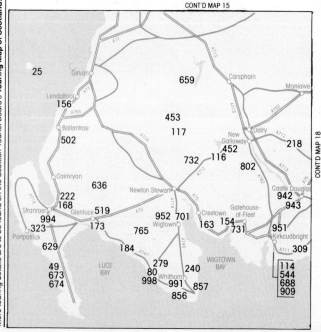

CONT'D MAP 15

CONT'D MAP 18

Map 18

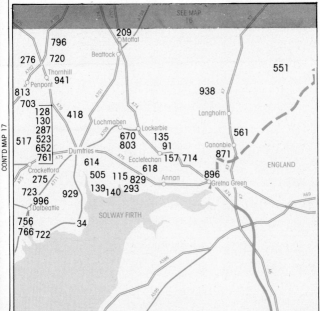

Abbotsford

1 Abbotsford House
Map 16

A7, 2½m SSE of Galashiels. Late Mar-end Oct, Mon-Sat 1000-1700, Sun 1400-1700. Adult: 70p, child: 35p, group rates.
(Mrs P Maxwell-Scott, OBE)
Sir Walter Scott's romantic mansion built 1817-22. Much as in his day, it contains the many remarkable historical relics he collected, armouries, the library with some 9,000 volumes and his study. He died here in 1832.

2 Abercairny Gardens
Map 8

Off A85, 4½m ENE of Crieff. Early Apr-end Sept, Wed only, dawn to dusk. Adult: 20p, child: 10p, groups by arrangement.
(Mr W S H Drummond Moray)
Extensive grounds with fine views; daffodils, azaleas and rhododendrons.

3 Abercorn Church
Map 13

Off unclassified road 2m N of A904 (signs for Hopetoun House). All year daily. Free.
Originally mediaeval church with additions, notably a lairds' loft. There are many fine gravestones in this attractive kirkyard.

4 Aberdeen Art Gallery and Museum
Map 7

Schoolhill. All year, Mon-Sat 1000-1700 (Thu 1000-2000), Sun 1400-1700. Free. (City of Aberdeen)
The Gallery contains a comprehensive collection of 20th-century British paintings and sculptures and many fine portraits including works by Raeburn. Regular exhibitions and recitals are held, and there is a small museum of applied art.

5 Aberdeen, Brig o' Dee
Map 7

Built in 1520-22 by Bishop Gavin Dunbar in James V's reign. Its seven arches span 400 feet and it formerly carried the main road to Deeside. The mediaeval solidity of the structure is enlivened by heraldic carvings.

6 Aberdeen, James Dun's House
Map 7

Schoolhill. All year, Mon-Sat 1000-1700. Free.
This former residence of James Dun, master and rector of Aberdeen Grammar School, now holds a museum for 'Children of all Ages'.

7 Aberdeen, Fishmarket
Map 7

On South Market Street.
Aberdeen is one of the major fishing ports of
Britain, exporting hundreds of tons of fish daily.
Every morning (Mon-Fri) the fishing fleets unload
their catches, which are auctioned off amid
intense bustle. Best visited around 0730-0930.

8 Aberdeen, Gordon Highlanders Regimental Museum
Map 7

Regimental Headquarters, Viewfield Road.
All year, Sun and Wed 1400-1700. Adult: 10p,
child: 10p.
Fine displays relating to the regiment's varied
campaigns. There are collections of uniforms,
colours and banners, silver and medals (with a
special Victoria Cross exhibition), and a library
with historical material and photograph albums.

9 Aberdeen, His Majesty's Theatre
Map 7

Rosemount Viaduct in city centre.
Aberdeen's main theatre, opened in 1906, seats
2,500. It offers a varied programme of
entertainment, including ballet, opera and
concerts.

10 Aberdeen, Marischal College
Map 7

Broad Street. Museum only: Mon-Fri 0900-
1700. (University of Aberdeen)
An imposing granite structure of the 19th
century. In the quadrangle, entered by a fine
archway, are older buildings of 1836-44, with the
graceful Mitchell Tower. The anthropological
museum houses local, classical, Egyptian and
Chinese antiquities, and a general ethnographic
collection.

11 Aberdeen, Mercat Cross
Map 7

Castle Street.
Built in 1686, and paid for out of Guild wine funds, the Cross is decorated with medallion heads of the Kings of Scotland.

12 Aberdeen, Provost Ross's House
Map 7

In the Shiprow. Undergoing extensive alteration. View from outside only.
A fine example of early Scottish domestic architecture, and one of Aberdeen's oldest houses (1593). Thought to have been built by the master-mason Andrew Jamesone, it has dormer windows, a projecting tower and arcading.

13 Aberdeen, Provost Skene's House
Map 7

Broad Street. All year, Mon-Sat 1000-1700. Adult: 10p, child: 2p.
Erected in the 16th century, this house bears the name of its most notable owner, Sir George Skene, Provost of Aberdeen 1676-1685. Remarkable painted ceilings and interesting relics.

14 Aberdeen (Old), Brig o' Balgownie
Map 7

Also known as the 'Auld Brig o' Don', this massive arch, 62 feet wide, spans a deep pool of the river and is backed by fine woods. It was built by Bishop Cheyne, c. 1320 and repaired in 1607. In 1605 Sir Alexander Hay endowed the bridge with a small property, which has so increased in value that it built the New Bridge of Don (1830), a little lower down, at a cost of £26,000, bore most of the cost of the Victoria Bridge, and contributed to many other public works.

15 Aberdeen (Old), King's College
Map 7

High Street. All year, weekdays 0800-1700, Sat 0800-1200. Free. (University of Aberdeen)
Founded 1494. The chapel, famous for its rich woodwork, is 16th-century and the notable 'crown' tower is 17th-century.

16 Aberdeen (Old), St Machar's Cathedral
Map 7

Chanonry. 0900-1700 (0900-2100 Apr-Sep). Free.
This granite cathedral was founded in 1157 on an earlier site, though the main part of the building dates from the mid-15th century. The west front with its twin towers is notable, and the painted wooden nave ceiling is dated 1520. The nave is in use as a parish church.

17 Aberdour Castle
Map 13

At Aberdour, A92, 10m E of Dunfermline. Opening standard. Adult:15p, child: 7p, group rates. (AM)
Overlooking the harbour at Aberdour, the oldest part is the tower, which dates back to the 14th century. To this other buildings were added in

succeeding centuries. A fine circular doocot stands nearby, and here also is St Fillans Parish Church, part Norman, part 16th-century.

18 Aberlady Church
Map 14

In Aberlady, A198, 7m SW of North Berwick. All reasonable times. Free.
Largely rebuilt 100 years ago, the church has a fortified 15th-century tower. In the chancel is the Aberlady Stone, part of a Celtic Cross, 8th century, and there are notable stained-glass windows.

19 Aberlemno Sculptured Stones
Map 7

At Aberlemno, B9134, 5m NE of Forfar. All times. Free. (AM)
In the churchyard is a splendid upright cross-slab with Pictish symbols; three other stones stand beside the road.

20 Abernethy Round Tower
Map 9

At Abernethy, A913, 9m SE of Perth. Under repair; view from outside only. (AM)
A round tower, 74 feet high, dating from the 11th century. Tradition has it that Malcolm Canmore did homage to William the Conqueror here. Beside it is a Pictish symbol stone. (See also No 110.)

21 Achamore House Gardens
Map 10

Isle of Gigha, off the Mull of Kintyre. 1 March-31 Oct, daily 1000-dusk. Adult: 40p, child: 20p. (Gardens only—house not open to the public.) Ferries from Tayinloan (no cars, and weather permitting) or West Loch Tarbert. (D W N Landale)
Rhododendrons, camellias and many semi-tropical shrubs and plants may be seen at these gardens developed over the past 30 years. (See also No 457.)

22 Achavanich Standing Stones
Map 3

E of Loch Rangag, off unclassified road 6m NW from Lybster. All reasonable times. Free.
A ritual site (c. 1850 BC) 100 feet by 225 feet, in the form of a truncated oval, open to the south east. Originally up to 60 slabs of local sandstone, the remainder still protrude 5 feet above ground.

Alford

Achnaba: see No 42.

23 Achray Forest Drive
Map 8

*Off A821, 4m N of Aberfoyle. Easter-end Sep,
daily 1000-1800. £1 per car.*
Scenic drive on Forestry Commission roads with
fine views of the Trossachs. Walks, picnic
places, play area and toilets.

Adam Smith Centre: see No 894

24 Adamston Agricultural Museum
Map 6

*Off A96, 2m SW of Huntly. All reasonable times,
by appointment, tel: Drumblade 231.
Admission by donation. (Hew McCall Smith)*
A collection of over 450 agricultural implements,
hand tools, kitchen equipment and farm
machinery, mostly from the northeast of
Scotland.

African Safari Park: see No 870.

25 Ailsa Craig
Map 17

Island in Firth of Clyde, 10m W of Girvan.
A granite island rock, 1,114 feet high with a
circumference of 2 miles. The rock itself is used
to make some of the finest curling stones and the
island has a gannetry and colonies of puffins,
guillemots and other seabirds.

26 Alexander III Monument
Map 13

*By A92 S of Kinghorn at Pettycur Promontory.
All times. Free.*
On the King's Crag, a monument marks the place
where Alexander III was killed in a fall from his
horse in 1286.

Achamore House Gardens

27 Alford Valley Railway
Map 7

Murray Park, Alford. From 1979.
Railway running on a short section of 2ft. gauge
track in the grounds of the park. Future
developments will continue the line to Alford
station.

Alloway

28 Alloway Kirk
Map 15

In Alloway, 2½m S of Ayr. All reasonable times. Free.
Ancient church, a ruin in Burns' day, where his father William Burnes is buried. Through its window, Tam saw the dancing witches and warlocks in the poem *Tam o' Shanter.*

29 Almondell Country Park
Map 13

Off A71 at East Calder, 12m SSW of Edinburgh.
In the valley of the River Almond, a network of paths and bridges, constructed by young people from all over the world through Enterprise Youth. Nature trails link with old drovers' roads over the Pentland Hills.

30 Alyth Folk Museum
Map 9

Off A94, 3m N of Meigle. All reasonable times. (Keys from Howes' Furnishers or tel: Alyth 2594.) Admission by Donation.
A collection of rural agricultural and domestic artefacts.

Am Fasgadh: see No 552.

31 An Cala
Map 10

B844 on Seil, 16m SW of Oban. Apr to Sep, Mon and Thu, 1400-1800. Adult: 20p, child (with adult): 5p. (Mrs H I Blakeney)
Cherries, azaleas, roses, water and rock gardens.

32 Angus Folk Museum
Map 9

Off A94, at Glamis, 5m SW of Forfar. 1 May-30 Sep, daily 1300-1730, and on request. Adult: 45p, child, 20p. (NTS)
Kirkwynd Cottages, a row of six 17th-century cottages with stone-slabbed roofs, containing relics of domestic and agricultural life in the county in the 19th century and earlier.

33 Antonine Wall
Map 12

From Bo'ness to Old Kilpatrick, best seen off A803 E of Bonnybridge, 12m S of Stirling. All reasonable times. Free. (AM)
This Roman fortification stretched from near Bo'ness on the Forth to Old Kilpatrick on the

Clyde. Built AD 138-143, it was a turf rampart with a ditch, and a fort about every two miles. It was abandoned before the end of the 2nd century. Remains are best preserved in the Falkirk/Bonnybridge area, notably Rough Castle (see also No 822) and at Old Kilpatrick.

34 Arbigland
Map 18

*By Kirkbean, off A710, 12m S of Dumfries. May-end Sep: Tue, Thu, Sun 1400-1800. Adult: 50p, child: 25p, groups by arrangement.
(Capt J B Blackett)*
These extensive woodlands, formal and water gardens are arranged round a sandy bay. John Paul Jones' birthplace is nearby, and his father was the gardener at Arbigland.

35 Arbroath Abbey
Map 9

In Arbroath. Opening standard. Adult: 20p, child: 10p, group rates. (AM)
Founded in 1176 by William the Lion, and dedicated to St Thomas of Canterbury, it was from here that the famous Declaration of Arbroath asserting Robert the Bruce as King was issued in 1320. Important remains of the cloisters survive: the abbot's house has been restored as a museum containing relics, maps, documents, etc.

Arbroath Abbey

36 Arbroath Art Gallery
Map 9

*Arbroath Library, Hill Terrace. All year, Mon-Sat 0930-1700. Free.
(Angus District Council)*
Changing exhibitions offer work of Angus artists and subjects of local interest.

37 Arbuthnot Museum and Art Gallery
Map 6

St Peter Street, Peterhead. All year, daily except Sun, 1000-1200, 1400-1700, Sat 1400-1700. Free.
The development of fishing and whaling, with Arctic exhibits, is featured. Local history and a new oil exhibition. The coin collection can be viewed by arrangement.

38 Arbuthnott Church
Map 7

Off B967, 10m SW of Stonehaven. All reasonable times. Free.
This church dates partly from 1242 and has a two-storeyed 16th-century chapel attached. The stained-glass windows depict Faith, Hope and Charity.

39 Arbuthnott House and Gardens
Map 7

Off B967, 10m SW of Stonehaven. By arrangement, tel: Inverbervie 226. Adult: 50p, child: 25p, group rates. Gardens only, Adult: 40p, child: 20p.
Home of the Arbuthnott family since 1206. The present 17th-century house has 18th-century additions and an extensive formal 17th-century garden.

40 Ardanaiseig Gardens
Map 10

E of B845, 22m E of Oban. 31 March-31 Oct, daily 1000-dusk. Adult: 30p, child: free. (Mr and Mrs J M Brown)
Rhododendrons, rare shrubs and trees. Magnificent view across Loch Awe.

41 Ardblair Castle
Map 8

On A923 1m W of Blairgowrie. By arrangement (tel: Blairgowrie 2155). Adult: 75p, child: 50p. (Mr L Blair-Oliphant)
Mainly 16th-century castle on 12th-century foundations, home of the Oliphant family. Jacobite relics and links with Charles Edward Stuart. Room containing relics of Lady Nairne (née Oliphant), author of 'Charlie is My Darling' and other songs.

42 Ardchattan Priory
Map 4

On the N side of lower Loch Etive, 7m NE of Oban. Open all times. Free. (AM)
One of three Valliscaulian houses founded in Scotland in 1230, and the meeting place in 1308 of one of Bruce's Parliaments, among the last at which business was conducted in Gaelic. Burned by Cromwell's soldiers in 1654, the remains include some carved stones. The gardens of Ardchattan House, adjoining the priory, are open Apr-Sep; admission charge. Achnaba Church, near Connel, has notable central communion pews.

43 Ardclach Bell Tower
Map 5

Off A939, 8½m SE of Nairn. Opening standard. Free; apply custodian. (AM)
A two-storey tower of 1655 whose bell summoned worshippers to the church and warned the neighbourhood in case of alarm.

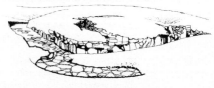

44 Ardestie and Carlungie Earth-Houses
Map 9

N of A92. Ardestie: about 6m E of Dundee, at junction with B962. Carlungie: 1m N on unclassified road to Carlungie. All times. Free. (AM)
Two examples of large earth-houses attached to surface dwellings. At Ardestie the gallery is curved and 80 feet in length; the Carlungie earth house is 150 feet long, and is most complex; used in first centuries AD.

Ardwell

45 Ardoch Roman Camp
Map 8

A822 at Braco, 10m S of Crieff. All reasonable times. Free. (Ardoch Estate)
One of the largest Roman stations in Britain, dating back to the 2nd century. There is a Roman fort and several camps in the surrounding area.

46 Ardrossan Castle
Map 15

Ardrossan, on a hill overlooking Ardrossan Bay. All year, all reasonable times. Free.
Mid 12th-century castle on a hill with fine views of Arran and Ailsa Craig. Castle was destroyed by Cromwell and only part of the north tower and two arched cellars remain.

47 Arduaine Gardens
Map 10

Arduaine, A816, 20m SSW of Oban. Apr-Oct, daily 0900-dusk. Adult: 30p, child: free. (Messrs E and H Wright)
Beautiful coastal garden, noted especially for rhododendrons and azaleas. Also magnolias and other rare and interesting trees and shrubs, rock garden and water garden.

48 Ardvreck Castle
Map 3

A837, 11m E of Lochinver, on Loch Assynt. All reasonable times. Free.
Built c. 1490 by the MacLeods, who in the mid-13th century obtained Assynt by marriage: the three-storeyed ruins stand on the shores of Loch Assynt. After his defeat at Culrain, near Bonar Bridge, in 1650, the Marquess of Montrose fled to Assynt but was soon captured and confined here before being sent to Edinburgh and execution.

Ardwell House Gardens

49 Ardwell House Gardens
Map 17

Ardwell, 11m SSE of Stranraer. Mar-Oct, daily 1000-1800. Admission by donation. (Mr and Mrs John Brewis)
Daffodils, rhododendrons, azaleas, roses, shrubs, crazy paving and pond. Fine trees. Best seen in April and May.

50 Argyll Forest Park
Map 11

W and NW from Loch Long almost to Loch Fyne: A815, B839, B828 and A83. (FC)
Three forests—Ardgartan, Glenbranter and Benmore—cover 60,000 acres of superb scenery. There are scores of forest walks as walkers may use virtually all the forest roads. Many leading through forests to high tops are arduous, but there are others, like the paths from the Younger Botanic Garden (see No 1001), by Loch Eck, which lead to Puck's Glen. The Arboretum at Kilmun should also be seen (No 608).

51 Argyll's Lodging
Map 12

Castle Wynd, Stirling. Seen from the outside.
This fine example of an old town residence was built c. 1632 by Sir William Alexander of Menstrie, later Earl of Stirling, who eleven years earlier helped to found Nova Scotia (New Scotland). It is now a youth hostel.
(See also No 713.)

52 Argyll and Sutherland Highlanders' Museum
Map 12

In Stirling Castle. Easter to end Sept, 1000-1730, Oct 1000-1600, Mon-Fri. Free.
Fine regimental museum, with a notable medal collection.

Armadale Castle: see No 193.

Arnol Black House: see No 649.

53 Arran Nature Centre
Map 10

On northern outskirts of Brodick, Arran, beneath the Castle. All year, daily 1000-1800. Adult: 20p, child: 10p.
Established in 1973 by local people to give information about the natural history of the island. Exhibition area, bookshop, craft shop, etc.

54 Athelstaneford Church
Map 14

Off B1343 4m N of Haddington. All reasonable times. Free.
A plaque by the church tells the story of the origins of St Andrew's cross as the Scottish flag.

55 Auchentoshan Distillery
Map 11

A82, 10m N of Glasgow. All year, Mon-Fri 0900-1200, 1400-1600. Free.
Guided tours show the brewing, distilling and warehousing of whisky, with a free dram at the end.

56 Auchindoun Castle
Map 6

In Glen Fiddich, 3m SE of Dufftown. All times; viewed from the outside only. Free. (AM)
A massive ruin on the summit of an isolated hill, enclosed by prehistoric earthworks. The corner stones were removed to Balvenie (see No 71). In Queen Mary's wars the castle was the stronghold of the redoubtable 'Edom o' Gordon'

Aultroy

who burned Corgarff (see No 214). Jacobite leaders held a council of war there after Dundee's death at Killiecrankie.

57 Auchindrain Museum
Map 10

On A83, 5½m SW of Inveraray.
Easter-Oct, weekdays 1000-1800, Sun 1400-1800 (other times by arrangement). Adult: 40p, child: 15p, group rates.
A fascinating example of a communal-tenancy farm, with traditional dwellings and barns dating from the late 18th and early 19th century. Furnishings and implements on display. Land farmed using traditional methods. Restaurant, craft shop and picnic places.

58 Auchinleck Church and Boswell Mausoleum
Map 15

In Auchinleck, A76, 17m E of Ayr. Seen from the outside at all times. For entry and guided tour, contact Mr G P Hoyle, 131 Main Street, Auchinleck (tel: Cumnock 20757); prior notice appreciated. Donations welcome.
(Auchinleck Boswell Society)
The ancient Parish Church, formerly a Celtic cell, was enlarged by Walter fitz Alan between 1145 and 1165, and again by David Boswell in 1641-43. It is now a museum of the Boswell family. The Boswell Mausoleum, attached, built by Alexander Boswell (Lord Auchinleck) in 1754, is the burial place of five known generations, including James Boswell, Dr Johnson's famous biographer. (Tour 1 hour). 1½ miles away is the Auchinleck Estate, containing James Boswell's Georgian home (not open). It was built by his father, Alexander Boswell, in 1757-79.

59 Auchterlonie's Golf Museum
Map 9

4 Pilmuir Links, St Andrews. May-Oct, Mon-Sat, 1000-1300, 1430-1730. Free.
A fine personal collection of golfing relics, photographs, clubs and balls, going back to the very beginning of golf.

60 Auld Kirk
Map 15

Off High Street, Ayr. All reasonable times. Free.
A fine church, dating from 1655, with notable lofts inside. Burns was baptised and sometimes attended church there.

Aultroy Cottage: see No 84.

61 Aviemore Centre
Map 5

Off A9, 32m S of Inverness. All year, daily 1000 onwards. Admission free (charges for facilities).
Leisure, sport and conference centre with wide range of recreational and entertainment facilities, including: cinema/theatre, swimming pool, ice rink, saunas, artificial ski slope, go-karts and many more. (See also Nos 62, 197 and 865.)

62 Aviemore Highland Craft Village
Map 5

By Aviemore Centre off A9, 32m S of Inverness. Daily opens 1000. Closes Jan-Feb 1700, Mar-Jun 1800, Jul-Aug 2000, Sep-Dec 1800. Free.
Traditional style village square where craftsmen work on a wide range of arts and crafts.

Avondale Castle: see No 915.

63 Bachelors' Club
Map 15

Tarbolton, B744, 7½m NE of Ayr off A758. 1 Apr-30 Sep. Daily 1000-1800; other times by arrangement. (Custodian: Mr Sam Hay, 7 Croft Street, Tarbolton. Tel: Tarbolton 424). Adult: 30p, child: 15p.
A 17th-century house where in 1780 Robert Burns and his friends founded a literary and debating society, the Bachelors' Club. In 1779, Burns attended dancing lessons here, and in 1781 he was initiated as a Freemason. Period furnishings, with reminders of Burns' life at Lochlea Farm.

64 Bachuil
Map 4

On Isle of Lismore, Argyll. (Ferry from Oban or Port Appin). Daily. By arrangement, tel: Lismore 256. Free.
(Alastair Livingstone of Bachuil)
The Bachuil Mor or Pastoral Staff of Saint Moluag is kept in the house, the Baron of Bachuil being its Hereditary Keeper.

65 Balbirnie Craft Centre
Map 9

On eastern outskirts of Glenrothes New Town. All year, Mon-Fri 0900-1800, Sat-Sun 1400-1800. Free.
Craftsmen designing and making furniture, chess sets and other high-quality articles. Glenrothes itself has fine examples of modern sculpture.

66 Balbithan House and Garden
Map 6

Unclassified road (Hatton of Fintry to Inverurie), 2½m NE of Kintore. Open by arrangement only, May-Sept, Adult: 50p, child: 10p. Tel: Kintore 2282.
(Mrs McMurtrie).
A fine 17th-century house with an interesting 'old-world' garden including old roses, yew hedges, and herbs. The house contains a small museum with a collection of Scottish kitchen antiques. There is usually an exhibition of paintings in the galleried dining room.

67 Balhousie Castle (Black Watch Museum)
Map 8

Facing North Inch Park, Perth. Entrance from Hay Street. Mon-Fri 1000-1200, 1400-1600 (1530 Oct-Mar). Free.
The castle houses the regimental headquarters and museum of the Black Watch (Royal Highland Regiment) and displays in chronological order the history of the famous Regiment from 1740 to the present time.

68 Balmerino Abbey
Map 9

On S shore of River Tay on unclassified road 5m W of Newport. View from outside only. Free.
Ruined Cistercian abbey founded in the 13th century by Alexander II. Houses nearby recall the last words of a Scottish soldier killed at Anzio in 1944.

69 Balmoral Castle
Map 7

On A93, 8m W of Ballater. Grounds only, May, Jun, Jul daily except Sun, 1000-1700 (not open when members of the Royal Family in residence). Adult: 35p, child: 10p.
(HM The Queen)
The family holiday home of the Royal Family for over a century. The earliest reference to it, as Bouchmorale, was in 1484. Queen Victoria visited the earlier castle in 1848; Prince Albert bought the 11,000-acre estate for £31,000 in 1852; the castle was rebuilt by William Smith of Aberdeen with modifications by Prince Albert, and was first occupied in 1855.

70 Balnakeil Craft Village
Map 3

1m W of Durness. Easter-end Sep, 0930-1800. Free.
Craftsmen working at pottery, boat-building, metalwork, weaving and many other crafts.

Balvenie Castle

71 Balvenie Castle
Map 6

At Dufftown, A941, 16m SSE of Elgin. Opening standard. Adult: 15p, child: 7p, group rates.
(AM)
Picturesque ruins of a 14th-century moated stronghold originally owned by the Comyns. Visited by Edward I in 1304 and by Mary Queen of Scots in 1562. Occupied by Cumberland in 1746. The corner stones came from Auchindoun (see No 56).

Banchory

72 Banchory Museum
Map 7

High Street. Jun-Sep, Mon, Tue, Wed, Fri, Sun 1400-1700. Sat 1000-1200, 1400-1700. Free.
A small display of local history in a room in the old Council Chambers.

73 Banff Museum
Map 6

On A947 at Banff. Jun-Sep, Wed, Fri, Sat, Sun 1400-1700. Free.
There is a fine display of birds of Britain in their settings and an interesting local history exhibition.

74 Bannockburn
Map 12

Off M80, 2m S of Stirling. Exhibition open Good Friday-30 Sep, Mon-Sat 1000-1800. (July-Aug 1000-1900, Sun 1100-1900). Exhibition: Adult: 65p, child: 30p. (NTS)
The 'Forging of a Nation' exhibition tells the story of the events leading up to the significant victory in Scottish history, in an audio-visual display. In June 1964 the Queen inaugurated the Rotunda and unveiled the equestrian statue, by the late C d'O Pilkington Jackson, of Robert the Bruce.

75 Barcaldine Castle
Map 4

On Loch Creran, 9m NE of Oban. Easter and July-Oct, Mon-Sat 1000-1600 (and by arrangement, tel: Ledaig 214). Adult: 50p, child: 25p. (Mr Campbell Godley)
A fortified keep built in 1590 by 'Black Duncan' and reputedly haunted.

76 Barguillean Garden
Map 10

3m W of Taynuilt on Glenlonan Road. Apr-Oct, daily, daylight hours. Adult: 30p, child: free. (Mr and Mrs Neil Macdonald)
Lochside gardens, featuring daffodils, rhododendrons, azaleas, flowering shrubs and heathers. Particularly attractive May-June.

77 Barochan Cross
Map 11

B789, 8m SE of Port Glasgow. At present under conservation. (AM)
A weathered Celtic cross, 11 feet high, attributed to the 12th century.

78 Barra Airport
Map 2

At north end of Isle of Barra.
On a magnificent shell beach, the airport is the only one in Britain where scheduled services are subject to tides.

79 Barrie's Birthplace
Map 7

9 Brechin Road, Kirriemuir. 1 May-30 Sep, Mon-Sat 1000-1230, 1400-1800. Sun 1400-1800. (Other times by arrangement. Miss O A G Bennell, tel: Kirriemuir 2646). Adult: 40p, child: 20p. (NTS)
Here in this white-washed cottage Sir J M Barrie

was born in 1860. Manuscripts, personal possessions and mementoes of actors and producers associated with his plays are shown.

80 Barsalloch Fort
Map 17

Off A749, 7½m WNW of Whithorn. All reasonable times. Free.
Remains of an iron-age fort on the edge of a raised beach bluff, 60-70 feet above the shore, enclosed by a ditch 12 feet deep and 33 feet wide.

81 Bass Rock
Map 14

Off North Berwick. Boat trips from North Berwick go round the Bass Rock.
A massive 350-feet-high rock whose many thousands of raucous seabirds include the third largest gannetry in the world.

82 Beauly Priory
Map 5

At Beauly, A9, 12m W of Inverness. Opening standard. Adult: 15p, child: 7p, group rates. (AM)
Ruins of a Valliscaulian Priory built in 1230. Notable windows and window-arcading.

83 Beech Hedge
Map 8

A93, just S of Meikleour, 12m NNE of Perth.
Listed as the highest of its kind in the world, the Beech Hedge was planted in 1746 and is now 600 yards long and 85 feet high.

84 Beinn Eighe National Nature Reserve
Map 4

Mid Apr-end Oct, daily, sunrise to sunset. W of A896/A832 junction at Kinlochewe (NCC)
The first National Nature Reserve in Britain, of great geological and natural history interest. Car park and nature trails on A832 NW of Kinlochewe. Aultroy Cottage Visitor Centre on A832, 1m nearer Kinlochewe. (See also No 956.)

85 Bell Obelisk
Map 11

Off A82 W of Bowling. All times. Free.
The obelisk at Douglas Point erected to commemorate Henry Bell, who launched the *Comet*, the first Clyde passenger steamer. Bowling is where the Forth and Clyde Canal enters the Clyde, and where the first practical steamboat, Symington's *Charlotte Dundas* was tried out in 1802 and in 1812.

86 Bell's Sports Centre
Map 8

On North Inch, Hay Street, Perth. All year, daily 0900-2230. Adult: 20p entrance + 30p for use of facilities. Child: 10p entrance + 15p for use of facilities.
The sports centre was opened in 1978 and in the dome-shaped building are facilities for a wide variety of sports.

87 Ben Lawers
Map 8

Off A827, 26m WSW of Aberfeldy. Visitor Centre open mid Apr-mid May, Mon-Sat 1100-1600, Sun 1000-1730; mid May-Sep, daily 1000-1730. Adult: 30p, child: 10p. (NTS)
Perthshire's highest mountain (3,984 feet) noted for its variety of rare alpine flowers and wild birds. There is a Visitor Centre, Nature Trail and a variety of guided walks in summer.

88 Ben Nevis
Map 4

Near Fort William.
Britain's highest mountain (4,406 ft, 1,344 m) and most popular mountain for both rock-climber and hillwalker. It is best seen from the north approach to Fort William, or from the Gairlochy Road, across the Caledonian Canal.

89 Bernera Barracks
Map 4

At Glenelg, on unclassified road W of A87 at Shiel Bridge. All times. Free.
The remains of Bernera Barracks, erected c 1722 and used continuously until after 1790.

Binns: see No 563.

90 Birnie Church
Map 3

Unclassified road off A941, 3m SE of Elgin. All year, daily. Free.
Small Romanesque church built in the early 12th century on the site of the church (c 550) of St Brendan the Navigator. Believed to be the oldest parish church in continuous use for worship in Scotland, and standing on a pre-Christian site (standing stones in churchyard).

Blackness Castle

Blackness

91 Birrens
Map 18

1m NE of Ecclefechan, S of Middlebie. All reasonable times. Free.
Fine example of ruined Roman fort which has been extensively excavated. There are defensive ditches and ramparts clearly visible and well-preserved (See also No 135).

Bishop's Palace: see No 330.

92 Blackhammer Cairn
Map 1

N of B9064, on the south coast of the island of Rousay (Orkney). All times. Free. (AM)
A long cairn bounded by a well-preserved retaining wall and containing a megalithic burial chamber divided into seven compartments or stalls; probably second millennium BC.

93 Black Watch Memorial
Map 8

On B846, N of Aberfeldy by Wade's Bridge. All times. Free.
The Black Watch Memorial, erected in Queen Victoria's Jubilee year (1887) is a large cairn surmounted by a kilted figure and commemorates the raising of the regiment of the Black Watch by General Wade in 1739.

Black Watch Museum: see No 67.

94 Blackness Castle
Map 13

B903, 4m NE of Linlithgow. Opening standard. Adult: 20p, child: 10p, group rates. (AM)
This 15th-century stronghold, once one of the most important fortresses in Scotland, was one of the four castles which by the Articles of Union were to be left fortified. Since then it has been a state prison in Covenanting times, a powder magazine in the 1870's, and more recently, for a period, a youth hostel.

Blair

95 Blair Castle
Map 8

On A9, 6m NNW of Pitlochry. Easter weekend and Apr, Sun-Mon. May to mid-Oct, daily. Mon-Sat 1000-1800, Sun 1400-1800. Adult: £1, child: 50p, group rates. (Duke of Atholl)
A white turreted baronial castle, seat of the Duke of Atholl, chief of Clan Murray. The oldest part is Cumming's Tower, 1269. Mary, Queen of Scots and Prince Charles Edward Stuart stayed here; when the castle was in Hanoverian hands, General Lord Murray laid siege to it on the Prince's behalf, making it the last castle in Britain to be besieged. The Duke is also the only British subject allowed to maintain a private army, the Atholl Highlanders. There are fine collections of furniture, portraits and Jacobite relics.

Blair Drummond Safari Park: see No 870.

96 Blantyre Obelisk
Map 11

Off B815 2m W of Erskine. All times. Free.
The tall monument is in memory of the 11th Lord Blantyre who was killed in the Brussels riots in 1830.

97 Boar Stone
Map 5

Knocknagael, off B861, 2m S of Inverness. All reasonable times. Free. (AM)
This roughly shaped slab, nearly 7 feet high, has incised at the top the mirror-case symbol; below is the figure of a boar.

98 Boath Doocot
Map 5

At Auldearn, 2m E of Nairn. All reasonable times. Adult: 10p (Donation box).
A 17th-century doocot (dovecote) on the site of an ancient castle where Montrose flew the standard of Charles I when he defeated the Covenanters in 1645. The plan of the battle is on display.

99 Bonawe Iron Furnace
Map 4

At Bonawe, 12m E of Oban, off A85. May be viewed from outside.
The restored remains of a charcoal furnace for iron-smelting, established in 1753, which worked until 1874. The furnace and ancillary buildings are in a more complete state of preservation than any other comparable site.

100 Bo'ness Museum
Map 12

In Bo'ness, 16m WNW of Edinburgh on A904 (adjacent to Kinneil House). May-Sept, Mon-Fri, 1000-1700. Free. (Falkirk District Council)
These converted 17th-century stables contain a museum of local industrial history, with displays of Bo'ness pottery, examples of local cast-iron work, salt pan implements, Roebuck and James Watt, etc. The lower floor houses a temporary exhibition area with changing displays. (See also No 620.)

101 Borthwick Castle
Map 13

Off A7, 13m SE of Edinburgh. Seen from outside only.
Built about 1430, the castle with its twin towers and two wings is one of the strongest and biggest of Scotland's tower houses. Mary, Queen of Scots visited the castle after her marriage to Bothwell.

Boswell Mausoleum: see No 58.

102 Bothwell Castle
Map 11

At Uddingston on A74, 7m SE of Glasgow. Opening standard. Adult: 15p, child: 7p, group rates. (AM)
Once the largest and finest stone castle in Scotland, dating from the 13th century and reconstructed by the Douglases in the 15th century. In a picturesque setting above the Clyde Valley.

103 Bowhill
Map 16

Off A708, 3m W of Selkirk. May-Sept, daily, 1400-1715. House and grounds: adult: 90p, child: 45p, group rates.
For many generations Bowhill has been the Border home of the Scotts of Buccleuch. Inside

the house, built in 1825, there is an outstanding collection of pictures, including works of Van Dyck, Reynolds, Gainsborough, Canaletto, Guardi, Claude Lorraine, Raeburn, etc.; porcelain; and furniture, much of which was made in the famous workshops of André Boulle in Paris.
In the grounds is an adventure woodland play area, a riding centre, garden and nature trails.

104 Bowmore Round Church
Map 10

Bowmore, Isle of Islay. All reasonable times. Free.
Designed by a French architect and built in 1769. It owes its circular shape to the common belief that no evil spirits could hide in any corners.

105 Braeloine Visitor Centre
Map 7

Glen Tanar, near Aboyne. Apr-Oct, daily, 1000-1700. By donation. (Hon. Mrs Bruce)
There are signposted walks and trails and an exhibition about the wildlife and the history of farming, forestry and land use on this fascinating Highland estate.

106 Braemar Castle
Map 8

A93, at Braemar. May to Oct, daily, 1000-1800. Adult: 50p, child: 20p. (Son et Lumière Aug and Sep.) (Farquharson of Invercauld)
This turreted stronghold built in 1628 by the Earl of Mar was burnt by Farquharson of Inverey in 1689. It was rebuilt about 1748 and garrisoned by Hanoverian troops. There is a round central tower, a spiral stair, barrel-vaulted ceilings and an underground pit prison.

107 Brandsbutt Stone
Map 6

A96, at Brandsbutt Farm, about 1m NW of centre of Inverurie. All times. Free. (AM)
A Pictish symbol stone with a well preserved Ogham inscription. Originally it formed one of a circle.

108 Branklyn Garden
Map 8

Dundee Road (A85), Perth. 1 Mar-31 Oct, daily 1000-sunset; or by arrangement (tel: Perth 25535).
Adult: 40p, child: 20p. (NTS). No dogs.
Described as the finest two acres of private

Brodick

garden in the country, this outstanding collection of plants, particularly alpines, attracts gardeners and botanists from all over the world.

109 Brechin Museum
Map 7

In Library, St Ninian's Square. All year, Mon-Fri 0930-1800, (Wed 1900) Sat 0930-1700. Free. (Brechin District Council)
Local history collection of Brechin and its surrounding district.

110 Brechin Round Tower
Map 7

At Brechin. Viewed from the churchyard. All reasonable times. (AM)
One of the two remaining round towers of the Irish type in Scotland, dating back to the 10th or 11th century. Now attached to the cathedral (c 1150, partially demolished 1807, restored 1900-02; interesting tombstones).
(See also Abernethy, No 20.)

111 Bridge of Carr
Map 5

Carrbridge. All times.
High and narrow single-arch bridge. Built by John Niccelsone, mason, in summer 1717, for Sir James Grant.

Broch of Gurness: see No 534.

Braemar Castle

112 Brodick Castle and Gardens
Map 10

1½m N of Brodick pier, Isle of Arran. Castle: Apr, Mon, Wed and Sat 1300-1700; 1 May-30 Sep, Mon-Sat 1300-1700, Sun 1400-1700. Gardens: all year, daily 1000-1700 (Castle and Gardens): Adult: 85p, child: 40p, group rates. (Gardens only): Adult: 50p, child: 25p (NTS)
This ancestral seat of the Dukes of Hamilton dates in part from the 13th century; it was extended in 1652 and 1844. The contents include silver, porcelain and fine paintings, sporting pictures and trophies. There are two gardens: the woodland garden (1923) is now one of the finest rhododendron gardens in Britain; the formal garden dates from 1710.

113 Brough of Birsay
Map 1

At Birsay, N end of mainland, 11m N of Stromness, Orkney. Opening standard, tides permitting. Adult: 15p, child: 7p, group rates. (AM)
The remains of a Romanesque church and a Norse settlement on an island accessible only at low tide. A replica of a Pictish sculptured stone discovered in the ruins is in the grounds. (Original in the National Museum of Antiquities, No 371.)

114 Broughton House
Map 17

High Street, Kirkcudbright. Nov-Mar, Sat, Sun, Mon 1400-1600. Apr-Oct, Mon-Sun 1100-1300, 1400-1700. Adult: 30p, child: 15p.
This early 18th-century mansion belonged to the late 19th-century artist E A Hornel. There is a display of his pictures, antique furniture, a library and an attractive garden.

115 Brow Well
Map 18

On B725 1m W of Ruthwell. All times. Free.
Ancient mineral well visited by Robert Burns in July 1786, when at Brow sea bathing under his doctor's orders.

116 Bruce's Stone
Map 17

6m W of New Galloway by A712. All reasonable times. Free. (NTS)
This granite boulder on Moss Raploch records a victory by Robert the Bruce over the English in March 1307, during the fight for Scotland's independence.

117 Bruce's Stone
Map 17

E side of Loch Trool, unclassified road off A714, 13m N of Newton Stewart. All reasonable times. Free.
A memorial stone, on a commanding viewpoint, which commemorates a victory by Bruce over the English.

118 Michael Bruce's Cottage
Map 9

Kinnesswood, off A911, 4m E of Milnathort. Apr-Sept, daily 1000-1800. (Keys at The Garage, Kinnesswood). Admission by donation. (Michael Bruce Memorial Trust).
A cottage museum in the birthplace of the Gentle Poet of Loch Leven (1746-1767), who wrote and improved some of the Scottish Paraphrases.

119 George Buchanan Obelisk
Map 11

On A875 at Killearn. All times. Free.
An obelisk in memory of George Buchanan (1506-1582) historian, scholar and tutor to Mary, Queen of Scots and James VI.

120 Buckie House
Map 9

High Street, Anstruther. March-end Oct, Mon-Sat 1030-1230, 1430-1730, Sun 1430-1530. Closed Wed. Nov-Feb, pm only. Free.
A three-storey merchant's house partly built in 1692 but largely 18th-century. The gable end and front of the house were decorated with shells in the 19th century. The house was restored by NTS and is now a dwelling house and art gallery.

121 Buckie Maritime Museum
Map 6

Cluny Place. May-Sep, Mon 1400-1600; Tues-Fri 1000-1200, 1400-1600; Sat 1000-1200. Free.
Exhibition of clothing, gear and models relating to the fishing industry. The Anson gallery houses water colours of the development of fishing in Scotland.

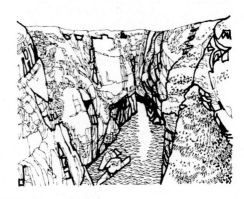

122 Bullers of Buchan
Map 6

Off A975, 7m S of Peterhead.
A vast chasm in the cliffs, 200 feet deep, *which no man can see with indifference* said Dr Johnson in 1773. A haunt of innumerable seabirds.

123 The Burg
Map 10

5m W on track from B8035 on N shore of Loch Scridain, Isle of Mull. Only accessible at low tide. Free. (NTS)·
Information from Miss McGillivray at Burg Farm.
The area contains MacCulloch's fossil tree, possibly 50 million years old, which can be reached at low water. Cars inadvisable beyond Tiroran. Five mile walk, very rough in places.

124 Burghead Well
Map 3

At Burghead, 8m NW of Elgin. Opening standard. Free. (AM)
This remarkable rock-cut structure within the wall of an Iron Age fort is probably an Early Christian Baptistry.

125 Burleigh Castle
Map 8

Off A911, 2m NE of Kinross. Opening standard. Free; key-keeper at farm opposite. (AM)
A fine tower house dating from about 1500.

Burns Cottage

The seat of the Balfours of Burleigh, several times visited by James VI.

Land o' Burns Centre: See No 639.

126 Burns Cottage and Museum
Map 15

B7024, at Alloway, 2m S of Ayr. Apr-Oct, weekdays 0900-1900; Sun (May, Sep and Oct only) 1400-1900 and Sun (Jun to Aug) 1000-1900. Adult: 30p, child: 15p (includes Burns Monument). (Trustees of Burns Monument)
In this thatched cottage built by his father, Robert Burns was born 25 January 1759, and this was his home until 1766. Adjoining the cottage is a leading museum of Burnsiana. This is the start of the Burns' Heritage Trail which may be followed to trace the places linked with Scotland's greatest poet.
(See No 639 and No 132.)

127 Burns Family Tombstones and Cairn
Map 7

Off A94 3m S of Stonehaven at Glenbervie Church. All times. Free.
The Burnes (Burns) family tombstones in the churchyard were restored in 1968 and a Burns memorial cairn is nearby.

128 Burns House, Dumfries
Map 18

Burns Street. House open Apr-Sep, Mon-Sat 1000-1300, 1400-1900; Sun 1400-1900; Oct-Mar, Mon-Sat 1000-1200, 1400-1700. Adult: 10p, child: 5p.
In November 1791 Robert Burns moved to Dumfries as an Exciseman and rented a three-room flat (not open to public) in the Wee Vennel (now Bank Street). In May 1793 he moved to a better house in Mill Vennel (now Burns Street), and here he died on 21 July 1796, though his wife Jean Armour stayed in the house until her death in 1834. The house has recently been completely refurbished and many relics of the poet are shown.

129 Burns House Museum, Mauchline
Map 15

Castle Street, Mauchline, 11m ENE of Ayr. All year, Mon-Sat 1000-1900, Sun 1400-1900. Adult: 5p, child: 2½p.
On the upper floor is the room which Robert Burns took for Jean Armour in 1788. It has been kept intact and is furnished in the style of that period. The remainder of the museum contains

Burns Monument

Burnsiana and a collection of folk objects. Close by is Mauchline Kirkyard (scene of *The Holy Fair*) in which are buried four of Burns' daughters and a number of his friends and contemporaries. Other places of interest nearby are 15th-century Mauchline Castle and Poosie Nansie's Tavern, scene of *The Jolly Beggars*.

130 Burns Mausoleum
Map 18

St Michael's Churchyard, Dumfries. All reasonable times. Free.
Burns was buried in St Michael's Churchyard, near to the house in Mill Vennel where he died in 1796 (see No 128). In 1815 his remains were removed to the present elaborate mausoleum.

131 Burns Memorial Tower
Map 15

At north end of Mauchline. All year, daily, 1000-1800. Adult: 10p, child 10p.
Two-storey tower with a museum of Burns relics, not far from Mossgiel Farm where Burns worked as a young man.

Burns Monument, Alloway

132 Burns Monument, Alloway
Map 15

B7024 at Alloway, 2m S of Ayr. Apr-mid Oct, daily, 0900-1900. Adult: 30p, child: 15p (including Burns Cottage). (Trustees of Burns Monument)
Grecian monument (1823) to the poet with relics dating back to the 1820's. Nearby is the attractive River Doon, spanned by the famous Brig o' Doon, a single arch (possibly 13th-century), central to Burns' poem, *Tam o' Shanter*. (See also No 932.)

133 Burns Monument and Museum, Kilmarnock
Map 15

Kay Park. Oct-Apr, Sat and Sun 1300-1700. May-Sep, daily 1300-1700. Adult: 3p, child: 3p.
The Monument is a statue by W G Stevenson, offering fine views over the surrounding countryside. The Kay Park Museum houses displays on the life and work of Burns, and has an extensive Burns library.

Burns Collection

134 Murison Burns Collection
Map 13

Dunfermline Central Library, Abbot Street. All year. Mon, Tue, Thu, Fri 1000-1300, 1400-1900; Wed 1000-1300, Sat 1000-1300, 1400-1700. Free.
A collection of Burns relics housed in a room in the first Carnegie library, built in 1883.

135 Burnswark
Map 18

2½m N of Ecclefechan. All reasonable times. Free.
A Roman artillery range and a native hill fort with extensive earthworks, thought to have been a series of Roman practice siege works. (See also No 91.)

136 Burntisland Museum
Map 13

Town house in High Street. By arrangement (Dilys Maywood, tel: Kirkcaldy 60732). Free.
A permanent display of the local history of Burntisland in the former Courtroom of the Council Chambers. The nearby church, with octagonal shape, is also interesting.

137 Bute Museum
Map 10

*Stuart Street, Rothesay. Apr-Sept, Mon-Sat 1030-1230, 1430-1630 (Jun-Sep, Sun 1430-1630); Oct-Mar, Tues-Sat 1430-1630. Adult: 20p, child: 10p.
(Buteshire Natural History Society)*
Exhibits relating to the county of Bute.

138 The Byre Theatre
Map 9

Abbey Street, St Andrews.
The original Byre Theatre was formed in a centuries-old cattle byre. It is now in a modern theatre and has its own resident repertory company.

139 Caerlaverock Castle
Map 18

Off B725, 9m S of Dumfries. Opening standard. Adult: 25p, child: 12p, group rates. (AM)
This seat of the Maxwell family dates back to 1220. In 1300, Edward I laid siege to it and in 1638 it capitulated to the Covenanters after a siege lasting 13 weeks. The castle is triangular with round towers. The heavy machicolation is 15th-century and over the gateway between two splendid towers can be seen the Maxwell crest and motto. The interior was reconstructed in the 17th century as a Renaissance mansion, with fine carving.

140 Caerlaverock National Nature Reserve
Map 18

B725, S of Dumfries, by Caerlaverock Castle. All year. Free. (NCC)
1,500 acres of salt marsh between the River Nith and the Lochar Water. A noted winter haunt of wildfowl, including barnacle geese. Access unrestricted, except in sanctuary area (600 acres).

Cairn Baan: see No 606.

Caledonian

141 Cairngorm Chairlift
Map 5

A951 from A9 at Aviemore, then by Loch Morlich to car park at 2,000 feet. All year, daily, 0900-1630, depending on weather. Prices vary according to journey.
(Cairngorm Chairlift Company Limited)
At the top of the chairlift is the highest restaurant in Britain, the Ptarmigan (3,500 feet above sea level), with magnificent views over Strathspey to the west, north and east.

142 Cairnpapple Hill
Map 12

Off B792, 3m N of Bathgate. Opening standard Apr-Sep; winter by arrangement with custodian at Torphichen Preceptory (No 955).
Adult: 15p, child: 7p, group rates. (AM)
Sanctuary and burial cairns. Originally a Neolithic sanctuary remodelled in the Early Bronze Age (c 1800 BC) as a monumental open-air temple in the form of a stone circle with enclosing ditch. Later (c 1500 BC) it was despoiled and built over by a Bronze Age Cairn, considerably enlarged several centuries later. Now excavated and laid out.

143 Caithness Glass
Map 3

Harrowhill, Wick. Mon-Fri 0900-1200, 1230-1630, Sat 0900-1200. By arrangement, tel: Wick 2286. Free.
Hand made glass blowing can be observed from the raw materials stage through all the processes to the finished article.

144 Caledonian Canal
Map 5

Built between 1803 and 1822 the canal runs across the highest parts of Britain through some of Scotland's most dramatic scenery almost in a straight line from Inverness to Corpach near Fort William. The canal stretches for 60 miles, 22 miles of it in man made cuttings, and 38 miles through natural lochs. There are a number of pleasure cruises available on the canal in the summer. (See also No 745.)

145 Cambuskenneth Abbey
Map 12

1m NE of Stirling. Opening standard: closed winter. Adult: 15p, child: 7p, group rates. (AM)
Ruins of an abbey founded in 1147 as a house of Augustinian Canons. Scene of Bruce's Parliament, 1326.

146 Cameron Cairn
Map 3

Near Poolewe, by Loch Ewe. All times, Free.
The cairn is in memory of Alexander Cameron the Tournaig bard who died in 1933 having spent his whole life by the loch.

147 Cameron Loch Lomond
Map 11

N from Balloch, A82, 18m NW of Glasgow. Early Easter-Sept, 1030-1800. £2.50 per car, group rates.
(Mr Patrick Telfer Smollett)
A wildlife park with a large leisure area including lochside picnic areas, gardens and play area, boating, water ski-ing, weekend events and many other attractions. Cameron House (open daily 1130-1800) has many fascinating displays, including an Oriental Room, a Nursery, the largest collection of different types of whisky bottles in the world (over 1,000), model aircraft, and many other treasures.

148 Cameronians (Scottish Rifles) Regimental Museum
Map 11, 12

129 Muir Street, Hamilton. All year, Mon, Tue, Thu, Fri 1000-1200, 1300-1700, Wed 1300-1700, Sat 1000-1700. Free.
Display of uniforms, medals, banners, silver and documents, relating to the regiment and also to Covenanting times.

Campbeltown Celtic Cross: see No 182.

149 Campbeltown Library and Museum
Map 10

Hall Street. All year, Mon, Tue, Thu, Fri 1000-1300, 1400-1700, 1800-2000; Sat 1000-1300, 1400-1700. Free.
Attractive red sandstone building given to the town in 1898, containing an excellent local history collection and describing the archaeology, geology and natural history of Kintyre.

150 Camphill Village Trust
Map 7

*Newton Dee Community, Bieldside. Mon-Fri
1000-1200, 1500-1700. Free.*
Sheltered workshops for the handicapped,
making soft toys and wood, metal, woven and
printed goods. There is also a large bakery and
two farms.

151 Canal Museum
Map 12

*The Basin, Union Canal, Linlithgow.
Apr-Sept, Sat and Sun 1400-1700.
Adult: 10p, child: 5p.*
Records, photographs, audio-visual display and
relics of the history and wildlife of the Union
Canal, in former canal stables, built c 1822 when
the Union Canal was opened.
(See also Nos 970 and 976.)

152 Canna, Isle of
Map 4

*Inner Hebrides. Ferry from Mallaig and Arisaig
(no cars).*
The island lies 3 miles west of Rhum. To the
north is Compass Hill (458 ft) whose rich iron
deposits in the basalt cliffs are said to affect the
magnetic compasses of passing ships. A
mutilated sculptured cross stands near Canna
Post office and there are remains of a small
Celtic nunnery, where the wall, mill and some
cells can still be seen. Accommodation is limited.

153 Cape Wrath
Map 3

12m NW of Durness.
The most northerly point of Scotland's north west
seaboard. A passenger ferry (summer only)
connects with a minibus service to the cape.

Cardoness Castle

154 Cardoness Castle
Map 17

*On A75, 1m SW of Gatehouse-of-Fleet. Opening
standard. Adult: 20p, child: 10p, group rates.
(AM)*
This 15th-century tower house was long the
home of the McCullochs of Galloway. It is four
storeys high, with a vaulted basement. Features
include the original stairway, stone benches and
elaborate fireplaces.

Carfin

155 Carfin Grotto
Map 12

Carfin Village, 2m N of Motherwell.
Daily. Outdoor devotions only on Sun (May-Oct)
at 1500. Free.
Grotto of Our Lady of Lourdes and a place of
pilgrimage.

156 Carleton Castle
Map 17

A77, 6m S of Girvan. All reasonable times. Free.
One in a link of Kennedy watchtowers along the
coast. Now a ruin, it was famed in ballad as the
seat of a baron who got rid of seven wives by
pushing them over the cliff, but was himself
similarly disposed of by May Cullean, his eighth
wife.

157 Carlyle's Birthplace
Map 18

A74 at Ecclefechan, 5½m SE of Lockerbie.
Good Friday-31 Oct, Mon-Sat 1000-1800.
Other times by arrangement (Mr J Swan, tel:
Ecclefechan 666). Adult: 25p, child: 10p. (NTS)
Thomas Carlyle (1795-1881) was born in this
little house built by his father and uncle, both
master masons, and itself of considerable
architectural interest. Parts of his
correspondence with Goethe are included in the
collection of his letters to be seen.

158 Carnasserie Castle
Map 10

Off A816, 9m N of Lochgilphead. All reasonable
times. Free. (AM)
The house of John Carswell, first Protestant
Bishop of the Isles, who translated Knox's
Liturgy into Gaelic, and published it in 1567, the
first book printed in that language. The castle
was captured and partly blown up during Argyll's
rebellion in 1685.

159 Carnegie Birthplace Memorial
Map 13

Moodie Street, Dunfermline. Daily 1100-1300,
1400-1900 (Sep-Apr 1700); Sun 1400-1800.
Free.
Weaver's cottage, birthplace in 1835 of Andrew
Carnegie, the multi-millionaire in USA who
showered immense benefits on his home town.
The cottage is now a museum.

160 Carradale House Gardens
Map 10

Off B842, 12½m NNE of Campbeltown.
Apr-Sep, daily 1000-1600. Adult: 20p,
child: free. (Naomi Mitchison)
Walled garden dating from about 1870; flowering
shrubs, rhododendrons, azaleas. Wild garden
with paths and iris pond. The remains of a vitrified
fort stand on an island (access by foot except at
high tide) south of the harbour at Carradale
village.

161 Carrick Castle
Map 11

*On W bank of Loch Goil, 5m S of Lochgoilhead.
All reasonable times. Free.*
Built in the 14th century and first recorded in
1511, the walls of this great rectangular keep are
entire though roofless. The Argylls kept their
writs and charters here, and used it as a prison.
Fortified in 1651 in expectation of a siege by
Commonwealth forces, it was burned by the Earl
of Atholl's troops in 1685.

162 Carsaig Arches
Map 10

*On shore 3m W of Carsaig, South Mull, 22m
SSW of Salen. All times. Free.*
A 3-mile walk from Carsaig leads to these
remarkable tunnels formed by the sea in the
basaltic rock. Reached only at low tide. On the
way is the Nun's Cave, with curious carvings; it is
said that nuns driven out of Iona at the time of the
Reformation sheltered here.

163 Carsluith Castle
Map 17

*A75, 7m W of Gatehouse-of-Fleet. Opening
standard. Free. (AM)*
A roofless 16th-century tower house on the
L-plan. The staircase wing is an addition, dated
1568.

164 Cartland Bridge
Map 16
On the A73 W of Lanark. All times. Free.
An impressive bridge built by Telford over a
gorge, carrying the Mouse Water.

Castle Balliol: see No 659.

165 Castle Campbell
Map 12

*In Dollar Glen, 1m N of Dollar. Opening
standard. Adult: 20p, child: 10p, group rates.
(AM)*
On a steep mound with extensive views to the
plains of the Forth, this castle was built towards
the end of the 15th century by the first Earl of
Argyll, and was at one time known as Castle
Gloom. It was burned by Cromwell's troops in the
1650's. The courtyard, great hall, and the great
barrel roof of the third floor are well worth seeing.
The 60 acres of woodland of Dollar Glen (NTS),
with paths and bridges, make an attractive walk
to the castle.

166 Castle Fraser
Map 7

3m S of Kemnay off unclassified road via Craigearn to Dunecht, 16m W of Aberdeen, Castle:1 May-30 Sep, Mon-Sat 1100-1715, Sun 1400-1715. Adult: 75p, child: 35p. Garden and grounds: All year, 0930-sunset. Grounds by donation. (NTS)
Perhaps the most spectacular of the Castles of Mar. It was begun about 1575, incorporating earlier building and was completed 1636. Two great families of master masons, Bel and Leiper, took part in the work. The great heraldic panel on the north side is signed 'J Bel'. Off the castle courtyard is an exhibition telling the story of the Castles of Mar.

Castle Girnigoe: see No 179.

Castle Gloom: see No 165.

167 Castle Jail Museum
Map 16

Castlegate, Jedburgh. Weekdays 1000-1200, 1300-1700, Sun 1300-1700. Adult: 10p, child: 5p. (Roxburgh District Council)
On the site of Jedburgh Castle, a 'modern' reform jail was built in 1825. Rooms have been interestingly reconstructed to re-create the 'reformed' system of the early 19th century.

168 Castle Kennedy Gardens and Lochinch Castle
Map 17

N of A75, 3m E of Stranraer. Apr to Sep, daily except Sat, 1000-1700. Adult: 35p, child: 10p. (Earl of Stair)
Lochinch Castle (1870), not open to the public, is the seat of the Earl of Stair. In spring and early summer the gardens are ablaze with rhododendrons. The notable pinetum was the first in Scotland.

169 Castle Menzies
Map 8

B846, Weem, 1m W of Aberfeldy. In process of restoration by Menzies Clan Society. May-Oct, Sat 1000-1230, 1400-1700, Sun 1400-1700; or by arrangement. Adult: 30p, child: 10p. (Menzies Clan Society)
Fine example of 16th-century Z-plan transitional fortified tower house with elaborately carved dormers added in 1577. Castle also houses Clan Menzies Museum.

170 Castle of Mey
Map 3

A836, 7m W of John o' Groats. Gardens only open 3 days in the year in aid of charity (contact Tourist Office, Wick). (HM The Queen Mother)
Built in 1568 by George, 5th Earl of Caithness, this castle remained in the Caithness family until the late 19th century. The present owner is Queen Elizabeth, the Queen Mother, who stays there at times.

171 Castle Moil
Map 4

Near Kyleakin pier, Skye. All reasonable times. Free.

Castle Sween

Earlier known as Dunakin, these rather scant ruins were once a lookout post and a fortress against raids by Norsemen. For centuries this keep was a stronghold of the MacKinnons of Strath. Now known as Castle Moil ('the roofless castle').

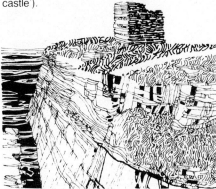

172 Castle of Old Wick
Map 3

Off A9, 1½m S of Wick. All reasonable times, except when adjoining rifle range is in use. Free. (AM)
On a headland above the sea, over a deep cleft in the rocks, this almost windowless square tower of the Cheynes, once known as Castle Oliphant, dates back to the 14th century.

173 Castle of Park
Map 17

Off A75, by Glenluce, 9m ESE of Stranraer. Not yet open to the public; may be viewed from the outside. (AM)
A tall, imposing castellated mansion, still entire, built by Thomas Hay of Park in 1590.

174 Castle Semple Collegiate Church
Map 11

At Castle Semple, 1½m NE of Lochwinnoch. Not open to the public. May be viewed from the outside. (AM)
The church is a rectangular structure. A square tower projects from the west gable. The apse is three-sided, each side having three windows of debased Gothic form.

Castle Sinclair: see No 179

175 Castle Stalker
Map 4

On a tiny island offshore from A828, 25m NNE from Oban. Mar-Sept, four days each month, by arrangement, tel: Upper Warlingham 2768. Adult: £1, child: 50p, including boat trip. (Major D R Stewart Allward)
This picturesque ancient home, c 1500, of the Stewarts of Appin, and associated with James V, has been restored in recent years.

176 Castle Sween
Map 10

On E shore of Loch Sween, 15m SW of Lochgilphead. All reasonable times. Free. (AM)
This is probably the oldest stone castle on the Scottish mainland, built in the mid-12th century. It was destroyed by Sir Alexander Macdonald in 1647.

Castle Tioram

177 Castle Tioram
Map 4

On an islet in Loch Moidart; unclassified road N of A861, 6m NNW of Salen. All reasonable times. Free.

The ancient seat of the Macdonalds of Clan Ranald, built in the early 14th century, well situated on a small island and accessible at low tide. It was burned by the orders of the then chief when he joined the 1715 Rising and feared that it might be taken by his enemies, the Campbells.

Castle Urquhart: see No 974.

178 Castlelaw Fort
Map 13

Off A702, 7m S of Edinburgh. Opening standard. Free. (AM)

A small Iron Age hill fort consisting of two concentric banks and ditches. In the older rock-cut ditch an earth-house is preserved. Occupied into Roman times (2nd century AD).

179 Castles Girnigoe and Sinclair
Map 3

3m N of Wick. Take airport road towards Noss Head Lighthouse. All times. Free.

Two adjacent castles on a cliff-edge above Sinclair's Bay, and one-time strongholds of the Sinclairs, Earls of Caithness. Girnigoe dates from the end of the 15th century; Sinclair from 1606-07. Both were deserted c 1679 and 20 years later were reported in ruins.

180 Cawdor Castle
Map 5

At Cawdor on B9090, 5m SW of Nairn. May-Sep, 1000-1700. Adult: £1, child: 50p, group rates. (Rt Hon The Earl Cawdor)

The old central tower of 1372, fortified in 1454, (a family home for over 600 years) is surrounded by 16th-century buildings, remodelled during the following century. Notable gardens surround the castle. Shakespeare's Macbeth was Thane of Cawdor, and the castle is one of the traditional settings for the murder of Duncan.

181 The Caterthuns
Map 7

5m NW of Brechin. All times. Free. (AM)

These remains of iron age hill forts stand on hills on either side of the road from Balrownie to Pitmudie, beyond Little Brechin. The Brown Caterthun has four concentric ramparts and ditches; the White Caterthun is a well-preserved hill fort with massive stone rampart, defensive ditch and outer earthworks.

182 Celtic Cross
Map 10

Main Street, Campbeltown.
This cross of unknown date but probably c 1500
has elaborate ornamentation and an inscription
in Lombardic letters.

183 Chambers Institution Museum
Map 16

*High Street, Peebles. Mon, Tue, Thu, Fri 0900-
1900. Wed 0900-1730. Free.*
Given by William Chambers, the publisher, in
1859, the museum room now houses items of
local history.

184 Chapel Finian
Map 17

*Off A747, 12½m WSW of Wigtown. All
reasonable times. Free. (AM)*
A small chapel or oratory probably dating from
the 10th or 11th century, in an enclosure about
50 feet wide.

185 Chapel of St Mahew
Map 11

*¼m N of Cardross, behind the golf course, and
4m NW of Dumbarton. All reasonable times.
Free.*
The first church was dedicated by St Mahew
(c 535), a prophet and disciple of St Patrick, but
the present building, restored in 1955, is the work
of Duncan Napier and dates from 1467.

186 The Chesters Fort
Map 14

1m S of Drem, East Lothian. All times. Free. (AM)
The Chesters is one of the best examples in
Scotland of an Iron Age Fort with multiple
ramparts.

Cawdor Castle

187 Church of the Holy Rude
Map 12

*St John Street, Stirling. Apr/May-Sept, daily
1000-1700. Free.*
The only church in Scotland still in use which has
witnessed a coronation, when in 1567, the infant
James VI, age 13 months, was crowned. John
Knox preached the sermon. The church dates
from 1414, and Mary Queen of Scots worshipped
there.

Church of St Moluag

188 Church of St Moluag
Map 2

*N end of the Isle of Lewis. To visit, apply to
'McLeod's' in Eoropie.
(Scottish Episcopal Church)*
Known in the Gaelic as Teampull mhor (big
temple) this chapel was probably built in the 12th
century. Now restored: service held every
Sunday.

189 Church of St Monan
Map 9

*In St Monans, A917, 12m S of St Andrews. All
reasonable times. Free.*
Built by David II (c 1362) in gratitude for his
recovery, at the tomb of St Moinenn, from a
wound. This church has a short square tower
surmounted by an octagonal steeple, with
characteristic little belfry windows. The interior,
lighted by beautiful windows, has a fine groined
roof. Well-restored in 1828.

190 Cille Barra
Map 2

*At Eoligarry, at N end of Isle of Barra. All times.
Free.*
The ruined church of St Barr, who gave his name
to the island, and the restored chapel of St Mary
formed part of a mediaeval monastery.
Preserved there are four grave stones, thought
to have come from Iona.

191 Clachan Bridge
Map 10

B884, 12m SW of Oban.
This picturesque single-arched bridge, built in
1791, which links the mainland with the island of
Seil, is often claimed to be the only bridge to
'span the Atlantic' (though there are others
similar). The waters are actually those of the
narrow Seil Sound, which joins the Firth of Lorne
to Outer Loch Melfort, but they can, with some
justification, claim to be an arm of the Atlantic.

192 Clackmannan Tower
Map 12

*On a hill W of Clackmannan (A907). No facilities
for entry whilst restoration work is in progress;
may be closely viewed from the outside.*
Before the partial collapse of this castle with its
14th-century tower, it was one of the most
complete of Scottish tower houses. In
Clackmannan itself, see the old Tolbooth, the
ancient 'Stone of Mannan' and the stepped Town
Cross.

193 Clan Donald Centre
Map 4

At Armadale Castle on A851, ½m N of Armadale Pier. Apr-Oct, Mon-Sat 1000-1700. Eves and Sun pm mid-season.
Adult: 25p, child: 10p, group rates.
The centre houses a museum of the history of the Macdonalds and the Lords of the Isles. Armadale Castle dates from the early 18th century and has associations with Flora Macdonald. It is surrounded by beautiful woodland gardens containing an Arboretum over 300 years old.

194 Clan Donnachaidh Museum
Map 8

Calvine, A9, 4m W of Blair Atholl. Apr-mid Oct, weekdays 1000-1730, Sun 1400-1730. Free.
Clan Donnachaidh comprises Reid, Robertson, MacConnachie, Duncan, MacInroy and others. Old and new exhibits include items associated with the Jacobite Risings of 1715 and 1745.

195 Clan Gunn Museum
Map 3

N of Latheron on A9, N of junction with A895.
Clan museum (opening in 1979) in the mid-18th-century Old Parish Church of Latheron.

196 Clan Macpherson Museum
Map 5

In Newtonmore on A9/A86, 15m S of Aviemore. May-Sep, Mon-Sat 1000-1200, 1400-1800. Free.
The museum of the clan with relics and memorials including the black chanter, green banner and charmed sword, Prince Charles Edward Stuart relics, and a magnificent silver centrepiece.

Clan Menzies Museum: see No 169.

197 Clan Tartan Centre
Map 5

By Aviemore Centre, off A9, 32m S of Inverness. Daily, Oct-Jun 1000-1800, Jul-Sep 1000-2030. Free.
Exhibition, reference library and audio-visual display. Computerized tracing of clan links, with commentary in four languages.

198 Jim Clark Memorial Trophy Room
Map 14

In Burgh Chambers, Newtown Street, Duns. Easter-end Sept, Mon-Sat 1000-1300, 1400-1800, Sun 1400-1800. Adult: 20p, child 10p.
A memorial to the late Jim Clark, twice world motor racing champion, with a large number of his trophies.

199 Clava Cairns
Map 5

Near Culloden, off B851, 6½m ESE of Inverness. All reasonable times. Free. (AM)
An extensive group of standing stones and cairns dating from the Bronze Age.

Cloch Lighthouse

200 Click Mill
Map 1

Off B9057, 2m NE of Dounby, Orkney. All reasonable times. Free. (AM)
The only working example of the traditional horizontal water mill of Orkney.

201 Clickhimin
Map 1

About ¾m SW of Lerwick, Shetland. Opening standard. Free. (AM)
This site was fortified at the beginning of the Iron Age with a stone-built fort. Later a broch (which still stands to a height of 17 feet) was constructed inside the fort.

202 Cloch Lighthouse
Map 11

A78, 3m SW of Gourock. Seen from the outside only.
This notable landmark stands at Cloch Point with fine views across the Upper Firth of Clyde estuary. The white-painted lighthouse was constructed in 1797.

203 Cobb Memorial
Map 5

Between Invermoriston and Drumnadrochit by A82. All times. Free.
A cairn commemorates John Cobb, the racing motorist, who lost his life in 1952 when attempting to beat the water speed record, with his jet speedboat, on Loch Ness.

204 Cobbie Row's Castle
Map 1

On the Island of Wyre, Orkney. Opening standard. Free. (AM)
Probably the earliest stone castle authenticated in Scotland. The *Orkneyinga Saga* tells how (c 1145) Kolbein Hruga built a fine stone castle in Wyre. It consists of a small rectangular tower, enclosed in a circular ditch. In a graveyard near the castle is St Mary's Chapel, a ruin of the late 12th century. It is a small rectangular structure of nave and chancel. The walls are built of local whinstone.

205 Coldingham Priory
Map 14

In Coldingham, A1107, 3m NW of Eyemouth. All reasonable times. Free.
Founded c 1098 by Edgar, King of Scots, the choir of this Benedictine Priory has been restored as the parish church. There are extensive ruins of other buildings adjacent.

206 Coldstream Museum
Map 16

Market Square. Easter-Sep daily, afternoons only. Adult: 20p, child: 10p.
Small museum rebuilt in 1863 in the original headquarters of the Coldstream Guards (founded 1659).

207 Collegiate Church of St. Nicholas
Map 13

Dalkeith. All reasonable times. Free.
Choir and apse of a 15th-century foundation endowed by the Douglas family. There is the notable tomb of Sir James Douglas, 1st Earl of Morton and his deaf and dumb Countess, Joanna, daughter of James I.

208 Columba's Footsteps
Map 10

W of Southend at Keil.
Traditionally it is believed that St Columba first set foot on Scottish soil near Southend. The footsteps are imprinted in a flat topped rock near the ruin of an old chapel.

209 Colvin Fountain
Map 18

Moffat. All times. Free.
The fountain, surmounted by a ram, signifies the importance of sheep farming in the district.

210 Colzium House and Park
Map 12

Off A803 at Kilsyth, 10m NE of Glasgow. All year, daily, dawn to dusk. House closed when booked for private functions. Free.
19th-century residence, with museum containing mainly local artefacts and a picture collection. Park contains a large collection of trees and shrubs and the ruins of Colzium Castle, destroyed by Cromwell. Walled garden.

211 Commando Memorial
Map 8

Off A82, 11m NE of Fort William.
An impressive sculpture by Scott Sutherland, erected in 1952 to commemorate the Commandos of the Second World War who trained in this area. Fine views of Ben Nevis and Lochaber.

212 Comrie Smiddy Museum
Map 8

*On A85, centre of Comrie Village.
('Smiddy House') Easter-Oct, Sat only,
1100-1300, 1430-1600. Free.
(A Wilson, MPS, FSA (Scot))*
Small private museum with collections of
everyday items from the past, displayed in the
'smiddy', the 'crofter's kitchen', and the
courtyard.

Corrieshalloch Gorge

213 Constabulary Garden
Map 5

*High Street, Nairn. 1 May-30 Sep, daily
1000-1800. Adult: 10p, child: 10p.
(Elizabeth, Countess Cawdor).*
A new small town garden featuring varieties of
shrubs.

214 Corgarff Castle
Map 7

*Off A939, 15m NW of Ballater. Opening
standard. Adult: 15p, child: 7p, group rates.
(AM)*
A 16th-century tower house, converted into a
garrison post and enclosed within a star-shaped
loopholed wall in 1748. The castle was burned in
1571 by Edom o' Gordon and the wife, family and
household of Alexander Forbes, the owner,
perished in the flames. (See also No 56.)

215 Corrieshalloch Gorge
Map 3

A835 at Braemore, 12m SSE of Ullapool. All times. Free. (NTS)
This spectacular gorge, 1m long and 200 feet deep, contains the Falls of Measach which plunge 150 feet. Suspension bridge viewpoint.

216 Corrimony Cairn
Map 5

At Glen Urquhart, 8m W of Drumnadrochit, Loch Ness. All times. Free. (AM)
This neolithic chambered cairn is surrounded by stone slabs, outside which is a circle of standing stones.

217 Corryvreckan Whirlpool
Map 10

Between the islands of Jura and Scarba.
This treacherous tide-race, very dangerous for small craft, covers an extensive area and may be seen from the north end of Jura or from Craignish Point. The noise can be heard from a considerable distance.

218 Corsock House Gardens
Map 17

Off A712, 10m N of Castle Douglas. Open in May, Sun 1430-1800, or by arrangement (tel: Corsock 250). Adult: 30p, child: 15p. (Mr F L Ingall)
Rhododendron and water garden, best seen mid April-mid June and in the autumn. House not open.

219 Coulter Motte
Map 16

At Coulter Railway Station, 2½m SW of Biggar (A702). Opening standard. Free. (AM)
Early mediaeval castle mound, originally moated and probably surmounted by a palisade enclosing a timber tower.

220 Coupar Angus Museum
Map 9

1 Cumberland Barracks, Coupar Angus. May-Sep. Tues-Sat 1300-1700. Free.
Exhibition of local history.

Cowane's Hospital: see No 533.

221 Craig Castle
Map 6

B9002 off A97, 12m SSW of Huntly (signposted). Open summer, by appointment only (contact Baroness of Craig, tel: Lumsden 202).
The oldest part of the castle is the keep, 60 feet high, which bears the date 1528, though possibly earlier. Of special interest are the courthouse and the coat of arms.

222 Craigcaffie Castle
Map 17

A77, 3½m NE of Stranraer. All reasonable times. Free.
The 13th-century foundations of this castle (a late 16th-century square tower) are said to have been laid on bags of wool, because of the boggy nature of the ground.

Craigellachie

223 Craigellachie Bridge
Map 6

Near A941, just N of Craigellachie, 12m SSE of Elgin.
One of Thomas Telford's most beautiful bridges. Begun in 1812, it carried the main road till 1973 when a new bridge was built alongside. It has a 150-feet main span of iron, cast in Wales, and two ornamental stone towers at each side.

224 Craigievar Castle
Map 7

N of junction of A974 and A980, 7m S of Alford. 1 May-30 Sep, daily (except Fri) 1400-1815. (Other days, parties of 12 or over, by arrangement, tel: Lumphanan 635). Adult: 80p, child: 40p. Grounds open all year, 0930-sunset.
This lovely castle was completed in 1626 by William Forbes of Aberdeen and has no later additions, its great tower standing alone. Its roof with turrets, crow-stepped gables, conical roofs, balustrading and corbelling contrasts remarkably with the severe lines of the rest of the building. Inside, there are superb, richly-moulded plaster ceilings.

225 Craignethan Castle
Map 16

2½m W of A72 at Crossford, 5m NW of Lanark. Opening standard. Adult: 15p, child: 7p, group rates. (AM)
This extensive and well-preserved ruin, chief stronghold of the Hamiltons who were supporters of Mary Queen of Scots, was repeatedly assailed by the Protestant party and partly dismantled by them in 1579. The oldest, central portion is a large tower house of an unusual and ornate design. Recent excavations have revealed possibly the earliest example in Britain of a *caponier*, a covered gun-looped passageway across a defensive ditch.

226 Craigston Castle
Map 6

Off B9105, 10m SE of Banff. By arrangement, tel: King Edward 228. (Mr Bruce Urquhart)
Seat of the Urquhart family since its building 1604-07. Can also be seen from the Aberdeen to Banff road.

227 Crail Museum
Map 9

62 Marketgate, Crail.
Opening in 1979 to house exhibits previously held in the Town House Museum.

228 Crail Tolbooth
Map 9

Marketgate, Crail.
The Tolbooth dates from the early 16th century, displaying a fish weather-vane, and a coat of arms dated 1602. In the striking Dutch Tower is a bell dated 1520, cast in Holland. There have been 18th and early 19th-century additions. In this picturesque fishing harbour and oldest Royal Burgh in the East Neuk of Fife, see also the Collegiate Church dating back to the 13th century, the Mercat Cross topped by a unicorn, and the attractive crow-stepped, red-tiled houses.

Crinan

229 Crarae Woodland Garden
Map 10

A83, 10m SW of Inveraray. Mar-Oct 0800-1800 daily, Adult: 40p, child: free.
(Sir Ilay Campbell of Succoth Bt)
Among the loveliest open to the public in Scotland, these gardens of Crarae Lodge, beside Loch Fyne and set in a Highland glen, are noted for rhododendrons, azaleas, conifers and ornamental shrubs.

230 Crathes Castle and Gardens
Map 7

Off A93, 3½m E of Banchory.
Castle: 1 May-30 Sep, Mon-Sat 1100-1715, Sun 1400-1715. Gardens: All year, daily 0930-dusk.
(Grounds): Car 60p May-Sep, other times free.
(Castle): Adult 75p, child 35p.
(Gardens): Adult 40p, child 20p. (NTS)
The double square tower of the castle dates from 1553 and the building, an outstanding example of a Scottish tower house, was completed in 1600. The notable interior includes the fascinating painted ceilings, dating from 1599, in the Chamber of the Nine Nobles, the Chamber of the Nine Muses, and the Green Lady's Room. The Queen Anne and Victorian wings, destroyed by fire in 1966, have been rebuilt and house the Visitor Centre. In the gardens with fine collections of trees and shrubs, yew hedges dating from 1702 enclose a series of small gardens.

231 Crathie Church
Map 7

Crathie, 8m W of Ballater. 1 Apr-31 Oct, Mon-Sat 1000-1500, Sun 1400-1800. Free. (Church of Scotland)
This small church, built in 1895, is attended by the Royal Family when in residence at Balmoral.

232 Crawford Centre for the Arts
Map 9

North Street, St Andrews. Gallery: All year, Mon-Sat 1000-1700, Sun 1400-1700. Gallery free.
New Arts Centre with exhibition galleries and drama studio.

233 Crichton Castle
Map 13

B6367, 7m SE of Dalkeith. Opening standard; closed Fri from Oct-May. Adult: 15p, child: 7p, group rates. (AM)
The keep dates from the 14th century, although today's ruins are mostly 15th/17th-century. This castle, elaborate in style, has an arcaded range, the upper frontage of which is wrought with faceted stonework, erected by the Earl of Bothwell in the 16th century. The little Collegiate Church, ½ mile north; dating from 1499 and still in use, is notable for its tower and barrel vaulting.

234 Crinan Canal
Map 10

Crinan to Ardrishaig, by Lochgilphead.
Constructed between 1793 and 1801 to carry ships from Loch Fyne to the Atlantic without rounding Kintyre. The nine-mile stretch of water with 15 locks is now almost entirely used by pleasure craft.

235 Croft House, Dunrossness
Map 1

At South Voe on unclassified road E of A970, 25m S of Lerwick, Shetland. May-Sep, daily 1000-1300, 1400-1700. Adult: 20p, child: 5p. (Shetland Islands Council)
This thatched croft complex comprising mid 19th-century croft house and steading have been carefully restored and all furnishings are authentic. There is a watermill nearby.

236 Croick Church
Map 3

On unclassified road up Strathcarron, 10m W of Ardgay. All reasonable times. Free.
A small Highland church, built by Telford, with remarkable inscriptions on the windows by crofters evicted in 1845.

237 Cross Kirk
Map 16

Peebles. Opening standard. Key from custodian in nearby house. Free. (AM)
The remains of a Trinitarian Friary, consisting of a nave and west tower. The foundations of the cloistered building have been laid bare.

Crossraguel Abbey

238 Crossraguel Abbey
Map 15

A77, 2m SW of Maybole. Opening standard. Adult: 15p, child: 7p, group rates. (AM)
A Cluniac monastery built in 1244 by the Earl of Carrick during the reign of Alexander II. The Abbey was inhabited by Benedictine monks from 1244 until the end of the 16th century, and the extensive remains are of high architectural distinction.

Croy Brae: see No 415.

239 Cruachan Hydro-Electric Power Station
Map 10

Off A85, 14m E of Oban. Easter-Oct, Mon-Fri 0930-1700, Jun-Aug, daily 0930-1700. Adult: 30p.
(North of Scotland Hydro Electricity Board)
In a vast cavern inside Ben Cruachan is a 400,000 kilowatt hydro-electric power station which utilises water pumped from Loch Awe to a reservoir 1,200 feet up the mountain. Visitor Centre, car park, guides and mini-bus tour.

240 Cruggleton Church and Castle
Map 17

Off B7063, 9m SSE of Wigtown. Summer months, any time. Church: keys from nearby farmer, Mr Fisher. Free.
The little church, just off the road, is Norman; the chancel arch doors and windows are 12th-century. An arch, the only remains of the castle, lies near the shore.

241 Robinson Crusoe Statue
Map 9

Lower Largo. All times. Free.
Statue to Alexander Selkirk (1676-1721) native of Largo, a sailor whose story of his time on Juan Fernandez Island is supposed to have suggested the Robinson Crusoe of Defoe.

242 Cullerlie Stone Circle
Map 7

Off A974, 1m S of Garlogie, 9m W of Aberdeen. All times. Free. (AM)
This stone circle of eight undressed boulders encloses an area on which eight small cairns were later constructed, probably of late second millennium BC.

243 Culloden Moor
Map 5

B9006, 5m E of Inverness. Site open all year. Visitor Centre, Good Friday-31 May and 1 Sep-mid Oct, Mon-Sat 0930-1830, Sun 1400-1830; 1 Jun-31 Aug, Mon-Sat 0930-2130, Sun 1400-1830. Visitor Centre (including audio-visual): Adult: 65p, child: 30p, group rates. (NTS)
Here Prince Charles Edward's cause was finally crushed at the battle on 16 April 1746. The battle lasted only 40 minutes; the Prince's army lost some 1,200 men, and the King's army 310. Features of interest include the Graves of the Clans, communal burial places with simple headstones bearing individual clan names alongside the main road; the great memorial cairn, erected in 1881; the Well of the Dead, a single stone with the inscription *The English were buried here*; Old Leanach farmhouse, now restored as a battle museum; and the huge Cumberland Stone from which the victorious Duke of Cumberland is said to have viewed the scene.

244 Culross Palace
Map 12

Culross, 7½m W of Dunfermline. Opening standard. Adult: 25p, child: 12p, group rates. (AM)
Culross, on the north shore of the River Forth, is a most remarkable example of a small town of the 16th and 17th centuries. Little changed in 300 years, it has been extensively restored. The small 'palace' was built between 1597 and 1611 by Sir George Bruce, who developed the sea-going trade in salt and coal from Culross. With crow-stepped gables and pantiled roofs, the 'palace' also has outstanding painted ceilings. Other buildings which must be seen include the Study (No 924), the Town House (No 958), the Ark and the Nunnery.

Culsh

245 Culsh Earth House
Map 7

Access by Culsh Farmhouse, near Tarland on B9119, 13m NE of Ballater. Opening standard. Free. (AM)
A well-preserved earth house of Iron Age date with roofing slabs intact over a large chamber and entrance.

246 Culzean Castle
Map 15

A719, 12m SSW of Ayr. 1 Apr-30 Sep, daily 1000-1730; 1-31 Oct, daily 1000-1600. Adult: £1 (Jul and Aug £1.20), child: 50p (Jul and Aug 60p), group rates. (NTS)
This splendid castle, one of Robert Adam's most notable creations, although built around an ancient tower of the Kennedys, dates mainly from 1777. Special features are the Round Drawing Room, the fine plaster ceilings and magnificent oval staircase. The Eisenhower Presentation explains the General's association with Culzean.

247 Culzean Country Park
Map 15

By Culzean Castle, A719, 12m SSW of Ayr. Grounds always open. Information centre, auditorium and exhibition Apr-30 Sep, daily 1000-1800; 1-31 Oct, daily 1000-1600. Pedestrians free; cars 60p; minibuses and caravans £1.50; coaches £4. (These charges apply 24 Mar-31 Oct only; vehicles except school coaches free other times). (NTS; Strathclyde Regional Council; Kyle and Carrick, Cunninghame, Cumnock and Doon Valley District Councils.)
In 1970 Culzean became the first country park in Scotland; in 1973 a Reception and Interpretation Centre with exhibition etc. was opened in the farm buildings designed by Robert Adam. The 565-acre grounds include a walled garden established in 1783, aviary, swan pond, camellia house and orangery. Ranger naturalist service with guided walks, talks and films in summer.

248 Cuween Hill Cairn
Map 1

A965, ½m S of Finstown, which is 6m WNW of Kirkwall. All reasonable times. Apply to key-keeper at nearby farmhouse. Free. (AM)
A low mound covering a megalithic passage tomb. Contained bones of men, dogs and oxen when discovered. Probably early second millennium BC.

249 Dalgairn House Garden
Map 9

Cupar. Jun-Aug, Sat and Sun 1400-1830. Adult: 20p, child: 10p. Car park: 10p. (Mr Roger Banks)
A unique 'shabby' garden with a fascinating collection of old-fashioned flowers, edible weeds and poisonous plants. Over 100 species are carefully labelled as to their uses.

Dean's

250 Dalkeith Arts Centre
Map 13

In centre of Dalkeith. All year, Mon Wed, Thur, Fri, Sat 1000-1530. Closed Tue and Sun. Free.
Gallery and exhibition area. Outdoor exhibition area for sculptures.

251 Dalkeith Park
Map 13

At E end of Dalkeith High Street, 7m S of Edinburgh on A68. Easter-end Oct, daily 1100-1800. Adult: 40p, child: 30p, group rates. (Duke of Buccleuch)
Woodland walks beside the river in the extensive grounds of Dalkeith Palace. Tunnel walk, adventure woodland play area, nature trails. 18th-century bridge and orangery.

252 Dalmeny Kirk
Map 13

Off A90, 7m W of Edinburgh. All year, daily. Free.
An attractive Romanesque church, built in the middle of the 12th century, with the Rosebery Aisle to the North, built in 1671 by Sir Archibald Primrose.

253 David Marshall Lodge
Map 8

Off A821, 1m N of Aberfoyle. Mid Mar-mid Oct, daily 1100-1900: 10p per car. (FC)
Visitor Centre and starting point for walks in the Queen Elizabeth Forest Park. It commands wide views over the upper Forth Valley to the Menteith Hills, Campsie Fells and Ben Lomond.
(See also No 23.)

254 Dawyck House Gardens
Map 16

B712, 8m SW of Peebles. Easter-end Sep, daily 1200-1700. Adult: 30p, child: 10p. Dogs on lead only. (Lt Col A N Balfour of Dawyck).
Rare trees, shrubs, rhododendrons and narcissi, among woodland walks. In the woods is Dawyck Chapel, designed by William Burn.

255 Dean Castle
Map 15

Dean Road, off Glasgow Road, Kilmarnock. Mid-May, mid-Sep, Mon-Fri 1400-1700, Sat and Sun 1000-1700 (and by arrangement, tel: Kilmarnock 34587). Free.
14th-century fortified keep and 15th-century palace, the ancestral home of the Boyd family. It contains an outstanding collection of mediaeval arms, armour, tapestries and musical instruments. Garden and nature trail.

256 The Dean's House
Map 8

Cathedral Square, Dunblane. Jun-Sept, Mon-Sat 1030-1230, 1430-1630. Donation box.
Former dwelling house, built 1624, of Dean James Pearson. There is also a cathedral museum and a fine library.

Deer

257 Deer Abbey
Map 6

*At Old Deer, B9029, off A950, 12m W of
Peterhead. Opening standard. Apr-Sep only.
Adult: 15p, child: 7p, group rates. (AM)*
Rather scant remains of a Cistercian monastery
founded in 1219.

Deer Museum: see Nos 452 and 956.

258 Delgatie Castle
Map 6

*Off A947, 2m E of Turriff. By arrangement,
tel: Turriff 3479 (Capt Hay of Hayfield).
Adult: 50p, child: 30p.*
Tower house home of the Hays of Delgatie
dating back to the 12th century with additions up
to the 17th century. Its contents include pictures
and arms; the notable painted ceilings were
installed c 1590. Mary Queen of Scots stayed
here for three days in 1562; a portrait hangs in
the room she used. Turnpike stair of 97 steps.

259 Deskford Church
Map 6

*Off B9018, 5m S of Cullen. Opening standard.
Free. (AM)*
This ruined building includes a rich carving which
bears an inscription telling that *this present
lovable work of sacrament house* was provided
by Alexander Ogilvy of Deskford in 1551.

260 Devil's Beef Tub
Map 16

A701, 6m N of Moffat.
A huge, spectacular hollow among the hills, at
the head of Annandale. In the swirling mists of
this out-of-the-way retreat Border reivers hid
cattle 'lifted' in their raids.

261 Devil's Mill and Caldron Linn
Map 12

*Off A823 at Rumbling Bridge. Free. All
reasonable times.*
Rumbling Bridge gives access to several
spectacular and picturesque gorges and falls.
The Devil's Mill and Caldron Linn are the best
known falls along the Devon River. The river is
spanned by two bridges here; one dates from
1713 and the other from 1816.

Devorgilla's Bridge: see No 761.

262 Dick Institute
Map 15

*Elmbank Avenue, off London Road, Kilmarnock.
Apr-Sep, Mon, Tue, Thu, Fri 1000-2000,
Wed and Sat 1000-1700; Oct-Mar, Mon-Sat
1000-1700. Free.*
The museum has an important collection of
geological specimens, local archaeology,
Scottish broad swords, firearms and natural
history. The Art Gallery has frequently changing
exhibitions.

Dornoch

263 Dingwall Town House
Map 3

Dingwall town centre. All times. Free.
Museum of local history in the Town House,
which dates from 1730. There is a special exhibit
of General Sir Hector MacDonald (1853-1903),
born near Dingwall, and recalling his
distinguished military career.

264 Dirleton Castle
Map 14

*A198, 7m W of North Berwick. Opening
standard. Adult: 25p, child: 12p, group rates.
(AM)*
Near the wide village green of Dirleton,
these beautiful ruins date back to 1225 with
15th/17th-century additions. The castle had an
eventful history from its first siege by Edward I
in 1298 until its destruction in 1650. The
'clustered' donjon dates from the 13th century
and the garden encloses a 17th-century bowling
green surrounded by yews.

265 Dogton Stone
Map 13

*Off B922, 5m NW of Kirkcaldy. All reasonable
times. Free. Entry by Dogton Farmhouse. (AM)*
An ancient Celtic Cross with traces of animal and
figure sculpture.

266 Dollar Glen
Map 12

Off A91, above the town. All times. Free. (NTS)
The wooded glen leads up to Castle Campbell,
which is set romantically above the deep ravines
of the glen and between the Burn of Sorrow and
the Burn of Care. The glen has a variety of steep
paths and bridges through spectacular woodland
scenery. (See also No 165.)

267 Dornoch Cathedral
Map 3

In Dornoch. All year, 0900-dusk. Free.
Founded 1224 by Gilbert, Archdeacon of Moray
and Bishop of Caithness, this little cathedral was
partially destroyed by fire in 1570, restored in the
17th century, in 1835-37, and again in 1924. The
fine 13th-century stonework is still to be seen.

268 Dornoch Craft Centre
Map 3

*Town Jail. All year, Mon-Fri 0900-1300,
1400-1700. Usually free; occasional charge for
special exhibitions.*
Weaving of tartans on Hattersley power looms,
knitting and soft toy making.

Doune

269 Doune Castle
Map 8

Off A84 at Doune, 8m NW of Stirling. Apr-Oct daily (excl Thu, Apr and Oct) 1000-1630. June-Aug 1000-1800. Adult: 40p, child: 20p. (Earl of Moray)

Splendid ruins of one of the best preserved mediaeval castles in Scotland, built late 14th or early 15th century by the Regent Albany. After his execution in 1424 it came into the hands of the Stuarts of Doune, Earls of Moray, in the 16th century, and the 'Bonnie Earl of Moray' lived here before his murder in 1592. The bridge in the village was built in 1535 by Robert Spittal, James IV's tailor, to spite the ferryman who had refused him a passage.

270 Doune Motor Museum
Map 8

Off A84, 1m from Doune village, adjacent to Doune Park Gardens. Apr-Oct 1000-1700, June-Aug 1000-1800. Adult: 60p, child (accompanied): free, (unaccompanied): 25p, group rates.
(Earl of Moray)

The Earl of Moray's collection of vintage and post-vintage cars.

271 Doune Park Gardens
Map 8

Off A84, 1½m NW of Doune. Apr-Oct 1000-1700, June-Aug 1000-1800. Adult: 50p, child (accompanied): free, (unaccompanied): 20p, group rates.
(Earl of Moray)

These 60 acres include an extensive walled garden, a pinetum dating from the 1860's and woodland walks. Rhododendrons, azaleas and flowering shrubs are features.

272 Dounreay Nuclear Power Development Establishment
Map 3

Dounreay, 10m W of Thurso. May-Sep, daily 0900-1600. Free. No dogs. Tours (free) by arrangement with Tourist Information Centre, Riverside, Thurso.
(United Kingdom Atomic Energy Authority)

An interesting exhibition giving visitors a general conception of the activities and works taking place at the establishment. Some conducted tours of the Prototype Fast Reactor.

273 Drochil Castle
Map 16

Off A72. 6m W of Peebles. By arrangement, tel: Aberlady 201. (Earl of Wemyss and March)
Built by James Douglas, Earl of Morton, who was executed in 1581. The castle was never completed and is now part of Drochil farm steading.

274 Drum Castle
Map 7

Off A93, 10m WSW of Aberdeen.
1 May-30 Sep, Mon-Sat 1100-1715, Sun
1400-1715. Adult: 75p, child: 35p. Grounds
open all year, 0930-sunset. (NTS)
A massive granite tower built towards the end of
the 13th century adjoins a mansion of 1619. The
Royal Forest of Drum was conferred in 1323 by
Robert the Bruce on his armour-bearer and
clerk-register, William de Irvine. The family
connection remained unbroken until the death of
Mr H Q Forbes-Irvine in 1975. The house stands
in pleasant grounds with lawns, rare trees and
shrubs, and inside are antique furniture and
silver, family portraits and relics.

275 Drumcoltran Tower
Map 18

Off A711, 8m SW of Dumfries. Opening
standard, apply key-keeper. Free (AM)
Situated among farm buildings, this is a good
example of a Scottish tower house of about the
mid-16th century, simple and severe.

276 Drumlanrig Castle
Map 18

Off A76, 3m N of Thornhill, Dumfriesshire. Daily
30 Apr-28 Aug; (castle) 1400-1800, (grounds)
1200-1800. Adult: 80p, child: 40p, group rates.
(Duke of Buccleuch).
Unique example of late 17th-century Scottish
architecture in local pink sandstone, built on the
site of earlier Douglas strongholds. Set in
parkland ringed by the wild Dumfriesshire hills.
Louis XIV furniture, and paintings by Rembrandt,
Holbein, Murillo, Ruysdael. Adventure woodland
play area and nature trail.

277 Druminnor Castle
Map 6

Off A97, 1m E of Rhynie, 10m S of Huntly.
28 May-31 Aug, Sun 1430-1730. Adult: 40p,
child: 20p. (A G D Forbes)
Restored 15th-century 'palace house', historic
home of the chiefs of the Forbes clan. There are
some fine rooms, mediaeval inscriptions and a
museum.

278 Drummond Castle Gardens
Map 8

Off A8022, 2½m S of Crieff. Apr-Oct, Wed and
Sun 1400-1800. Adult: 40p, child: 20p.
(Earl of Ancaster).
The oldest tower, now an armoury, dates from
the 15th century, but most of the old castle once
attacked by Cromwell was dismantled in 1745.
There is a multiple sundial dated 1630 and
notable formal Italian garden.

279 Drumtrodden
Map 17

Off A714, 8m SSW of Wigtown. All times. Free.
(AM)
A group of cup-and-ring markings of Bronze Age
date on a natural rock face. 400 yards south is an
alignment of three adjacent stones.

Dryburgh

280 Dryburgh Abbey
Map 16

Off A68, 6m SE of Melrose. Opening standard. Adult: 25p, child: 12p, group rates. (AM)
One of the four famous Border abbeys, founded in the reign of David I by Hugh de Morville, Constable of Scotland. Though little save the transepts has been spared of the church itself, the cloister buildings have survived in a more complete state than in any other Scottish monastery, except Iona and Inchcolm (see Nos 586 and 570). Much of the existing remains are 12th/13th century. Sir Walter Scott is buried in the church.

281 Dryhope Tower
Map 16

Off A708 near St Mary's Loch, 15m W of Selkirk. All reasonable times. Free.
A stout little tower originally four storeys high, rebuilt c 1600. Birthplace of Mary Scott, *The Flower of Yarrow* who married the freebooter Auld Wat of Harden, 1576—ancestors Sir Walter Scott was proud to claim.

282 Duart Castle
Map 4

Off A849, on E point of Mull. May-Sep, Mon-Fri 1030-1800; Jul and Aug, daily 1030-1800, Sun 1430-1800. Adult: 50p, child: 25p. (Lord Maclean K.T.)
The keep, dominating the Sound of Mull, was built in the 13th century. A royal charter of 1390 confirmed the lands, including Duart, to the Macleans. The clan supported the Stuarts and the castle, extended in 1633, was taken and ruined by the Duke of Argyll in 1691. During the 1745 Rising, Sir Hector Maclean of Duart was imprisoned in the Tower of London and his estate forfeited, not to be recovered until 1911 when Sir Fitzroy Maclean restored it.

283 Duff House
Map 6

At Banff. Opening standard, Apr-Sep only. Adult: 15p, child: 7p, group rates. (AM)
Although incomplete, William Adam's splendid and richly detailed mansion is among the finest works of Georgian baroque architecture in Britain. There is an interpretative exhibition.

284 Dufftown Museum
Map 6

The Tower, The Square, Dufftown. Daily, May-Sept 1000-1300, 1400-1700, 1800-1900. Free.
Exhibition of local photographs, whisky making and civic regalia. There are relics of Mortlach Church.

285 Duffus Castle
Map 3

Off B9012, 4m NW of Elgin. Opening standard.
Free; apply to key-keeper. (AM)
Massive ruins of a fine motte and bailey castle,
surrounded by a moat still entire and water-filled.
A fine 14th-century tower crowns the Norman
motte. The original seat of the de Moravia family,
the Murrays, now represented by the dukedoms
of Atholl and Sutherland.

286 Dumbarton Castle
Map 11

Dumbarton, off A814 on Dumbarton Rock.
Opening standard. Adult: 20p, child: 10p, group
rates. (AM)
Though mainly modern barracks, a dungeon, a
12th-century gateway and a sundial gifted by
Mary Queen of Scots are preserved. It was from
Dumbarton that Queen Mary left for France in
1548, at the age of five.

287 Dumfries Museum
Map 18

The Observatory, Dumfries. Apr-Sep,
Mon and Wed to Sat, 1000-1300, 1400-1700,
Sun 1400-1700; Oct-Mar, Mon and Wed-Sat
only 1000-1300, 1400-1700. Free.
(Nithsdale District Council)
This regional museum for the Solway area has
recently been refurbished and contains a wide
variety of interesting exhibits. It is based on an
18th-century windmill and has a camera
obscura.

Dumgoyne Distillery: see No 515

Duart Castle

288 Dun Carloway Broch
Map 2

A858, 15m WNW of Stornoway, Isle of Lewis.
Opening standard. Free. (AM)
One of the best preserved Iron Age broch towers
in the Western Isles. Still standing about 30 feet
high.

289 Dun Dornadilla Broch
Map 3

20m N of Lairg. A836, then on Loch Hope road.
All times. Free. (AM)
A notable example of a prehistoric broch.

Dun Telve and Dun Troddan: see No 509.

290 Dunadd Fort
Map 10

W of A816, 4m NNW of Lochgilphead. All reasonable times. Free. (AM)
On an isolated once-fortified hillock, Dunadd was once the site of the ancient capital of Dalriada (c 500-800), from which the Celtic Kingdom of Scotland sprang. On its highest rock is carved a fine figure of a boar and the sign of a footprint; this is probably where the early kings were invested with royal power.

Dunakin: see No 171.

291 Dunaverty Rock
Map 10

At Southend, dominating beach and golf course. All times. Free.
Formerly the site of Dunaverty Castle, a Macdonald stronghold. In 1647, about 300 people were put to death there by Covenanters under General Leslie. The rock is known locally as 'Blood Rock'.

292 Dunblane Cathedral
Map 8

In Dunblane, A9, 6m N of Stirling. Opening standard, except summer when 1400-1700 on Sun. Free. (AM)
The existing building dates mainly from the 13th century. The nave was unroofed after the Reformation, but the whole building was restored in 1892-95.

Dunblane Cathedral Museum: see The Dean's House, No 256.

Henry Duncan Cottage Museum

293 Henry Duncan Cottage Museum
Map 18

In Ruthwell, 6½m W of Annan. All year; custodian on call at all reasonable times. Free. (Trustee Savings Bank of South of Scotland)
The cottage was the first Savings Bank, founded by Dr Henry Duncan in 1810. The museum with its interesting exhibition, is a mine of information abut the early days of the Savings Bank movement.

294 Duncansby Head
Map 3

The NE point of mainland Scotland, 18m N of Wick.
The lighthouse on Duncansby Head commands a fine view of Orkney, the Pentland Skerries, and the headlands of the east coast. A little to the south are the three Duncansby Stacks, huge stone 'needles' in the sea. The sandstone cliffs are severed by great deep gashes (geos) running into the land. One of these is bridged by a natural arch.

295 Dundee, Barrack Street Museum
Map 9

City centre. All year, Mon-Sat 1000-1700. Free. (City of Dundee District Council).
A fine collection illustrating the history of old Dundee, with particular sections devoted to ships and shipping, and schools and education.

296 Dundee, Bonar Hall
Map 9

University of Dundee, near Park Place, between Hawkhill and Nethergate. All year, Mon-Fri 0900-1700. Free.
Auditorium and galleries with changing exhibitions of pictures and photographs from the University collection, and local history.

297 Dundee, Broughty Castle Museum
Map 9

4m E of city centre. 1000-1730, Sun, Jun-Sep daily except Fri 1400-1700. Free.
(City of Dundee District Council)
Many whaling relics from Dundee, formerly an important whaling base, including harpoons, darts, knives, axes, boat models and scrimshaw. Also displays relating to the history of the Castle, Broughty Ferry and Monifieth; arms and armour; and the ecology of the Tay.

298 Dundee, Camperdown
Map 9

Off A923, near junction with A972, 3m NW of city centre.
A mansion of c 1829 for the 1st Earl of Camperdown, son of Admiral Lord Duncan, victor of the Battle of Camperdown, 1797. Part of the house holds the Spalding Golf Museum (see No 305). There is a Field Study Centre and a wide range of outdoor activities in the extensive parkland.

299 Dundee, Central Museum and Art Gallery
Map 9

Albert Square. Weekdays, 1000-1730. Free.
(City of Dundee District Council)
Contains regional collections of archaeological and other material; Flemish, Dutch, French and British paintings, particularly the Scottish Schools.

300 Dundee, Claypotts Castle
Map 9

*S of A92, 3m E of city centre. Opening standard,
Adult: 15p, child: 7p, group rates. (AM)*
Now in suburban surroundings, this is one of the
most complete of old tower houses, with many
turrets. It bears the dates 1569 and 1588 and
was forfeited by the Douglases in 1689.

301 Dundee, Mills Observatory
Map 9

*Balgay Hill, north side of the city.
Apr-Sep, Mon-Fri 1400-2100, Sat 1400-1700;
Oct-Mar, Mon-Fri 1400-2200, Sat 1400-1600
(weather permitting). Adult: 5p, child: 2p,
(City of Dundee District Council)*
A public astronomical observatory with
telescopes, display apparatus, lecture room
fitted with projection equipment, and small
planetarium.

302 Dundee, Old Steeple
Map 9

*Kirkstile, Nethergate. Mon-Thu and Sat,
1300-1700. Sun 1400-1700. Adult: 5p, child: 2p,
family: 8p. (City of Dundee District Council)*
The Old Steeple, or St Mary's Tower, is the
oldest part of the City Churches in the centre of
Dundee. The building, which once comprised
four churches, was largely destroyed by fire in
1871; but the steeple, 156 feet high and built in
the 15th century, survived and is considered one
of the finest of its type in Scotland. Displays
relating to the history of the Tower and the city
churches, stained-glass windows, bell ringing
and the ancient Royalty.

303 Dundee, Orchar Gallery
Map 9

*Beach Crescent, Broughty Ferry. All year,
Sat and Sun 1400-1700. Free.*
The gallery displays paintings and watercolours,
mostly by Scottish artists of the 19th century, and
includes 36 etchings by Whistler.

304 Dundee Repertory Theatre
Map 9

Lochee Road. Sep-Jun.
Theatre housed in converted church, built in
1840, now a listed building.

305 Dundee, Spalding Golf Museum
Map 9

At Camperdown House, off A923, 3m NW of city centre. June-Sept, Mon-Sat 1300-1700 (closed Fri); Sun 1400-1700. Free.
A fine collection of clubs, illustrations and equipment showing the development of golf to the present day.

306 Dundee, Unicorn
Map 9

Victoria Dock, just E of Tay Road Bridge. Apr-Oct, Mon-Thu 1100-1300, 1400-1700. Sat 1100-1300, 1400-1700. Adult: 25p, child: 15p. (The Unicorn Preservation Society)
The *Unicorn* is a 46-gun wooden frigate now in the course of restoration. She was launched at Chatham in 1824 and is Britain's oldest ship afloat. Displays on board of the history of the *Unicorn*, ship-building and the Royal Navy.

307 Dundee, Wishart Arch
Map 9

East Port. All times. Free.
The only remaining town gate in Dundee, dating back to the 16th century. George Wishart, the Reformation leader (1513-46), is said to have preached from here during the Plague of 1544.

308 Dundonald Castle
Map 15

At Dundonald, 4½m SW of Kilmarnock, off A759. Not open to the public; may be viewed from the outside. (AM)
Most of the tower and much of the barmkin wall survive of this castle, standing on an isolated hill. King Robert II, the first Stuart king, died here in 1390, as did his son Robert III in 1406.

309 Dundrennan Abbey
Map 17

A711, 7m SE of Kirkcudbright. Opening standard. Adult: 20p. child: 10p, group rates. (AM)
A Cistercian house founded in 1142 whose ruins include much late Norman and transitional work. Here it is believed Mary Queen of Scots spent her last night in Scotland, 15 May 1568.

310 Dunfermline Abbey
Map 13

Monastery Street, Dunfermline. Apr-Sep, Mon-Sat 0930-1200, 1300-1700, Sun 1400-1600. Oct-Mar, Mon-Sat 0930-1200, 1300-1600, Sun 1400-1600. Free.
This great Benedictine house owes its foundation to Queen Margaret, wife of Malcolm Canmore (1057-93) and the foundations of her modest church remain beneath the present nave, a splendid piece of late Norman work. At the east end are the remains of St Margaret's shrine, dating from the 13th century. Robert the Bruce is buried in the choir, his grave marked by a modern brass. Of the monastic buildings, the ruins of the refectory, pend and guest-house still remain. The guest-house was later reconstructed as a royal palace, and here Charles I was born.

311 Dunfermline Museum
Map 13

Viewfield, Dunfermline. Jun-Sep, Mon-Sat (exc Tue) 1100-1700, Sun 1300-1700, Oct-May, Wed-Sat, 1100-1700, Sun 1300-1700. Free. (Dunfermline District Council)
The museum, housed in a Victorian villa, has an interesting local history collection, particularly of weaving and linen damask articles, the industry that made Dunfermline famous. A new natural history room has been established and special exhibitions are on show regularly.

312 Dunglass Collegiate Church
Map 14

On estate road, W of A1 (sign-posted Bilsdean) 1m N of Cockburnspath. All reasonable times. Free. (AM)
Founded in 1450, the church consists of nave, choir, transepts, sacristy and a central tower; richly embellished interior, in an attractive estate setting.

313 Dunimarle Castle
Map 12

N shore of the Forth, on unclassified road ¼m W of Culross. Apr-Oct, Wed, Thu, Sat and Sun, 1400-1800. Adult: 20p, child: 10p, group rates. (Erskine of Torrie Institute)
The 19th-century castle contains a museum and notable paintings. Also pleasant gardens and grounds.

314 Dunkeld Bridge
Map 8

Over the River Tay at Dunkeld. All times, Free.
One of Thomas Telford's finest bridges, built in 1809.

315 Dunkeld Cathedral
Map 8

High Street, Dunkeld, 15m NNW of Perth. Opening standard. Free. (AM)
Founded in the 9th century, this cathedral is in a beautiful setting by the Tay. The choir has been restored and is in use as the parish church. The nave and the great north-west tower date from the 15th century.

316 Dunkeld Little Houses
Map 8

Dunkeld, 15m NNW of Perth. Visitor Centre: Good Friday-30 Sep, Mon-Sat 1000-1800, Sun 1400-1800. Free.
The houses date from the rebuilding of the town after the Battle of Dunkeld, 1689. Charmingly restored by NTS and Perth County Council as private homes, they are not open to the public but may be seen from the outside and information on them gained from the Visitor Centre, and audio-visual presentation at Dunkeld.

317 John Dunlop Plaque
Map 15

2m E of Irvine on A71 at Dreghorn. All times. Free.
John B Dunlop (1840-1921), born at Dreghorn, was a veterinary surgeon, and is remembered particularly for his invention of the pneumatic tyre in 1888.

318 Dunmore Pineapple
Map 12

N of Airth, 7m E of Stirling off A905, then B9124.
Viewed from the outside only.
(NTS, leased to the Landmark Trust)
This curious structure, built as a 'garden conceit'
and shaped like a pineapple, stands in the
grounds of Dunmore Park, and bears the date
1761. It is the focal point of the garden and is
available for holiday and other short lets.

319 Dunnet Head
Map 3

B855, 12m NE of Thurso.
This bold promontory of sandstone rising to
417 feet is the northernmost point of the Scottish
mainland with magnificent views across the
Pentland Firth to Orkney and a great part of the
north coast to Ben Loyal and Ben Hope. The
windows of the lighthouse are sometimes broken
by stones hurled up by the winter seas.

320 Dunnottar Castle
Map 7

Off A92, S of Stonehaven. All year,
Mon-Sat 0900-1800, Sun 1400-1700. Closed
Fri, Oct-Apr. Adult: 30p, child: 10p, group rates.
(Dickinson Trust Ltd)
An impressive ruined fortress on a rocky cliff
160 feet above the sea, a stronghold of the Earls
Marischal of Scotland from the 14th century.
Montrose besieged it in 1645. During the
Commonwealth wars, the Scottish regalia were
hidden here for safety. Cromwell's troops
occupied the castle but in 1652 this treasure was
smuggled out by the wife of the minister at
Kinneff, 7 miles south, and hidden under the
pulpit in his church. (See also No 619.)

321 Dunrobin Castle
Map 3

Off A9, 12½m NNE of Dornoch.
May-Sep, Mon-Sat 1030-1730, Sun 1300-1730.
Adult: 90p, child: 50p, group rates.
(Countess of Sutherland).
Magnificently set in a great park overlooking the
sea, Dunrobin Castle was originally a square
keep built about 1275 by Robert, Earl of
Sutherland, from whom it got its name Dun
Robin. For centuries this was the seat of the
Earls and Dukes of Sutherland. The present
outward appearance results from extensive
changes made in 1856. Fine paintings are
among the miscellany of items to be seen.

322 Dunsgiath Castle
Map 4

At Tokavaig, on unclassified road 20m SSW of Broadford, Isle of Skye. All reasonable times. Free.
Well-preserved ruins of a former Macdonald stronghold.

323 Dunskey Castle
Map 17

On cliff, 1m S of Portpatrick. Free. (Mr E S Orr Ewing).
Ruined 15th-century castle. Great care should be taken on the cliffs.

324 Dunstaffnage Castle
Map 4

Off A85, 4m N of Oban. Opening standard. Free. (AM)
A fine, well-preserved example of a 13th-century castle with curtain wall and round towers.

325 Dunvegan Castle
Map 4

Dunvegan, Isle of Skye. Easter-mid Oct, 1400-1700. (Jun-Sep, 1030-1700). Closed Sun. Adult: 60p, child: 30p, group rates. (J Macleod of Macleod)
Historic stronghold of the Clan Macleod, set on the sea loch of Dunvegan, still the home after 700 years of the Chiefs of Macleod. Possessions on view, books, pictures, arms and treasured relics, trace the history of the family and clan from the days of their Norse ancestry through thirty generations to the present day. Boat trips from the castle jetty to the seal colony.

326 Durness Old Church
Map 3

At Balnakeil, ½m W of Durness, near Craft Village. All reasonable times. Free.
Built in 1619, now a ruin.

327 Dwarfie Stane
Map 1

On island of Hoy, Orkney. All times. Free. (AM)
A huge block of sandstone in which a burial chamber has been quarried. No other tomb of this type is known in the British Isles. Probably c 2000-1600 BC.

328 Dyce Symbol Stones
Map 7

At Dyce Old Church, 5m NW of Aberdeen. All reasonable times. Free. (AM)
Two fine examples of Pictish symbol stones.

329 Eagle Stone
Map 5

By A834 NE of Strathpeffer. All reasonable times. Free.
An eagle is the crest of Clan Munro and the stone commemorates a successful action by the Munros against the Macdonalds in 1411. The ancient seer, Brahan, foretold that ships would anchor to the stone if it fell three times. It has fallen twice, but is now well protected.

Eassie

330 Earl Patrick's Palace and Bishop's Palace
Map 1

Kirkwall, Orkney. (Both) Opening standard.
Adult: 15p, child: 7p, group rates. (AM)
Earl Patrick's Palace has been described as *the*
most mature and accomplished piece of
Renaissance architecture left in Scotland; it was
built in 1607. The Bishop's Palace nearby dates
back to the 13th century, with a 16th-century
round tower.

331 Earl's Palace, Birsay
Map 1

At Birsay, N end of Mainland, 11m N of
Stromness, Orkney. All times. (AM)
The impressive remains of the palace built in the
16th century by the Earls of Orkney.

332 Eas Coul Aulin
Map 3

At the head of Loch Glencoul, 3m W of A894.
The tallest waterfall in Britain, dropping 658 feet
(200 metres). There are occasional cruises to the
waterfall and it may also be seen from the
Kylesku Ferry.

333 Eassie Sculptured Stone
Map 9

In Eassie Kirkyard, 7m WSW of Forfar.
All reasonable times. Free. (AM)
A fine example of an early Christian monument,
elaborately carved.

Eden

334 Eden Castle
Map 6

Off A947, 5½m S of Banff. All reasonable times. Free.
The ruin of the family home (built 1676) of the Nicholases. A reputed reason for its downfall is that the wife of a tenant asked the laird to control her wayward son, which he did by drowning him in the nearby river, and was subsequently cursed.

335 Eden Court Theatre
Map 5

Bishops Road, Inverness.
An 800-seat multi-purpose theatre, conference centre and art gallery, completed in 1976, on the banks of the River Ness. Part of the complex is the 19th-century house built by Bishop Eden. There is a wide variety of shows and exhibitions throughout the year.

336 Edinburgh, Acheson House
Map 13

Canongate, Royal Mile. All year. Daily except Sun, 1000-1700. Free.
A mansion of 1633-34 entered through a small courtyard and now the Scottish Craft Centre, which shows and sells the work of Scotland's leading craftsmen, including pottery, weaving, silver, woodwork, textiles, hand-crafted glass and jewellery.

337 Edinburgh, Alexander Graham Bell Plaque
Map 13

16 South Charlotte Street. All times. Free.
Plaque commemorating the birthplace of Alexander Graham Bell (1847-1922), inventor of the telephone.

338 Edinburgh, Bəːclay Church
Map 13

Bruntsfield Place. All reasonable times. Free.
A remarkable church begun in 1861 and considered to be one of the finest works of F. T. Pilkington.

339 Edinburgh, Braidwood and Rushbrook Fire Museum
Map 13

McDonald Road, off Leith Walk. Visits by arrangement with Fire Brigade Headquarters, (tel: 031-229 7222). Free.
(Lothian & Borders Fire Brigade)
Guided tours round the museum, with its collection of old uniforms, equipment and engines, subject to the availability of a Fireman Guide.

340 Edinburgh Brass Rubbing Centre
Map 13

Canongate Tolbooth, Royal Mile. Apr-Dec, Monday to Saturday, 1000-1700. Admission: free.
A charge is made for every rubbing, which includes cost of materials and a royalty to the churches where applicable.
Rubbings of the brass commemorating Robert the Bruce and the Burghead Bull, a Pictish incised stone c AD 700 are among the selection available. Instruction and materials supplied.

Edinburgh Castle

341 Edinburgh, Calton Hill
Map 13

Off Regent Road. (Edinburgh District Council) 350 feet above sea level, with magnificent views. The monumental collection on top includes a part-reproduction of the Parthenon, the 120-feet-high Nelson Monument of 1806-16 (Apr-Sep, Mon-Sat 1000-1800; Oct-Mar, Mon-Sat 1000-1500; Adult: 20p) and the old Observatory buildings of 1774 and 1818 (Fri from 2000 or by arrangement with Mr G Taylor, 121 Mayfield Rd., Edinburgh.

Edinburgh, Camera Obscura: see No 376.

342 Edinburgh, Canongate Kirk
Map 13

On the Canongate, Royal Mile. Open on request; apply the Manse, Reid's Court near the church.
The church, built by order of James VII and II in 1688, is the Parish Church of the Canongate and also the Kirk of Holyroodhouse and Edinburgh Castle. The church silver dates from 1611. Restored in 1951, the church contains much heraldry. The burial ground contains the graves of Adam Smith, the economist, 'Clarinda', friend of Robert Burns, and Robert Fergusson, the poet.

343 Edinburgh, Canongate Tolbooth
Map 13

Canongate, Royal Mile. Jun-Sep, weekdays 1000-1800; Oct-May, weekdays 1000-1700; Sun during Festival 1400-1700. Free.
Built in 1591 with outside stair and a turreted tower, this is now a museum including a collection of Highland dress and tartans. Temporary exhibitions are held throughout the year.

344 Edinburgh Castle
Map 13

Castle Rock, top of the Royal Mile. May-Oct 0930-1800, Sun 1100-1800; Nov-Apr 0930-1705, Sun 1230-1620. War Memorial and precincts: free. Museum and historic apartments: Adult: 40p (1 May-31 Oct); 20p (1 Nov-30 Apr); child: 20p (1 May-31 Oct); 12p (1 Nov-30 Apr).
One of the most famous castles in the world, whose battlements overlook the Esplanade where the floodlit Military Tattoo is staged, late August to early September. Edinburgh Castle stands on a rock which has been a fortress from time immemorial. The oldest part of the buildings which make up the castle is Queen Margaret's

Chapel, built in the 11th century. In addition to the Great Hall built by James IV, with fine timbered roof, and the Old Palace, which houses the Regalia of Scotland and the Military Museum, the castle also holds the Scottish National War Memorial, opened in 1927.

Edinburgh, Charlotte Square: see No 351.

345 Edinburgh, Craigmillar Castle
Map 13

A68, 3½m SW of city centre. Opening standard. Adult: 20p, child: 10p, group rates. (AM)
Imposing ruins of a massive 14th-century keep enclosed in the early 15th century by an embattled curtain wall; within are the remains of the stately ranges of apartments dating from the 16th and 17th centuries. The castle was burnt by Hertford in 1544. There are strong connections with Mary Queen of Scots, who frequently stayed here. While she was in residence in 1566 the plot to murder Darnley was forged.

346 Edinburgh, Cramond
Map 13

5m NW of city centre, on the shores of the Firth of Forth.
This picturesque 18th-century village is situated at the mouth of the River Almond. See particularly the Roman fort and mediaeval tower, the kirk, kirkyard and manse, the old schoolhouse and the iron mills. Conducted walks around the village start from Cramond Kirk (Jun-Sep, Sun, 1500, free).

347 Edinburgh Crystal Works
Map 13

Eastfield, Penicuik. By arrangement, tel: Penicuik 72244. Mon-Thu 1400 & 1415. Free.
Demonstration of the production of high-grade crystal.

Edinburgh, Dean Village

348 Edinburgh, Dean Village
Map 13

Bell's Brae, off Queensferry Street, on Water of Leith.
There was grain milling in this notable 'village' of Edinburgh for over 800 years. The view downstream through the high arches of Dean Bridge is among the most picturesque in the city. A walk along the waterside leads to St Bernard's Well, an old mineral source (open by arrangement, tel: 031-557 1415).

349 Edinburgh, Richard Demarco Gallery
Map 13

61 High Street. All year, Tue-Sat 1000-1800. Free. (Richard Demarco)
Continuous art exhibitions and varying theatre programmes.

350 Edinburgh, Fruit Market Gallery
Map 13

29 Market Street. All year. Mon-Sat 1000-1730. Free. (City of Edinburgh)
The gallery has changing exhibitions throughout the year, including photos, sculptures, paintings etc. (See also Nos 373 & 380.)

351 Edinburgh, Georgian House
Map 13

No 7 Charlotte Square. Good Friday-26 Oct, Mon-Sat 1000-1700, Sun 1400-1700; 1 Nov-31 Jan, Sat 1000-1630, Sun 1400-1630. Closed 20/21 and 27/28 Dec and Feb and Mar. Adult: 75p, child 35p. (NTS)
The lower floors have been furnished as they might have been by their first owners, showing the domestic surroundings and reflecting the social conditions of that age. Charlotte Square itself was built at the end of the 18th century and is one of the most outstanding examples of its period in Europe. Bute House, said to be Robert Adam's masterpiece, is the official residence of the Secretary of State for Scotland. The west side of the square is dominated by the green dome of St George's Church, now West Register House. (See No 406.)

352 Edinburgh, Gladstone's Land
Map 13

Lawnmarket, Royal Mile. Good Fri-26 Oct, Mon-Sat 1000-1700, Sun 1400-1700; 1 Nov-31 Jan, Sat 1000-1630, Sun 1400-1630. Closed 20/21 and 27/28 Dec and Feb and Mar. Adult: 50p, child: 25p (NTS)
Completed in 1620, the six-storey tenement contains remarkable painted ceilings, and has been refurbished as a typical home of the period.

353 Edinburgh, Greyfriars Bobby
Map 13

Corner of George IV Bridge and Candlemaker Row. All times. Free.
Statue of Greyfriars Bobby, the Skye terrier who, after his master's death in 1858, watched over his grave in the nearby Greyfriars Churchyard for fourteen years. (See No 360.)

354 Edinburgh, Heart of Midlothian
Map 13

High Street, close to the W door of St. Giles Cathedral. All times. Free.
A heart-shaped design in the cobblestones, marking the site of the Old Tolbooth, built 1466, which was stormed in the 1736 Porteous Riots and demolished in 1817.

355 Edinburgh, George Heriot's School
Map 13

Lauriston Place. May be viewed from the grounds. Gates close 1630.
Now a school, the splendid building was begun in 1628, endowed by George Heriot, goldsmith and jeweller to James VI and I, the 'Jingling Geordie' of Scott's novel *Fortunes of Nigel.*

356 Edinburgh, High Kirk of St Giles
Map 13

On the Royal Mile. Mon-Sat 1000-1700, 1900 in Summer, and Sunday pm. Free. (Thistle Chapel: Adult: 30p, child: 5p).
There has been a church here since the 9th century. Of the present building, the tower is late 15th-century. At one time, there were four churches here, and yet another part served as a prison. See also the exquisite Thistle Chapel.

357 Edinburgh, Hillend
Map 13

Biggar Road, S outskirts of Edinburgh. Charge for chairlift: Adult: 35p, child: 15p. Session tickets for skiers are also available.
(Lothian Regional Council)
The largest artificial ski slope in Britain. Facilities include chairlift, drag-lift, ski-hire and tuition. Fine views from top of chairlift (available to non-skiers) of the Pentland Hills, over Edinburgh and beyond.

358 Edinburgh, Huntly House
Map 13

Canongate, Royal Mile. Jun-Sep, weekdays 1000-1800; Oct-May, weekdays 1000-1700; Sun during Festival 1400-1700. Free.
Built in 1570, this fine house was later associated with members of the Huntly family. It is now a city museum illustrating Edinburgh life down the ages, and contains important collections of Edinburgh silver and glass and Scottish pottery.

359 Edinburgh, King's Theatre
Map 13

2 Leven Street.
Opened 1906. A memorial stone laid by Andrew Carnegie and a plaque commemorating the occasion may be seen in the theatre.

360 Edinburgh, Kirk of the Greyfriars
Map 13

Greyfriars Place, S end of George IV Bridge. Mon-Sat by arrangement, tel: 031-225 1900, with additional facilities during the Festival; Sun, normally open for public worship. Free.
The kirkyard is on the site of a 15th-century Franciscan Friary, inaugurated in 1562. The Kirk, dedicated on Christmas Day, 1620, was the scene of the Adoption and Signing of the National Covenant on 28 February, 1638. 1400 Covenanters were imprisoned in the kirkyard in 1679. (See No 701.)

361 Edinburgh, John Knox's House
Map 13

*High Street, Royal Mile. All year, Mon-Sat 1000-
1700. Adult: 25p. child: 15p, group rates.*
Attractive old house, with timber galleries, built
possibly c 1490. This was probably John Knox's
residence from c 1566 to his death in 1572.

Edinburgh, Lady Stair's House: see No 400.

362 Edinburgh, Lamb's House
Map 13

*Burgess Street, Leith. By arrangement,
tel: 031-554 3131. Free. (NTS)*
The restored residence and warehouse of
Andrew Lamb, a prosperous merchant of the
17th century. Now an old people's day centre.

363 Edinburgh, Lauriston Castle
Map 13

*N of A90 at Cramond Road South, 4m WNW of
city centre. Apr-Oct, daily except Fri 1100-1300,
1400-1700; Nov-Mar, Sat and Sun only,
1400-1600. Adult: 20p, child: 10p, group rates.*
The original 16th-century tower, built by
Sir Archibald Napier, father of the inventor of
logarithms, has been much extended to become
a gracious house with paintings and old furniture.
John Law (1671-1729), founder of the first Bank
of France and author of the disastrous
'Mississippi Scheme' of 1717-20, spent his early
years in this castle, now administered by the City
of Edinburgh. The grounds include croquet
lawns.

364 Edinburgh, Magdalen Chapel
Map 13

*Cowgate, off the Grassmarket. By arrangement,
tel: 031-225 1836. Free.
(Scottish Reformation Society)*
This 16th-century chapel, temporarily the
chaplaincy for Heriot-Watt University, is notable
for its stained-glass windows.

365 Edinburgh, Meadowbank Stadium
Map 13

193 London Road.
Sports complex, opened in 1970, was the venue
for the Commonwealth Games of that year, and
is now used for a wide variety of major sporting
events throughout the year, with facilities for over
30 sports. Temporary membership is available to
visitors on application to the Sports Centre.

366 Edinburgh, Mercat Cross
Map 13

*High Street, opposite City Chambers. All times.
Free.*
Royal proclamations are still read from the
platform of the mediaeval cross, restored in 1885
by W. E. Gladstone.

367 Edinburgh, Museum of Childhood
Map 13

*High Street, Royal Mile. Jun-Sep, Mon-Sat
1000-1800; Oct-May, Mon-Sat 1000-1700;
Sun (during Festival) 1400-1700. Adult: 25p,
child: 10p.*
This unique museum has a fine collection of toys,
dolls, dolls' houses, costumes and nursery
equipment.

368 Edinburgh, Museum of Lighting
Map 13

*In Mr Purves' Lighting Emporium and Museum
Shop, 59 St Stephen Street. All year,
Sat 1400-1800 and by arrangement,
tel: 031-556 4503. Free. (W M Purves)*
Small private collection of domestic transport
and marine lamps and equipment of the oil and
gas era.

369 Edinburgh, National Gallery of Scotland
Map 13

*The Mound. Mon-Sat 1000-1700 (extended
hours during Festival); Sun 1400-1700. Free.*
One of the most distinguished of the smaller
galleries of Europe, the National Gallery of
Scotland contains a comprehensive collection of
old masters, impressionist and Scottish
paintings. This includes masterpieces by
Raphael, El Greco, Rembrandt, Constable,
Titian, Velasquez, Raeburn, Van Gogh and
Gauguin. Drawings, watercolours and original
prints. (Turner, Goya, Blake etc) are shown on
request (Mon-Fri 1000-1230, 1400-1630).

370 Edinburgh, National Library of Scotland
Map 13

George IV Bridge. All year. (Reading room) Mon-Fri 0930-2030, Sat 0930-1300. (Exhibition) Mon-Fri 0930-1700, Sat 0930-1300; Sun 1400-1700 (Sep-Apr). Free.
Founded in 1682, this is one of the four largest libraries in Great Britain. The Map Room annexe is at 137 Causewayside.

371 Edinburgh, National Museum of Antiquities
Map 13

East End of Queen Street. All year, weekdays 1000-1700 (Festival period 1000-1800); Sun 1400-1700. (Festival period 1100-1800). Free.
An intriguing and comprehensive collection of the history and everyday life of Scotland from the Stone Age to modern times.

Edinburgh, Nelson Monument: see No 341.

372 Edinburgh, Netherbow Arts Centre
Map 13

43 High Street. All year, Mon-Sat 1000-1600 (Wed 1000-1400). Free.
(Church of Scotland Home Board)
A modern three-storey building in the style of a mediaeval town house, with three barrel-vaulted arches, courtyard and metal gates: offering a wide variety of exhibitions, theatre, and concerts.

373 Edinburgh, New 57 Gallery
Map 13

29 Market Street. Above Fruit Market Gallery. Oct-10 Sep, Mon-Sat 1030-1730. Free. (City of Edinburgh)
The gallery is run by a committee of artists and was founded in 1957. It has changing exhibitions of contemporary art by young Scottish artists.

374 Edinburgh, New Fountain Brewery
Map 13
Scottish & Newcastle Breweries Ltd, Gilmore Park. By arrangement, tel: 031-556 2591 Ext. 301. Free.
A tour of the complete brewing process and high Speed Can Line, in the most fully automated brewery in Europe.

375 Edinburgh, New Town Conservation Centre
Map 13

13A Dundas Street. Mon-Fri 0900-1700. Free.
The headquarters of the committee which promotes the conservation of the Georgian New Town. There is a display of conservation work in progress, a conservation reference library, and an exhibition of architecture. Tours and guided walks are arranged.

376 Edinburgh, Outlook Tower and Camera Obscura
Map 13

Castle Hill, between the Castle and the Lawnmarket. All year, daily 0930-1800. Adult: 50p, child: 30p, group rates.
(University of Edinburgh, leased to Landmark.)
The camera throws a fascinating image of Edinburgh on to a white concave table top. Exhibition.

377 Edinburgh, Palace of Holyroodhouse
Map 13

Foot of the Royal Mile. May-Oct 0930-1800,
Sun 1100-1800; Nov-Apr 0930-1715, Sun
1230-1630. Last ticket sold 45 mins before
closing times. The Palace is also closed during
Royal and State Visits, and for periods before
and after visits; check dates in May to July.
Adult: 40p (summer), 25p (winter); child: 20p
(summer), 12p (winter).
The Palace of Holyroodhouse is the official
residence of the Queen in Scotland. The oldest
part is built against the monastic nave of
Holyrood Abbey, little of which remains. The rest
of the palace was reconstructed by the architect
Sir William Bruce for Charles II. Here Mary
Queen of Scots lived for six years; here she met
John Knox; here Rizzio was murdered, and here
Prince Charles Edward Stuart held court in 1745.
State apartments, house tapestries and
paintings: the picture gallery has portraits of
over 100 Scottish kings, painted by De Wet in
1684-86.

378 Edinburgh, Parliament House
Map 13

Behind the High Kirk of St Giles, Royal Mile. By
written request to: The Librarian, Signet Library,
Parliament House, Parliament Square,
Edinburgh. Free.
Built 1632-39, this was the seat of Scottish
Government till 1707, when the governments of
Scotland and England became united. Now the
supreme Law Courts of Scotland. See the Great
Hall, with fine hammer beam roof, and portraits
by Raeburn and other major Scottish artists.

379 Edinburgh, Philatelic Bureau
Map 13

In the Post Office, Waterloo Place.
Mon-Thu 0900-1630; Fri 0900-1600;
Free.
Display of stamps and historic relics of postal
services.

380 Edinburgh, Printmakers Workshop Gallery
Map 13

29 Market Street. Above Fruit Market Gallery.
All year. Mon-Sat 1000-1730. Free.
(City of Edinburgh)
There are regular exhibitions of contemporary
prints from the gallery workshop, as well as from
other leading printmakers in Scotland. Exchange
exhibitions with printmakers from further afield
are also held.

381 Edinburgh, Register House
Map 13

*E end of Princes Street. Mon-Fri 0900-1645,
Sat (Historical Search Room only) 0900-1230.
(Exhibition: 1000-1600). Free.*
This fine Robert Adam building, founded 1774, is
the headquarters of the Scottish Record Office
and the home of the national archives of
Scotland. In front is a notable statue of the Duke
of Wellington (1852). (See also No 406.)

382 Edinburgh, Royal Botanic Garden
Map 13

*Inverleith Row; Arboretum Road (car parking).
Daily 0900 (Sun 1100) to one hour before
sunset, summer; 0900-dusk, winter. Free.
Plant houses 1000 (Sun 1100) to 1700, summer;
1000 (Sun 1100) to dusk, winter. During
Festival, opens at 1000 on Sun.*
The Royal Botanic Garden has a world famous
rock garden and probably the biggest collection
of rhododendrons in the world. The unique
exhibition plant houses show a great range of
exotic plants displayed as indoor landscapes
and a plant exhibition hall displays many aspects
of botany and horticulture. Here also is the
Scottish National Gallery of Modern Art, No 396.

383 Edinburgh, Royal Lyceum Theatre
Map 13

Grindlay Street.
A fine Victorian theatre, recently extensively
renovated, offering, with the Little Lyceum
nearby, a wide variety of plays.

384 Edinburgh, Royal Observatory
Map 13

Blackford Hill. Visitor Centre opening 1979.
Comprising both the Department of Astronomy
of the University of Edinburgh and an
establishment of the Science Research Council,
the Observatory specialises in the development
of advanced technologies.

385 Edinburgh, Royal Scottish Academy
Map 13

*At the foot of the Mound, on Princes Street.
Open for its Annual Exhibition late Apr-July,
and for Festival exhibitions; 1000-2100, Sun
1400-1700. Adult: 50p, child: 20p.*

386 Edinburgh, Royal Scottish Museum
Map 13

*In Chambers Street. 1000-1700 weekdays,
Sun 1400-1700. Free.*
A national museum in a fine Victorian building.
Houses the national collections of decorative
arts of the world, archaeology and ethnography,
natural history, geology, technology and
science. Special exhibitions, lectures, gallery
talks, films and other activities for adults and
children.

387 Edinburgh, Royal Scots Dragoon Guards Museum
Map 13

*The Castle. All year, daily. 0930-1645,
Free.*
Display of pictures, badges, brassware and other
historical relics of the regiment.

388 Edinburgh, St Cecilia's Hall
Map 13

The Cowgate, off the Grassmarket.
Sat 1400-1700. Adult: 20p.
(University of Edinburgh)
The elegant Georgian hall, built in 1762 by
Robert Milne, originally the concert hall for the
Edinburgh Music Society, contains the Russell
collection of early keyboard instruments, many of
which are unique.

389 Edinburgh, St. Cuthbert's Church
Map 13

Lothian Road. All reasonable times. Free.
An ancient church, the 'West Kirk', rebuilt
by Hippolyte Blanc in 1894. The tower is
18th-century, and there is a monument to Napier
of Merchiston, inventor of logarithms.

390 Edinburgh, St Cuthbert's Co-operative
Association Transport Collection
Map 13

Grove Street, off Dundee Street.
By written request to Transport Manager, Mon-
Fri 1300-1700. Free.
An extensive collection of horse-drawn
carriages.

391 Edinburgh, St John's Church
Map 13

W end of Princes Street. All reasonable times.
Free.
An impressive 19th-century church, the nave
of which was built in 1817 by William Burn.
(See No 340.)

392 Edinburgh, St Mary's Cathedral
Map 13

In Palmerston Place
Built 1879. The western towers were added in
1917. The central spire is 276 feet high and the
interior is impressive. Nearby is the charming
Easter Coates House, built in the late 17th
century with stone filched from the old tower. It is
now St Mary's Music School.

393 Edinburgh, Scott Monument
Map 13

In Princes Street. Apr-Sep, Mon-Fri
0900-1800; Oct-Mar, Mon-Fri 0900-1500.
Adult: 20p, child: 20p.
Completed in 1844, a statue of Sir Walter Scott
and his dog Maida, under a canopy and spire
200 feet high, with 64 statuettes of Scott
characters. Fine view of the city from the top.

394 Edinburgh, Scottish Arts Council Gallery
Map 13

19 Charlotte Square. All year, Mon-Sat 1000-
1800; Sun 1400-1800. Usually free.
The gallery features monthly exhibitions of
paintings, sculpture, etc.

Edinburgh, Scottish Craft Centre: see No 336.

395 Edinburgh, Scottish Genealogy Society
Map 13

9 Union Street. All year, Wed 1530-1830.
Library facilities for members of the society.

396 Edinburgh, Scottish National Gallery of Modern Art
Map 13

Inverleith House, in the Royal Botanic Garden; car park in Arboretum Road. Winter: Mon-Sat 1000-sunset. Summer: Mon-Sat 1000-1800. Sun 1400-1800. Sun during Festival, 1100-1800. Free.
The temporary home for Scotland's collection of 20th-century painting, sculpture and graphic art, with masterpieces by Derain, Matisse, Braque, Moore, Hepworth, Picasso and Giacometti; and work by Hockney, Caulfield and Sol LeWitt. Also Scottish School.

397 Edinburgh, Scottish National Portrait Gallery
Map 13

E end of Queen Street. Weekdays 1000-1700, (extended hours during Festival), Sun 1400-1700.
Illustrates the history of Scotland through portraits of the famous men and women who contributed to it in all fields of activity from the 16th century to the present day, such as Mary Queen of Scots, James VI and I, Flora Macdonald, Robert Burns, Sir Walter Scott, David Hume and Ramsay MacDonald. The artists include Raeburn, Ramsay, Reynolds and Gainsborough.

398 Edinburgh, Scottish National Zoological Park
Map 13

Entrance from Corstorphine Road (A8), 4m W of city centre. Summer: 0900-1900. Winter: 0900-1700 (or dusk if earlier) 0930 opening on Sun. Adult: £1.20, child: 60p, group rates.
Established by The Royal Zoological Society of Scotland in 1913, this is one of Britain's leading zoos, with a large and varied collection of mammals, birds and reptiles displayed in extensive grounds on Corstorphine Hill. Edinburgh Zoo is widely known for its large breeding colony of Antarctic Penguins, and the Carnegie Aquarium is one of the finest in Britain.

399 Edinburgh, Scottish Record Office
Map 13

*HM General Register House, E end
of Princes Street. All year, Mon-Fri. Search
rooms: 0900-1645, Sat 0900-1230. Exhibitions:
1000-1600. Free.*
Historical search rooms and exhibitions housed
in one of Robert Adam's finest buildings. There is
a branch repository at West Register House in
Charlotte Square. (See also Nos 381, 406.)

400 Edinburgh, Lady Stair's House
Map 13

*Off Lawnmarket, Royal Mile. Jun-Sep,
weekdays 1000-1800; Oct-May, weekdays
1000-1700; Sun during Festival 1400-1700.
Free.*
Built in 1622, this is now a museum of Burns,
Scott and Stevenson.

401 Edinburgh, Swanston Cottage
Map 13

*Swanston Village, at end of Swanston Road, 4m
S of city centre. Off A702. By written
arrangement with Director of Administration,
Edinburgh District Council, High Street. Free.
(Edinburgh District Council)*
The house where Robert Louis Stevenson and
his family spent their summers from 1867 to 1881.
The village nearby has an attractive group of
thatched whitewashed cottages around a green.

402 Edinburgh, Talbot Rice Art Centre
Map 13

*Old College, South Bridge. Mon-Sat
1000-1700. Free.*
The Torrie Collection and travelling exhibitions
are on public display in this fine building, part of
the University of Edinburgh, begun by Robert
Adam in 1789 and completed by William Playfair
around 1830.

403 Edinburgh, Transport Museum
Map 13

*In Shrubhill Works, Leith Walk. Mon-Fri 0930-
1630, Sat 0900-1230. Groups by arrangement
(Sat pm), tel: 031-225 3941. Free.*
Full scale and model exhibits of transport in the
city over the centuries.

404 Edinburgh, Traverse Theatre Club
Map 13

*112 West Bow, Grassmarket
All year, Tues-Sun 1000-2300.*
One of Britain's best-known experimental
theatres, housed in a building 200 years old just
off the Grassmarket.

Edinburgh, University of Edinburgh: see
No 402.

405 Edinburgh, Wax Museum
Map 13
*High Street, Royal Mile. 1 Apr-30 Sep,
1000-1900. 1 Oct-31 Mar, 1000-1700.
Adult: £1, child: 40p group rates.*
Models of prominent figures in Scottish history,
including Mary Queen of Scots, Bonnie Prince
Charlie, Robert Burns and William Wallace. Also
a Chamber of Horrors, featuring such characters

as Burke and Hare, and Deacon Brodie; as well as a 'Never, Never Land' with fairy-tale characters.

406 Edinburgh, West Register House
Map 13

W side of Charlotte Square. Mon-Fri. Exhibitions: 1000-1600, Search Rooms: 0900-1645, Sat 0900-1230. Free.
Formerly St George's Church, 1811, this now holds the more modern documents of the Scottish Record Office (see No 399). Permanent exhibition on many aspects of Scottish history, including the Declaration of Arbroath, 1320.

407 Edinburgh, White Horse Close
Map 13

Off Canongate, Royal Mile.
A restored group of 17th-century buildings off the High Street. The coaches to London left from White Horse Inn (named after Queen Mary's palfrey), and there are Jacobite links.

408 Edinshall Broch
Map 14

On the NE slope of Cockburn Law, off A6112 4m N of Duns. All times. Free. (AM)
Listed among the ten Iron Age brochs known in lowland Scotland, its dimensions are exceptionally large. The site was occupied into Roman times.

409 Edrom Norman Arch
Map 14

Off A6105, 3m ENE of Duns. All reasonable times. Free. (AM)
Fine Norman chancel arch from church built by Thor Longus c 1105, now standing behind recent parish church.

410 Edzell Castle and Garden
Map 7

Off B966, 6m N of Brechin. Opening standard. Adult: 15p, child: 7p, group rates. (AM)
The beautiful pleasance, a walled garden, was built by Sir David Lindsay; the heraldic and symbolic sculptures are unique in Scotland, and the flower-filled recesses in the walls add to the outstanding formal garden, which also has a turreted garden house. The castle itself, an impressive ruin, dates from the early 16th century, with a large courtyard mansion of 1580.

411 Eglinton Castle
Map 15

2m N of Irvine. Open from dawn to dusk. Free.
Built in 1796, with a central tower 100 feet high,
the castle was the site of the Eglinton tournament
in 1839. The gardens are also open.

412 Eigg, Isle of
Map 4

*Inner Hebrides. Ferry from Mallaig and Arisaig
(no cars).*
The island of Eigg lies to the southeast of Rhum
and is 5m by 2½m. It is distinguished by the
Sgurr of Eigg (1289 ft), a mass of black, glassy
pitchstone towering to a height of 400 ft above its
high-lying base. The principal residence on Eigg
is a colonial-style house with palms in the
gardens. A cave near the SE shore of the island
was the scene of a 16th-century clan feud
tragedy; 200 Macdonalds were suffocated by
smoke from a fire lit at the entrance to the cave
where they were hiding. (See also Nos 815, 726
and 152.)

413 Eilean Donan Castle
Map 4

*Off A87, 9m E of Kyle of Lochalsh. Easter-Sep,
daily 1000-1230, 1400-1800. Adult: 40p. (Mr J D
H MacRae)*
On an islet (now connected by a causeway) in
Loch Duich, this picturesque castle dates back to
1220. It passed into the hands of the Mackenzies
of Kintail who became Earls of Seaforth. In 1719
it was garrisoned by Spanish Jacobite troops and
was blown up by an English man o'war. Now
completely restored, it incorporates a war
memorial to the Clan Macrae, who held it as
hereditary Constables on behalf of the
Mackenzies.

Eilean Donan Castle

414 Elcho Castle
Map 8

*On River Tay, 4m SE of Perth. Opening
standard. Adult: 15p, child: 7p, group rates.
(AM)*
A preserved fortified mansion notable for its
tower-like jambs or wings and for the wrought-
iron grills protecting its windows. An ancestral
seat of the Earls of Wemyss; another castle, on
or very near the site, was a favourite hide-out of
William Wallace.

415 Electric Brae
Map 15

*A719 9m S of Ayr (also known as Croy Brae).
All times. Free.*
An optical illusion is created so that a car appears
to be going down the hill when it is in fact going
up.

416 Elgin Cathedral
Map 6

*North College Street, Elgin. Opening standard.
Adult: 20p, child: 10p, group rates. (AM)*
When entire, this was perhaps the most beautiful
of Scottish cathedrals, known as the Lantern of
the North. It was founded in 1224, but in 1390 it
was burned by the Wolf of Badenoch. Much
13th-century work still remains; the nave
and chapter house are 15th-century. There is a
6th-century Pictish slab in the choir.

417 Elgin Museum
Map 6

*High Street, Elgin. Mid Mar-mid Oct,
Mon and Wed-Sat 1000-1230, 1400-1700;
Tue 1000-1300; mid Oct-mid Mar, Wed and Sat
only, 1000-1400. Adult: 20p, child: 10p, group
rates. (Moray Society)*
The museum houses a varied collection which
includes fossils, notably from Old Red
Sandstone, Burghead Bulls, prehistoric
weapons, costumes and local domestic items.

418 Ellisland Farm
Map 18

*Off A76, 6½m NNW of Dumfries. All reasonable
times. Free. (Ellisland Trust)*
Robert Burns took over this farm in June 1788,
built the farmhouse, and tried to introduce new
farming methods. Unsuccessful, he became an
Exciseman in September 1789; in August 1791
the stock was auctioned, and he moved to
Dumfries in November 1791. Some of the poet's
most famous works were written at Ellisland,
including *Tam o'Shanter* and *Auld Lang Syne*.
The Granary houses a display showing Burns as
a farmer.

419 Eriskay
Map 2

*Island 3m by 1½m, 5m NE of Barra, Western
Isles. Ferry from Ludag.*
Tiny island where Prince Charles Edward Stuart
first set foot on Scottish soil, 23 July 1745, and off
the shore of which, in 1941, the SS *Politician*
foundered with 20,000 cases of whisky on board,
an incident made famous by the book *Whisky
Galore*.

Erskine

420 Erskine Bridge
Map 11

Connecting M898 and A82 across Clyde.
Opened in 1971, the high bridge is the last to
cross the river and superseded the old ferry.

421 Eynhallow Church
Map 1

*On island of Eynhallow, Orkney. All reasonable
times. Free. (AM)*
A 12th-century church, now largely in ruins.
Close by is a group of domestic buildings, also
ruined.

422 Fair Isle
Map 1

*Most isolated inhabited island in Britain, halfway
between Orkney and Shetland. Twice-weekly
mailboat sailings in summer from Shetland and
scheduled and charter flights from Shetland.
(NTS)*
Home of internationally-famous Bird
Observatory, open March to November.
Important breeding ground for great and Arctic
skuas, storm petrel, fulmar, razorbill, puffin, etc.
The Observatory, on main bird migration routes,
notes some 300 species. The island itself is
notable for Fair Isle knitwear in intricate colourful
patterns, a traditional skill of the womenfolk.

423 Falconer Museum
Map 3

*Off Main Street, Forres, 12m W of Elgin.
May, 1000-1300, 1400-1700. Jun,
1000-1300, 1400-1800. Jul-Aug, 1000-1300,
1400-1900. Sept, 1000-1300, 1400-1800. Free.
(Moray District Council)*
A varied collection which includes shells, fossil
fish, birds, weapons, flints and arrowheads from
Culbin and the Hugh Falconer exhibit.

424 Falkirk Museum
Map 12

*Falkirk Town Centre. All year Mon-Sat 1000-
1700. Free.
(Falkirk District Council)*
A varied collection of local pottery, clocks,
weapons and Victoriana.

425 Falkland Palace and Gardens
Map 9

*A912, 11m N of Kirkcaldy. 1 Apr-31 Oct,
Mon-Sat 1000-1715, Sun 1400-1715. Adult:
(palace and gardens) £1, (gardens only) 50p;
child (palace and gardens) 50p, (gardens only)
25p; group rates. (NTS)*
A lovely Royal Palace in a picturesque little town.
The buildings of the Palace, in Renaissance
style, date from 1501-1541. This was a favourite
seat of James V, who died here in 1542, and of
his daughter Mary Queen of Scots. The Royal
Tennis Court of 1539 is still played on. The
gardens are small but charming.

426 Falls of Glomach
Map 4

Unclassified road off A87, 18m E of Kyle of Lochalsh. (NTS)
One of the highest falls in Britain, 370 feet, above wild Glen Elchaig. From west end of Loch na Leitreach, Glen Elchaig (approach from Ardelve), a 1½-hour arduous climb. Or from Croe Bridge on Loch Duich, a 7m long-distance walkers' path through the hills via Dorusduain. Stout footwear essential.

Falls of Measach: see No 215.

427 Falls of Shin
Map 3

A836, 5m N of Bonar Bridge.
Spectacular falls through a rocky gorge famous for salmon leaping.

Farr Church: see No 918.

428 Farigaig Forest Centre
Map 5

Off B862 at Inverfarigaig, 17m S of Inverness. Easter-end Oct 0930-1900. Free. (FC)
A Forestry Commission interpretation centre in a converted stone stable, showing the development of the forest environment in the Great Glen.

429 Fasque
Map 7

Approx. 2m N of Fettercairn on Edzell to Banchory road (B974). May-Sep daily (except Fri) 1330-1700 and evenings for parties by arrangement, tel: Fettercairn 201. Adult: 80p, child: 50p.
Built between 1820 and 1828, the house was bought in 1829 by Sir John Gladstone, father of W E Gladstone, the Victorian Prime Minister. There are impressive public rooms and a remarkable collection of documents and relics relating to the history of the estate.

430 Fast Castle
Map 14

Off A1107, 4m NW of Coldingham.
The scant, but impressive remains of a Home stronghold, perched on a cliff above the sea. Care should be taken on the cliffs.

431 Fettercairn Arch
Map 7

In Fettercairn, On B966 3m E of Lawrencekirk. All times. Free.
Stone arch built to commemorate the visit by Queen Victoria and the Prince Consort in 1861.

432 Fife Folk Museum
Map 9

At Ceres, 3m SE of Cupar. Apr-Oct, Mon-Sat (except Tue) 1400-1700, Sun 1430-1730. Adult: 20p, child: 10p.
(Central & North Fife Preservation Society)
Situated in the 17th-century Weigh House, near an old bridge in an attractive village, this museum is a growing collection in a unique setting, showing the domestic and agricultural past of Fife. Nearby is the attractive Ceres Church (1806) with a horse-shoe gallery.

Finavon

433 Finavon Castle
Map 7

A94, 7½m SW of Brechin: directions from Doocot Shop, Finavon. All reasonable times. Free. (Mrs S Mazur)
A stronghold with foundations dating back to c 1300, added to in 1593. The castle collapsed in the 18th century through undermining by the Lemno Burn.

434 Finavon Doocot
Map 7

Off A94, 5m NE of Forfar, opposite Finavon Shop. (Key with Finavon Doocot Shop.) Daily, 1000-1800. Adult 25p, child:10p. (Angus Historic Buildings Society)
A two-chamber lean-to doocot containing over 2,100 nesting boxes, the largest in Scotland. There is an exhibition of the doocots of Angus.

Fingal's Cave

435 Fingal's Cave
Map 4

On the uninhabited island of Staffa, 8m off the W coast of Mull. Seen by steamer and boat trips from Oban and Mull.
A huge cave, 227 feet long and some 66 feet high from sea level, flanked by black pillared walls and columns. The basaltic rock formations of Staffa, where there are other curious caves, are famous. Fingal's Cave inspired Mendelssohn's *The Hebrides* overture.

436 Finlarig Castle
Map 8

S point of Loch Tay near Killin, 22m WSW of Aberfeldy. All reasonable times. Free.
This one-time seat of the Breadalbanes has a beheading pit, thought to be the only one left in Scotland.

437 Finlaystone
Map 11

Off A8 W of Langbank, 17m W of Glasgow. Mon-Sat 0900-1700, Sun 1400-1700. (Woods) Adult: 30p, child: 20p. (Gardens) Adult: 15p, child: 15p. (House) by arrangement, tel: Langbank 285 (Mr George MacMillan)
Family estate with woodland walks, garden centre, jogging trail, formal gardens and summer Ranger. The house has some fine rooms, Victorian relics, and an international collection of dolls shown in the billiard room.

438 Flodden Monument
Map 16

Town Centre, Selkirk. All times. Free.
The monument was erected in 1913 on the
400th anniversary of the battle and is inscribed
'O Flodden Field'.

439 Floors Castle
Map 16

*B6089, 2m NW of Kelso. Early May-late Sep,
daily except Fri and Sat; grounds and gardens
1230-1730, house 1330-1730. Adult: 85p,
child: 45p, group rates. (Duke of Roxburghe)*
A large and impressive mansion, built by William
Adam in 1721, with additions in the 1840s by
William Playfair. A holly tree in the park is said to
mark the spot where James II was killed by the
bursting of a cannon in 1460.

440 Fogo Church
Map 16

Off B6460 3m SW of Duns. All reasonable times.
The attractive church has an outside staircase
giving access to the private laird's loft dating from
1671.

441 Fordyce
Map 6

Unclassified road off A98, 4m SE of Cullen.
A tiny village built round a small 16th-century
castle. Adjacent are the remains of the old
church with an interesting belfry.

442 Fort Augustus Abbey
Map 5

*A82, at S end of Loch Ness. Guided tours daily
at 1030, 1140, 1530, 1615, 1700 and by
arrangement, tel: Fort Augustus 6232. Free.
(The Benedictines)*
This former fort takes its name from William
Augustus, Duke of Cumberland, who made it his
headquarters after the Battle of Culloden in
1746. A Benedictine Abbey, started in 1876, now
occupies the much-adapted buildings of the old
fort.

443 Fort Charlotte
Map 1

*Lerwick, Shetland. Opening standard. Free.
(AM)*
A fort roughly pentagonal in shape with high
walls containing gun ports pointing seawards.
Designed by John Mylne and begun in 1665 to
protect the Sound of Bressay, it was burned in
1673 with the town of Lerwick by the Dutch, but
repaired in 1781.

444 Fort George
Map 5

*B9039, off A96, 8m W of Nairn. Opening
standard. Adult: 25p, child: 12p, group rates.
(AM)*
Begun in 1748 as a result of the Jacobite
rebellion, this is one of the finest late artillery
fortifications in Europe. There is also the
Regimental Museum of the Queen's Own
Highlanders. (See No 797.)

445 Forth Bridges
Map 13

Queensferry, 10m W of Edinburgh.
For over 800 years travellers were ferried across
the Firth of Forth. Queensferry was named from
Queen Margaret who regularly used this
passage between Dunfermline and Edinburgh in
the 11th century. The ferry ceased in 1964 when
the Queen opened the Forth Road Bridge, a
suspension bridge then the longest of its kind in
Europe (1,993 yards). Also here is the rail bridge
of 1883-90, one of the greatest engineering feats
of its time. It is 2,765 yards long.

446 Forth/Clyde Canal
Map 12

Opened in 1790, the Canal linked industrial
towns of West Central Scotland with the east
coast at Grangemouth. When the Union Canal
opened this link was extended via Falkirk to the
heart of Edinburgh. The route of the Canal is
close to that of the Antonine Wall.

447 Fortingall Yew
Map 8

Fortingall, 9m W of Aberfeldy.
The great yew in the churchyard, possibly the
oldest in Britain, is claimed to be over 3,000
years old, and the attractive village is said to be
the birthplace of Pontius Pilate.

Fortrose Cathedral

448 Fortrose Cathedral
Map 5

*At Fortrose, 8m SSW of Cromarty. Opening
standard. Free. (AM)*
The existing portions of this 14th-century
cathedral are complete and include vaulting and
much fine detail.

449 Foulden Tithe Barn
Map 14

*A6105, 5m NW of Berwick-upon-Tweed. May
be viewed from the roadside. (AM)*
A two-storeyed tithe barn, with outside stair and
crow-stepped gables.

450 Fowlis Wester Sculptured Stone
Map 8

Off A85, 5m NE of Crieff in centre of village. (AM)
An 8th-century Pictish stone with remarkably
clear carvings. Opposite is St Bean's Church.
(See No 836.)

451 Fyvie Church
Map 6

Off A947, 7m NW of Old Meldrum. By arrangement, tel: Fyvie 230 (The Manse). Free.
An attractive church with notable stained glass, Celtic stones and 17th-century panelling inside. 'Mill of Tifty's Annie' is buried in the churchyard, and nearby a cross marks the site of a 12th-century monastery.

452 Galloway Deer Museum
Map 17

On A712, by Clatteringshaws Loch, 6m W of New Galloway. Apr-Sep, daily 1000-1700. Free. (FC)
The museum, in a converted farm steading, has a live trout exhibit as well as many features on deer and other aspects of Galloway wildlife, geology and history. Bruce's Stone (No 116) on Moss Raploch, is a short walk away.

453 Galloway Forest Park
Map 17

Off A714, 10m NW of Newton Stewart. (FC)
Covering some 150,000 acres, a magnificent area of hills, trails, forests and lochs, including Lochs Doon and Trool, and Clatteringshaws. Merrick (2,765 feet) is a notable feature of the landscape. (See also Nos 452 and 802.)

454 Gargunnock Garden
Map 11

Gargunnock, off A811, 6m W of Stirling. Apr, May, Jun, Sep & Oct, Wed (except 1st Wed in Apr & Sep), 1300-1700. Admission by donation, minimum 10p. (Miss Stirling of Gargunnock)
Small shrub and flower garden beside 16th-18th century house (not open). Drive and small woodland walk. Narcissi, azaleas, rhododendrons, flowering shrubs and trees, autumn colours.
Gargunnock House open by written arrangement only.

455 Garvamore Bridge
Map 5

6m W of Laggan Bridge, on unclassified road 17m SW of Newtonmore.
This two-arched bridge at the south side of the Corrieyarrick Pass was built by General Wade in 1735.

456 Gifford Church
Map 14

Gifford, B6369, 5m SSE of Haddington. All reasonable times. Free.
The Dutch-looking church dates from 1708, and in it is preserved a late mediaeval bell, and also a 17th-century pulpit. A tablet near the church commemorates the Rev John Witherspoon (1723-94), born at Gifford, principal of Princeton University, USA, and the only cleric to sign the American Declaration of Independence.

457 Gigha, Isle of
Map 10

Ferry from West Loch Tarbert and Tayinloan (no cars).
The fertile island lies off the west coast of Kintyre. There is a ruined church at Kilchattan dating back to the 13th century, and Achamore House Gardens, noted for semi-tropical plants, are open in the summer. Accommodation is limited. (See also No 21.)

458 Gladstone Court Street Museum
Map 16

A702 in Biggar, 13m W of Peebles. Easter-Oct, daily 1000-1230, 1400-1700. Sun 1400-1700: other times by arrangement, tel: Biggar 20005. Adult: 20p, child: 10p, group rates.
(Biggar Museum Trust)
An indoor street museum of shops and windows. Grocer, photographer, dressmaker, bank, school, library, ironmonger, chemist, china merchant, telephone exchange, etc. An open-air museum is being created and a 17th-century farmhouse rebuilt.

459 Glamis Castle
Map 9

A928, 5m SW of Forfar. Easter, May- 1st Oct, Sun-Thu 1300-1700 (mid Jul-Sep, Sun-Fri 1300-1700); other times by arrangement, tel: Glamis 242. Adult: £1, child: 50p, group rates.
(Earl of Strathmore and Kinghorne)
This famous Scottish castle, childhood home of Queen Elizabeth the Queen Mother and birthplace of Princess Margaret, owes its present aspect to the period 1675-87. But portions of the high, square tower with walls 15 feet thick are much older. There has been a building on the site from very early times, and Malcolm II is said to have died there in 1034. The oldest part of today's castle is Duncan's Hall, and there are links with Shakespeare's *Macbeth*. There are also fine collections of china, tapestry and furniture, and a massive sundial in the grounds.

460 Glasgow Art Gallery and Museum
Map 11

In Kelvingrove Park. Weekdays 1000-1700, Sun 1400-1700.
The first municipal art collection in the UK has outstanding Flemish, Dutch and Italian canvases, including magnificent works by Giorgione and Rembrandt, as well as a wide range of French Impressionist and British pictures. Other major halls include sculpture, costume, silver, pottery and porcelain and a connoisseur's collection of arms and armour.

461 Glasgow, Botanic Gardens
Map 11

Entrance from Great Western Road (A82). Gardens 0700-dusk; Kibble Palace 1000-1645; Main Range 1300 (Sun 1200)-1645. Closes 1615 Oct-Mar. Free.
The glasshouses contain a wide range of tropical plants including orchids and begonias. The Kibble Palace, an outstanding Victorian glasshouse, has a unique collection of tree ferns and other plants from temperate areas of the world. Outside features include a Systematic

Garden, a Herb Garden and a Chronological Border.

462 Glasgow, Calderpark Zoo
Map 11

6m E of city centre on A74 (Glasgow/Carlisle). Daily, 0930-1900 or dusk, whichever is earlier. Adult: 70p, child: 30p, group rates.
A medium-sized zoo undergoing a major expansion and improvement programme. Animals exhibited include rhinos, elephant, lions, cheetahs, black panthers, leopards, polar bears, zebras, camels, monkeys, reptiles, birds, lemurs, llamas, deer and wallabies.

463 Glasgow, Ca d'Oro Building
Map 11

Union Street and Gordon Street.
An elaborate building of 1872, still in use, with iron window tracery giving a cathedral-like effect.

464 Glasgow, Cathcart Castle
Map 11

In Linn Park. All reasonable times. Free.
Ruins of a 15th-century castle now in a city park. Nearby is the Queen's Knowe, associated with Mary, Queen of Scots.

465 Glasgow Cathedral
Map 11

At E end of Cathedral Street. Apr-Sep, weekdays 1000-1900, Sun 1300-1800; Oct-Mar, weekdays 1000-1730. Sun 1300-1800. Free. (AM)
The Cathedral, dedicated to St Mungo, is the only unmutilated survivor of the great Gothic churches of south Scotland. Parts date from the late 12th century, though several periods (mainly 13th century) are represented in its architecture. The splendid crypt, consecrated in 1197, is the chief glory of the cathedral, which is now the Parish Church of Glasgow.

466 Glasgow, Citizens' Theatre
Map 11

Gorbals. Sept-May.
Opened in 1878 originally as a Music Hall and now a listed building.

467 Glasgow, City Chambers
Map 11

George Square. Mon-Fri, guided tours at 1030 and 1430 or by arrangement, tel: 041-221 9600. Sometimes restricted owing to Council functions. Free.
Built in Italian Renaissance style, and opened in 1888 by Queen Victoria. The interiors, particularly the function suites and the staircases, reflect all the opulence of Victorian Glasgow.

468 Glasgow, Collins Exhibition Hall
Map 11

University of Strathclyde, off George Street, Glasgow. All year except Aug, Mon-Sat 1000-1700. Free.
Modern exhibition hall with year-round programme of exhibitions, mainly visual arts, sometimes including historical subjects.

469 Glasgow, Crookston Castle
Map 11

4m SW of city centre. Opening standard.
Adult: 15p, child: 7p, group rates. (AM)
On the site of a castle built by Robert Croc in the
mid-12th century, the present tower house dates
from the early 15th century. Darnley and Mary
Queen of Scots stayed here after their marriage
in 1565.

470 Glasgow, Custom House Quay
Map 11

*N shore of the Clyde, between Glasgow Bridge
and Victoria Bridge.*
By Victoria Bridge is moored the *Carrick* (1864)
and there is a fine view of Carlton Place on the
opposite bank. The Quay is part of the Clyde
Walkway, an ambitious project to give new life to
the riverside.

471 Glasgow, Egyptian Halls
Map 11

Union Street.
A remarkable building by Alexander 'Greek'
Thomson dating from 1871-73, notable for its
detached curtain walls of glass.

Glasgow, Fossil Grove: see No 501.

472 Glasgow, Gardner's Warehouse
Map 11

Jamaica Street.
Built in 1855-56, the warehouse, still in use
today, was a pioneering example of the use of
iron framing and glass to produce a simple,
functional yet elegant building.

473 Glasgow, George Square
Map 11

The heart of Glasgow with the City Chambers
(see No 467) and statues of Sir Walter Scott,
Queen Victoria, Prince Albert, Robert Burns,
Sir John Moore, Lord Clyde, Thomas Campbell,
Dr Thomas Graham, James Oswald, James
Watt, William Gladstone and Sir Robert Peel.

474 Glasgow, Greenbank
Map 11

*Flenders Road. All year (garden) daily
1000-1700; (garden advice centre) Mon-Fri
1000-1700. 1 Apr-1 Oct: also Sat and Sun
1430-1700. Adult: 30p,. child (with adult): 15p.*
A colourful garden featuring shrub roses and
annuals with an advice centre specially suited to

the owners of small gardens. Lectures,
demonstrations and talks are given. The
Georgian house, built in 1763, is not open to the
public.

475 Glasgow, Haggs Castle
Map 11

*100 St Andrew's Drive. Mon-Sat 1000-1715,
Sun 1400-1700. Free. (Glasgow District
Council)*
Built in 1585 by John Maxwell of Pollok, the
castle was acquired by the city in 1972, and, after
restoration, was developed as a museum of
history for children. As well as the exhibitions,
there are workshops where every Saturday,
there are museum-based activities for children.
The gardens have been landscaped and include
herb and vegetable plots and a knot garden.

476 Glasgow, Hunterian Museum
Map 11

*Glasgow University, 2m NW of city centre.
Mon-Fri 0900-1700, Sat 0900-1200. Free.*
Opened in 1807. Exhibits include geological,
archaeological and ethnological items. Scientific
instruments are exhibited in the Natural
Philosophy Building. The anatomical and
zoological collections, and manuscripts and
early printed books, can be seen on application.

477 Glasgow, King's Theatre
Map 11

Bath Street, Glasgow.
This 1,800-seat theatre dates back to 1904, and
preserves the style and elegance of the
Edwardian period. Now carefully modernised, it
has become one of the best-equipped civic
theatres in Scotland.

478 Glasgow, Langside Memorial
Map 11

Battle Place, Queens Park. All times. Free.
Commemorates the Battle of Langside in 1568,
where Mary, Queen of Scots' forces were
defeated.

479 Glasgow, Charles Rennie Mackintosh Society
Map 11

*Springbank Street, Queens Cross. Tue and Thu
1200-1730, Sun 1430-1700 and by
arrangement, tel: 041-946 6600. Free.*
Queens Cross, a Mackintosh church, and now
the headquarters of the Charles Rennie
Mackintosh Society. There is a small exhibition.

480 Glasgow, Merchants' House
Map 11

*W side of George Square. May-Sep, Mon-Fri
1400-1600. Free. The hall and ante-rooms may
be seen by arrangement, tel: 041-221 8272
(The Merchants' House of Glasgow)*
This handsome building occupies one of the best
sites in the city. Built in 1874 by John Burnet, it
contains the Glasgow Chamber of Commerce,
the oldest in Britain, the fine Merchants' Hall, with
ancient relics and good stained-glass windows,
and the House's own offices.

481 Glasgow, Mitchell Library
Map 11

*North Street. Mon-Fri 0930-2100, Sat
0930-1700. Free. (Glasgow District Council)*
Founded in 1874, this is the largest public
reference library in Scotland, with stock of nearly
one million volumes. Its many collections include
probably the largest on Robert Burns in the
world.

482 Glasgow, Museum of Transport
Map 11

*25 Albert Drive. All year. Weekdays 1000-1700,
Sun 1400-1700. Free. (Glasgow District
Council)*
The museum presents a large collection of
trams, buses, motor cars (including the oldest
car in Scotland), horse-drawn vehicles, railway
locomotives, fire engines and bicycles, in
addition to a wealth of special displays and
models, including a working model railway. Of
particular note is the new gallery, housing a fine
collection of ship models.

483 Glasgow, Necropolis
Map 11

Behind Glasgow Cathedral.
Remarkable and extensive burial ground laid out
in 1833, with numerous elaborate tombs of
19th-century illustrious Glaswegians and others;
see particularly the Menteith Mausoleum of
1842.

484 Glasgow, People's Palace
Map 11

*In Glasgow Green. Weekdays 1000-1700,
Sun 1400-1700.*
Opened in 1898, the building is Glasgow's local
history museum and tells the story of the city from
1175 onwards.

485 Glasgow, Pollok House
Map

*2060 Pollokshaws Road (A736). All year, Mon-
Sat 1000-1700, Sun 1400-1700. Free.
(Glasgow Museums and Art Galleries).*
The house was built to William Adam's design in
1752, with additions by Sir Rowland Anderson
between 1890 and 1908. Containing the Stirling
Maxwell collection of paintings, it stands in a
varied landscape of garden, park and
woodlands. The fine collection of Spanish
paintings is complemented by Spanish glass and
a selection of European and Oriental furniture,
pottery, porcelain and other decorative arts; also
some important paintings by William Blake.

486 Glasgow, Provan Hall
Map 11

*At Auchinlea Road, 4m E of city centre.
All year, daily except Tues, 1000-1900. Entry by
donation. (NTS)*
A well-restored 15th-century house said to be
the most perfect example of a simple pre-
Reformation house remaining in Scotland. It was
restored in 1935, and is now part of Auchinlea
Park.

487 Glasgow, Provand's Lordship
Map 11

By Glasgow Cathedral. Apr-Sep 1000-1700,
Oct-Mar 1100-1600. Daily (except Sun).
Adult: 15p, child: 5p.
The oldest house in the city (1471); James II,
James IV and Mary Queen of Scots all stayed
here. Now a museum with 17th-century furniture.

488 Glasgow, Regimental Headquarters of the Royal Highland Fusiliers
Map 11

518 Sauchiehall Street, Glasgow. Mon-Fri
0900-1630. Free.
The exhibits in this regimental museum include
medals, badges, uniforms and records which
illustrate the histories of The Royal Scots
Fusiliers, The Highland Light Infantry and The
Royal Highland Fusiliers.

489 Glasgow, Rouken Glen
Map 11

Thornliebank. All reasonable times. Free.
One of Glasgow's most attractive parks with
lovely shaded walks and a waterfall.

490 Glasgow, St Andrew's
Map 11

St Andrews Square, off Saltmarket. All
reasonable times. Free.
A fine church, 1739-56, with magnificent interior
plaster work and mahogany gallery fronts.

491 Glasgow, St David's 'Ramshorn' Church
Map 11

Ingram Street. All reasonable times. Free.
Impressive church built in 1824 with a graveyard
containing the graves of many notable citizens
including David Dale, creator of New Lanark.
(See No 748.)

492 Glasgow, St Vincent Street Church
Map 11

St Vincent Street. All reasonable times. Free.
Church by Alexander 'Greek' Thomson of varied
styles high on a plinth. There is an open air
theatre on the south side.

493 Glasgow School of Art
Map 11

In Renfrew Street. Mon-Fri 1000-1200, 1400-
1600 and by arrangement, tel: 041-332 9797.
A fine example of the work of Charles Rennie
Mackintosh, designed in 1896, and built between
1897 and 1909.

494 Glasgow, Scottish Design Centre
Map 11

St Vincent Street. Mon-Fri 0930-1700,
Sat 0900-1700. Free.
On show here are an average of 500 items
selected from the Design Index of 10,000 British
manufactured consumer and other products.

495 Glasgow, Stirling's Library
Map 11

Ingram Street. All reasonable times. Free.
Formerly known as the Royal Exchange, and
before that the Cunningham Mansion, the
present building, used as a library, was designed
in 1827 and has a particularly rich interior.

496 Glasgow, The Stock Exchange—Scottish
Map 11

St George's Place. Visitor's Gallery. All year,
Mon-Fri 1000-1245, 1400-1530. A 'French
Venetian' building of 1877. Free.

497 Glasgow, Strathclyde Police Headquarters Museum
Map 11

Pitt Street. All year, Mon-Fri 0930-1630;
by arrangement, tel: 041-204 2626. Free.
A small museum showing the history of the police
service in Scotland. Articles are on show from a
variety of crime cases.

498 Glasgow, Templeton's Carpet Factory
Map 11

Off Glasgow Green. View from outside only.
Free.
Victorian factory built to copy the design of the
Doge's Palace in Venice with ornate decoration
of coloured glazed brick, battlements, arches
and pointed windows.

499 Glasgow, Theatre Royal
Map 11

Hope Street.
A fine Victorian theatre, now elegantly restored
as the home of Scottish Opera. Performances
also by Scottish Ballet.

500 Glasgow, Third Eye Centre
Map 11

350 Sauchiehall Street. Tue-Sat 1000-1730,
Sun 1400-1730. Free.
Changing programme of exhibitions, music,
poetry reading and other events.

501 Glasgow, Victoria Park and Fossil Grove
Map 11

Victoria Park Drive North, facing Airthrey
Avenue. Mon-Sat 0900-dusk. Free.
Cornish elms, lime trees, formal flower garden
and arboretum. Within the park is famous Fossil
Grove, with fossil stumps and roots of trees
which grew here 230 millions years ago.

502 Glenapp Castle Gardens
Map 17

A77, 15m SSW of Girvan. 23 Apr-end Sep, daily
1000-1700 except Sat. Adult: 25p, child: 10p,
group rates. (Earl and Countess of Inchcape)
The Scottish Baronial mansion built by David
Bryce in 1870 has extensive gardens, including
terraces, woodland walks and formal walled
garden.

Glenelg

503 Glenarn Gardens
Map 11

*Rhu, 10m NW of Dumbarton. Daily Mar-Aug,
dawn-dusk. Adult: 40p, child: 20p.
(Mr J F A Gibson)*
A woodland garden with a large variety of
different shrubs, including rhododendrons,
azaleas and magnolias.

504 Glenbuchat Castle
Map 7

Off A97, 14m W of Alford.
Not open to the public: may be viewed from
outside. (AM)
This ancient seat of the Gordons on upper
Donside is a fine example of a Z-plan castle.

505 Glencaple
Map 18

On B725, 5m S of Dumfries.
One of two small quays on the banks of the Nith
which Burns visited regularly in his capacity as
Exciseman. (See No 614.)

506 Glen Coe and Dalness
Map 4

A82, 10m N of Tyndrum, runs through the glen.
The finest and perhaps the most famous glen in
Scotland through which a main road runs. Scene
of the Massacre of Glencoe, 1692, and centre for
some of the best mountaineering in the country
(not to be attempted by the unskilled). Noted for
wildlife which includes red deer, wildcat, golden
eagle, ptarmigan etc. NTS owns 14,200 acres of
Glen Coe and Dalness. Ski centre, chairlift and
ski tows (weekends and New Year and Easter
holiday periods only, other times by charter
arrangements) at White Corries (see No 988).
Visitor Centre open Good Friday-mid May and
mid Sep-mid Oct daily 1000-1700; mid May-mid
Sep, daily 1000-1900. Gives general
information, particularly on walks. Adult: 10p.

507 Glencoe and North Lorn Folk Museum
Map 4

*In Glencoe village, off A82, on S shore of
Loch Leven. May-Sep, Mon-Sat 1000-1730.
Adult: 15p, child: 10p.*
Historic relics, many connected with Prince
Charles Edward Stuart, also domestic
implements, weapons, costumes, photographs,
dolls' houses and dolls, agricultural tools, dairy
and slate quarrying equipment are included in
this museum housed in a number of thatched
cottages.

508 Glendronach Distillery
Map 6

*On B9001, between Huntly and Aberchirder,
19m N of Inverurie. All year, Mon-Fri 1000 or
1400 (by arrangement only,
tel: Forgue 202). Free.*
Visitor Centre and guided tour around malt
whisky distillery dating from 1856.

509 Glenelg Brochs
Map 4

*Unclassified road from Eilanreach, 12m W of
Shiel Bridge. All times. Free. (AM)*
Two Iron Age brochs, Dun Telve and Dun
Troddan, have walls still over 30 feet high.

Glenesk

510 Glenesk Folk Museum
Map 7

16m NNW of Brechin. Easter weekend and Sun from Easter; daily Jun-Sep 1400-1800. Adult: 30p, child: 15p.
A series of displays shows everyday life in Glenesk from c 1800 to the present day.

511 Glenfarclas Distillery
Map 5

Off A95, 17m WSW of Keith and 17m NE of Grantown-on-Spey. All year, Mon-Fri 0900-1630. Groups by arrangement, tel: Ballindalloch 209. Free.
Tours of a well-known malt whisky distillery, visual exhibition and museum of old illicit distilling equipment in Reception Centre.

512 Glenfiddich and Balvenie Distilleries
Map 6

Just N of Dufftown, 10m SW of Keith. All year, Mon-Fri 1000-1230, 1400-1630. Free.
The malting, mashing, fermenting, distilling, maturing and bottling of malt whisky are shown.

513 Glenfinnan Monument
Map 4

A830, 18½m W of Fort William. Good Fri-31 May, 1 Sep-mid Oct, daily 0930-1800; Jun-Aug, daily 0930-2000. Adult: 30p, child: 15p. (NTS)
The monument commemorates the raising of Prince Charles Edward Stuart's standard at Glenfinnan on 19 August 1745 as a rallying point for the clans in the '45 Rising. It was erected by Macdonald of Glenaladale in 1815; a figure of a Highlander surmounts the tower. The Visitor Centre tells of the Prince's campaign from Glenfinnan to Derby and back to the final defeat at Culloden.

514 Glengarioch Distillery
Map 6

15m NW of Aberdeen at Oldmeldrum. Free. By arrangement, tel: Oldmeldrum 706/7/8
Display of the whole process of producing single malt Scotch whisky.

515 Glengoyne Distillery
Map 11

Off A81, 10m N of Dumgoyne, Glasgow. (Lang Bros.) Free. By arrangement, tel: 041-332 6361.
Distilling of Scotch whisky.

516 Glen Grant and Caperdonich Distilleries
Map 6

Rothes. (Glen Livet and Glen Grant Distilleries Ltd.) Daily 1000-1600. Closed mid Jul-end Aug. Visits by arrangement, tel: Rothes 243 or 327. Adults and children over 12 years.
Production of malt whisky is shown.

517 Glenkiln
Map 18

Unclassified road 10m WNW of Dumfries, by the reservoir. All times. Free.
In lonely country around Glenkiln Reservoir stand Henry Moore's King and Queen and other sculptures by Epstein, Rodin etc.

518 Glenlivet Distillery Visitor Centre
Map 5

B9008, 5m N of Tomintoul. Apr-mid Oct, Mon-Fri 1000-1600. Free.
Guided tours of distillery. Exhibition of ancient tools connected with the industry and an old whisky still.

519 Glenluce Abbey
Map 17

Off A75, 2m N of Glenluce. Opening standard. Adult: 15p, child: 7p, group rates. (AM)
A fine vaulted chapter house, founded in 1192 by Roland, Earl of Galloway for the Cistercian order, is of architectural interest.

520 Glenmore Forest Park
Map 5

7m E of Aviemore, off A951. (FC)
Over 12,000 acres of pine and spruce woods and mountainside on the north-west slopes of the Cairngorms, with Loch Morlich as its centre. This is probably the finest area in Britain for wildlife, including red deer, reindeer, wildcat, golden eagle, ptarmigan, capercailzie etc. Remnants of old Caledonian pinewoods. Well-equipped caravan sites and hostels open all year, canoeing, sailing, fishing, swimming, forest trails and hillwalking, and an Information Centre.

Glenrothes: see No 65.

Glen Roy: see No 775.

521 Glenruthven Mills
Map 8

Robert White & Co (1929) Ltd, Abbey Road, Auchterarder, ¼m SE of A9. All year, Mon-Fri 0900-1700. Free.
Demonstration of the weaving of cloth using a working steam engine to drive the machinery.

522 Glenshee Chairlift
Map 8

Off A93, 10m S of Braemar. Daily, 0900-1700. Charge for chairlift.
Ascends the Cairnwell mountain (3,059 feet) from the summit of the highest main road pass in Britain (2,199 feet).

523 Globe Inn
Map 18

Off High Street, Dumfries. Normal public house hours.
Burns' favourite howff (pub) where his chair, inscribed window pane and other relics can still be seen and enjoyed in a convivial atmosphere.

524 Goatfell
Map 10

3½m NNW of Brodick, Arran.
At 2,866 feet this is the highest peak on Arran. NTS property includes Glen Rosa and Cir Mhor, wth grand walking and climbing. The golden eagle may occasionally be seen, along with hawks, harriers etc.

525 Grangemouth Museum
Map 12

Victoria Library, Bo'ness Road, Grangemouth. All year Mon-Sat 1000-1700. Free. (Falkirk District Council)
This display concentrates on Central Scotland canals, including canal tools and a model lock. Also exhibits relating to *Charlotte Dundas*, the world's first practical steamship, and to modern Grangemouth.

526 Grain Earth House
Map 1

Hatson, Kirkwall, Orkney. Opening standard, on application to key-keeper. Free. (AM)
A bean-shaped Iron Age souterrain with an entrance stair leading to an underground passage and chamber.

Granny Kempock's Stone: see No 598.

527 Great Glen Exhibition
Map 5

Centre of Fort Augustus beside the canal. Jun-mid Sept, Mon-Sat 1000-1800, Sun 1400-1800. Adult: 30p, child: 15p.
An open-plan museum and audio-visual show which tells the history of the Great Glen. One room is devoted to information about Loch Ness and the monster

528 Greenknowe Tower
Map 16

½m W of Gordon on A6089, 9m NW of Kelso. Opening standard. Apply custodian. Free. (AM)
A fine turreted tower house of 1581, still retaining its iron yett (gate).

529 Greenlaw Church
Map 16

A697, 11m NW of Coldstream. All reasonable times. Free.
The church dates from 1675 and has a tall square tower of 1696.

Gretna: see No 896.

530 Grey Cairns of Camster
Map 3

6m N of Lybster on Watten Road (off A9). All reasonable times. Free. (AM)
Two megalithic chambered cairns.
(c 3000-2000 BC.)

531 Greyfriars House Gardens
Map 6

Queen St at Institution Road, Elgin. May-Jul,
Sun 1400-1900. Adult: 15p. (Major G C Yool)
About five hundred medium and small flowering
trees; about a hundred of these are considered
by experts to be 'tender'.

532 Grey Mare's Tail
Map 16

Off A708, 10m NE of Moffat. (NTS)
A spectacular 200-feet waterfall formed by the
Tail Burn dropping from Loch Skene. The area is
rich in wild flowers and there is a herd of wild
goats.
NB: Visitors should keep to the path to the foot of
the falls: there have been serious accidents to
people scrambling up and care should be
exercised.

Grotto of Our Lady of Lourdes: see No 155.

533 Guildhall
Map 12

St John Street, Stirling. May-Sep, Mon-Fri
1000-1300, 1400-1700; Oct-Apr, Mon-Fri
1000-1300, 1400-1530. Admission by donation.
The Guildhall, or Cowane's Hospital, was built
between 1634 and 1649 as an almshouse for
elderly members of the Guild of Merchants. It
contains portraits of former Deans of Guild,
weights and measures and an old scaffold. John
Cowane, who financed the project, was a Stirling
merchant who made a fortune trading with
Holland.

534 Gurness Broch
Map 1

Off A966, 11m NNW of Kirkwall, Orkney.
Opening standard. Adult: 15p, child: 7p, group
rates. (AM)
An Iron Age broch still over 10 feet high,
surrounded by stone huts and within a deep
ditch. Later inhabited in Dark Age and Viking
times.

535 Gylen Castle
Map 10

On the island Kerrera, 1m W of Oban.
Passenger ferry from Oban. All reasonable
times. Free.
The castle, dating from 1587 and once a
MacDougal stronghold, is now in ruins.

536 Haddington
Map 14

17m E of Edinburgh.
One of the best-conserved towns in the country,
Haddington preserves a very complete
mediaeval street plan and 129 of its buildings
are scheduled as of special architectural or
historic interest. A 'Walk around the Town'
(booklet available locally) includes the Town
House (1748) designed by William Adam; the
17th-century Nungate Bridge; 18th-century
Poldrate Mill; St Mary's Parish Church, late 14th
and 15th-century; and the High Street, with its
attractive facades and shop fronts. (See also No
854.)

537 Haddington Museum
Map 14

In Haddington Library, Newton Port.
Mon, Tue, Thu and Fri 1000-1900; Wed
1000-1200; Sat 1000-1600. Closed Sun. Free.
An interesting display of local historical items in a
small room in the 19th-century former meeting
house, now used as a local public library.

538 Haddo House
Map 6

Off B9005, 7½m NW of Ellon. Early May to late
Sep, Mon-Sat 1100-1800, Sun 1400-1800.
Adult: 85p. child: 40p. (NTS)
A Georgian house built in 1732 by William Adam
on the site of a former house, home of the
Gordons of Haddo, Earls and Marquesses of
Aberdeen, for over 500 years. The Haddo House
Theatre has notable opera and concert
productions.

Hailes Castle

539 Hailes Castle
Map 14

Off A1, 5m E of Haddington. Opening standard.
Adult: 15p, child: 7p, group rates. (AM)
These extensive ruins date from the
13th/15th century. There is a fine 16th-century
chapel. Here Bothwell brought Mary Queen of
Scots on their flight from Borthwick Castle in
1567.

540 Halliwell's House
Map 16

In main square, Selkirk. Mon-Wed, Fri and
Sat. 1000-1700; Thu 1000-1300. Donations.
(Mr F H Robson)
A museum of ironmongery.

541 Hamilton District Museum
Map 11

½m SW of M74 at A7283 interchange.
All year. Mon-Fri 1000-1200, 1300-1700, Sat
1000-1700. Free.
Interesting local history museum with fine
transport and farm equipment sections.

Hawick

542 Hamilton Mausoleum
Map 11

Hamilton, 11m SE of Glasgow. Daily 0900-one hour before dusk. By arrangement, tel: Hamilton 66155. Adult: 15p, child: 7p.
Created in 1840 by the 10th Duke of Hamilton, with a remarkable echo. Note the huge bronze doors. The Mausoleum stands within the Strathclyde Country Park which has a wide variety of facilities. (See also No 916.)

543 Handa Island Nature Reserve
Map 3

Handa Island, 3m NW of Scourie. Access: day visits by local boatmen from Tarbet. Apr-mid Sep, Mon-Sat 1000-1700, Adult: 20p, child: 10p. Accommodation in well-equipped bothy available to members of RSPB only (contact RSPB, 17 Regent Terrace, Edinburgh). Warden on island. (RSPB)
An island seabird sanctuary with vast numbers of fulmars, shags, gulls, kittiwakes and auks. Arctic and great skuas on moorland.

544 Harbour Cottage Gallery
Map 17

Kirkcudbright. July-Sep, Mon-Sat 1030-1230, 1400-1700. Adult: 10p, child: 5p. (Harbour Cottage Trust)
Exhibitions of paintings and sometimes crafts in a picturesque whitewashed building beside the River Dee.

545 Keir Hardie Statue
Map 15

Cumnock town centre. All times. Free.
Bust outside the Town Hall to commemorate James Keir Hardie (1856-1913), an early socialist leader, and founder of the Independent Labour Party in 1893.

546 Harestanes
Map 16

At Monteviot, off A68 4m N of Jedburgh. Easter to Sept. Admission charge. (Marquis of Lothian)
An interpretation centre, based on the old home farm of a large country estate. The major theme is the use of woodlands and timber utilisation and there are walks through the estate and pinery.

547 John Hastie Museum
Map 15

Strathaven. May-Sep, Mon-Fri 1400-1700, Sat 1400-1900. Free.
Museum of local history set in Strathaven Park.

548 Hawick Museum and Art Gallery
Map 16

In Wilton Lodge Park, on western outskirts of Hawick. Apr-Oct, Mon-Sat 1000-1700, Sun 1400-1700. Nov-Mar, Mon-Sat 1000-1600. Adult: 20p, child: 10p.
(Roxburgh District Council)
In the ancestral home of the Langlands of that Ilk is an unrivalled collection of local and Scottish Border relics, natural history, art gallery, etc. Situated in 107-acre Wilton Lodge Park, open at all times: riverside walks, gardens, greenhouses, recreations and playing fields.

549 Heatherbank Museum and Library of Social Work
Map 11

163 Murdoch Road, Milngavie, 8m NW of Glasgow. All year, by arrangement, tel: 041-956 2687. Free.
The only museum of social work in the world. There are 2500 slides of the 19th and early 20th century and 5000 volumes in the reference library.

550 The Hermitage
Map 8

Off B898 2m W of Dunkeld. All reasonable times. Car park 15p.
A picturesque folly, built in 1758 and restored in 1952. It is set above the wooded gorge of the River Bran. There are nature trails in the area.

551 Hermitage Castle
Map 18

Off A6399, 16m NE of Langholm. Opening standard. Adult: 20p, child: 10p, group rates. (AM)
This grim 13th-century castle was a stronghold of the de Soulis family and, after 1341, of the Douglases. It has had a vivid, sometimes cruel history; to here Mary Queen of Scots made her exhausting ride from Jedburgh in 1566 to meet Bothwell, a journey which almost cost her her life. The building consists of four towers and connecting walls, outwardly almost perfect.

552 Highland Folk Museum
Map 5

A9 at Kingussie, 12m SW of Aviemore near Kincraig. All year. Apr-Oct, Mon-Sat 1000-1800, Sun 1400-1800. Nov-Mar, Mon-Fri 1000-1500. Adult: 45p, child: 10p, group rates. (Highland Regional Council)
The open air museum includes an 18th-century shooting lodge, a "Black House" from Lewis, a Clack Mill, and exhibits of farming equipment. Indoors, the farming museum has fine displays of a barn, dairy, stable and an exhibition of Highland tinkers; and there are special features on weapons, costume, musical instruments and Highland furniture.

553 Highland Mary's Monument
Map 15

At Failford, on A758 3m W of Mauchline. All times. Free.
The monument commemorates the place where, it is said, Robert Burns parted from his 'Highland Mary', Mary Campbell. They exchanged vows, but she died the following autumn.

554 Highland Mary's Statue
Map 11

Dunoon, near pier. All times. Free.
The statue of Burns' Highland Mary at the foot of the Castle Hill. Mary Campbell was born on a farm near Dunoon, and consented to become Burns' wife before he married Jean Armour.

555 Highland Wildlife Park
Map 5

Off A9, 7m SW of Aviemore. 1000-1800, closed winter season. £3.00 per car.
(Highland Wildlife Park Limited)
This notable wildlife park features breeding groups of Highland animals and birds in a beautiful natural setting. Drive-through section has red deer herd, bison, Highland cattle, etc. Aviaries display capercailzie, ptarmigan, eagles; also wolves, wildcats and nearly 60 other species. There is an exhibition on 'Man and Fauna in the Highlands', and a children's animal park.

556 The Hill House
Map 11

Upper Colquhoun Street, Helensburgh. 1 Apr-31 Oct: Mon 1230-1700, Tue 1230-1900, Wed 0930-1700. Sat and Sun 1400-1800, closed Thu and Fri. 1 Nov-31 Mar: Mon and Tue 1230-1700, Wed 0930-1700, Sat and Sun 1300-1700, closed Thu and Fri. Adult:50p, child/OAP: 25p.
Designed and built for W W Blackie Esq in 1902-03 by Charles Rennie Mackintosh with Mackintosh furniture and other items.

557 Hill o' Many Stanes
Map 3

3¼m ENE of Lybster. All reasonable times. Free. (AM)
Neolithic or Bronze Age site with almost 200 stones of no great size set out in 22 parallel rows.

558 Hill of Tarvit
Map 9

A916, 2m S of Cupar. (House) Easter weekend, 1 May-30 Sep, daily except Friday 1400-1730. (Garden) All year, 1000-dusk. Adult: 85p, child: 40p. Garden only: Adult: 30p, child: 15p (NTS)
A mansion of 1696 remodelled by Sir Robert Lorimer in 1906, with a collection of furniture, tapestries, porcelain and paintings.

559 The Hirsel
Map 16

Off A697, 7½m NE of Kelso. Grounds all reasonable times. Free. (Lord Home of the Hirsel, K.T.)
A wildlife preserve with rhododendrons and woodland and a small loch, adjoining the grounds of a private house. Estate information centre.

560 James Hogg Monument
Map 16

By Ettrick 1m W of B7009. All times. Free.
A monument on the site of the birthplace of
James Hogg. (1770-1835) known as "The Ettrick
Shepherd", friend of Scott. His grave is in the
nearby church.

561 Hollows Tower
Map 18

*A7, 5m S of Langholm. All reasonable times.
Free.*
Also known as Holehouse, the tower dates from
the 16th century and has walls 6 feet thick. It was
once the home of the 16th-century Border
freebooter, Johnny Armstrong.

562 Hopetoun House
Map 13

*W of South Queensferry. May-Sep, daily 1100-
1700. Adult: £1, child: 50p, group rates.
(Marquess of Linlithgow)*
This splendid Scottish country house is the home
of the Hope family, Earls of Hopetoun and later
Marquesses of Linlithgow. Started in 1696 to the
designs of Sir William Bruce, it was rebuilt and
enlarged in 1721-54 by William Adam and his
sons, John and Robert. Notable portraits include
Rubens, Van Dyck, Rembrandt and Canaletto.
The extensive grounds include deer parks with
fallow and red deer, St Kilda Sheep and
ornamental birds. Also sea walk, formal rose
garden, educational day centre and stables
museum featuring 'Horse and Man in Lowland
Scotland'.

563 The House of the Binns
Map 13

*Off A904, 4m E of Linlithgow. Easter,
1 May-Sep, daily (except Fri) 1400-1730. (Park)
1000-1900. Adult: 75p, child: 35p, group rates.
(NTS)*
Occupied for more than 350 years, The Binns
dates largely from the time of General Tam
Dalyell, 1599-1685, and reflects the early
17th-century transition in Scottish architecture
from fortified stronghold to gracious mansion.
There are magnificent plaster ceilings, fine views
across the Forth and a visitor trail.

Huntingtower

564 Hume Castle
Map 16

B6364, 6m N of Kelso. All year Mon-Fri 1000-1700, Sun 1400-1700, Adult: 15p. Key from Breadalbane Guncraft, below Castle. (Dept of Agriculture and Fisheries)
On a hilltop 600 feet above sea level, this castle, once the seat of the Earls of Home, dates originally back to the 13th century. It capitulated in 1651 to Cromwell, and was largely destroyed. In 1794 the Earl of Marchmont restored it as a sham antique with battlemented walls. Fine views.

565 Hunter Monument
Map 11

East Kilbride town centre. All times. Free.
The monument commemorates the Hunter brothers, 18th century anatomists.

566 Hunterston Castle, House and Gardens
Map 15

Off A78, 2½m NNW of West Kilbride. 7 Jun-17 Sep, Wed-Sun, 1400-1700. Admission charge. (Hunterston Estates Ltd)
A 15th-century castle, 18th-century family mansion and a large walled garden and kitchen garden.

567 Huntingtower Castle
Map 8

Off A85, 3m WNW of Perth. Opening standard. Adult: 15p, child: 7p, group rates. (AM)
A 15th-century castellated mansion until 1600 known as Ruthven Castle. This was the scene of the Raid of Ruthven in 1582; James VI, then 16, accepted an invitation from the Earl of Gowrie to his hunting seat and found himself in the hands of nobles who demanded the dismissal of the royal favourites. When the king tried to escape, his

way was barred by the Master of Glamis. The Ruthven conspirators held power for some months, but the Earl was beheaded in 1584.

568 Huntly Castle
Map 6

Castle Street, Huntly. Opening standard. Adult: 20p, child: 10p, group rates. (AM)
An imposing ruin which replaced mediaeval Strathbogie Castle which, until 1544, was the seat of the Gay Gordons, the Marquesses of Huntly, the most powerful family in the north until the mid-16th century. There are elaborate heraldic adornments on the castle walls. The castle, now in a wooded park, was destroyed by Moray in 1452, rebuilt, then rebuilt again in 1551-54, burned 40 years later and again rebuilt in 1602.

569 Huntly Museum
Map 6

In the Library, Main Square, Huntly. All year, Tues-Sat 1000-1200, 1400-1600. Free. (North East of Scotland Library Service)
Permanent local history exhibitions and temporary thematic exhibitions twice a year.

570 Inchcolm Abbey
Map 13

On Inchcolm Island in the Firth of Forth; check at Aberdour about boat hire. Opening standard. Adult: 15p, child: 7p, group rates. (AM)
The monastic buildings, which include a fine 13th-century octagonal chapter house, are the best preserved in Scotland.

571 Inchkenneth Chapel
Map 4

On the island of Inchkenneth, in Loch na Keel, west of Mull. All reasonable times. Free. (AM)
A unicameral chapel of the West Highland type.

Inverallochy

572 Inchmahome Priory
Map 11

On an island in the Lake of Menteith, A81, 4m E of Aberfoyle. Access by boat from lakeside, Port of Menteith, Apr-Sep 0930-1900; Oct-Mar 0930-1600. (Ferry normally suspended during winter months, depending on weather conditions; tel: Stirling 62421.) Adult: 25p, child: 12p (inclusive of ferry), group rates. (AM)
The ruins of an Augustinian house, founded in 1238, where the infant Mary Queen of Scots was sent for refuge in 1547.

573 The 'Indian Temple'
Map 3

Above Evanton village on Fynish Hill off A9. All times. Free.
Erected by General Sir Hector Munro (1726-1805), as a means of easing local unemployment. The structure is said to represent the gateway to an Indian town Sir Hector captured in 1781.

Industrial Museum: see No 627

574 Ingasetter
Map 7

North Deeside Road, Banchory. Mon-Fri 0830-1700. Free.
Film and tour explaining the growing and distilling of lavender and manufacture of other toilet preparations.

575 Inishail Chapel
Map 10

On an islet in Loch Awe, 10m N of Inveraray; a boat can be hired from Lochawe village, on B840.
In c 1257 this chapel was dedicated to St Findoc. Lying on the grass are two fine carved slabs (14th or 15th century).

576 Innerpeffray Library
Map 8

B8062, 4m SE of Crieff. May-end Sep, Mon-Wed, Fri and Sat 1000-1300, 1400-1700; Sun 1400-1600. Oct-Apr, Mon-Wed, Fri and Sat 1000-1300, 1400-1600. Sun 1400-1600.
The oldest library still in existence in Scotland, founded 1691, housed in a late 18th-century building. The nearby church was built in 1508.

Inchcolm Abbey

577 Inverallochy
Map 6

On B9107 4m E of Fraserburgh.
Small, attractive village with rows of low fishermen's cottages in an area traditionally famous for its fishing.

578 Inveraray Bell Tower
Map 10

In Inveraray. May-Sep, daily 1000-1300, 1400-1700. Adult: 25p, child: 10p.
(Scottish Episcopal Church of All Saints)
The 140-feet high granite tower houses Scotland's finest ring of bells and the world's second-heaviest ring of ten bells. The bells are chimed to melodies daily. Excellent views.

579 Inveraray Castle
Map 10

½m N of Inveraray. Apr-end Jun, daily (exc Fri) 1000-1230, 1400-1800, Sun 1400-1800; end Jun-Oct, daily 1000-1800, Sun 1400-1800. Adult: £1, child: 50p, group rates.
(Argyll Estates)
Inveraray has been the seat of the chiefs of Clan Campbell, Dukes of Argyll, for centuries. The present castle was started in 1743 when the third Duke engaged Roger Morris to build it. Subsequently the Adam family, father and sons, were also involved. The magnificent interior decoration was commissioned by the fifth Duke from Robert Mylne. In addition to many historic relics, there are portraits by Gainsborough, Ramsay and Raeburn. The extensive damage caused by the fire in 1975 has now been impressively restored.

Inveraray Castle

580 Inveresk Lodge Garden
Map 13

S of Musselburgh, A6124, 7m E of Edinburgh. All year, Mon, Wed, Fri 1000-1630 (and also Sun, when house is occupied). Adult: 30p, child: 15p. (NTS)
This garden of a 17th-century house (not open to the public) displays a range of plants suitable for the small garden. Good shrub rose border and selection of climbing roses.

581 Inverewe Gardens
Map 3

On A832, 6m NE of Gairloch. (Gardens) All year, dawn-dusk. (Visitor Centre) 1 Apr-mid Oct, Mon-Sat 1000-1830 (or dusk if earlier), Sun 1300-1830 (or dusk). Adult: 95p, child: 45p, group rates. (NTS)
Plants from many countries flourish in this garden created by Osgood Mackenzie over 100 years ago, giving an almost continuous display of colour throughout the year. Eucalyptus, rhododendron and many Chilean and South African plants are represented in great variety, together with Himalayan Lilies and giant forget-me-nots from the South Pacific.

Irvine

582 Inverkeithing Museum
Map 13

1m N of Forth Road Bridge. All year.
Wed-Sun 1000-1230, 1430-1700. Free.
(Dunfermline District Council)
The museum, showing the history of the Old
Royal Burgh, is housed in the Old Friary, founded
in 1384.

583 Inverness Museum and Art Gallery
Map 5

Castle Wynd, Inverness. Weekdays 0900-1700.
Free. (Inverness District Council)
The museum interprets the social and natural
history, archaeology and culture of the
Highlands, with fine collections of Highland
silver, bagpipes, and Jacobite relics. Special
exhibitions, performances and talks.

584 Inverpolly National Nature Reserve
Map 3

Off A835, 12m NNE of Ullapool. (NCC)
A remote, almost uninhabited area of bog,
moorland, woodland, cliffs and summits. Car
park, nature/geological trail and Information
Centre at Knockan Cliff, 12m N of Ullapool;
geological and wildlife interest. (Open May-Sep,
Mon-Fri 1000-1730).

585 Inverurie Museum
Map 6

Inverurie. All year, Mon-Fri 1400-1700,
Sat 1000-1200. Free.
(North East of Scotland Library Service)
Permanent display of local archaeology and
thematic exhibitions three times a year. Just
outside the town, on B993, is a 60 foot high
motte, The Bass.

586 Iona
Map 10

Off the SW tip of Mull; A849 to Fionnphort, then
ferry. Also steamer trips from Oban.
In 563 St Columba with 12 followers came to this
little island to found a monastery from which his
monks travelled over much of Scotland
preaching Christianity to the Picts. The
monastery, often attacked up to the 9th century
by Norse raiders, was replaced in 1203 but,
along with the cathedral, fell into decay.
Restoration started early this century.
The monastery is the home of the Iona
Community, founded by Dr George Macleod in
1938, who have done much restoration of the
Cathedral, which has a beautiful interior and
interesting carvings. For centuries Iona was the
burial place of Scottish kings and chiefs. The
oldest surviving building is St Oran's Chapel,
c 1080 (restored). The remains of the 13th-
century nunnery are to be seen, and outside the
cathedral is 10th-century St Martin's Cross,
14 feet high and elaborately carved.

587 Irvine Burns Club Museum
Map 15

Wellwood, 28 Eglinton Street. Sat pm and by
arrangement, tel: Irvine 74511. Free.
A Burns museum, library and burgh museum.

588 Isle of May
Map 9

Island in the Firth of Forth, 5½m SE of Crail.
Sailings from Anstruther, parties only, Apr-end
Oct. Tel: Kirkcaldy 51587.
Lighthouse dates from 1816. There is a bird
observatory and field station and a national
nature reserve. St Adrian's Chapel, now ruined,
was established in the 12th century.

589 Italian Chapel
Map 1

St Margaret's Hope, Lamb Holm, Orkney.
All times. Free.
(POW Chapel Preservation Committee)
Using a Nissen hut, Italian prisoners-of-war in
1943 created this beautiful little chapel out of
scrap metal, concrete and other materials.

Jail Museum: see No 167.

590 Jarlshof
Map 1

Sumburgh Head, 28m S of Lerwick, Shetland.
Opening standard. Adult: 20p, child: 10p, group
rates. (AM)
One of the most remarkable archaeological sites
in Europe with the remains of three extensive
village settlements occupied from Bronze Age to
Viking times, together with a medieval farmstead
and the 16th-century house of the Earls Robert
and Patrick Stewart.

Kellie Castle and Gardens,
Pittenweem

591 Jedburgh Abbey
Map 16

High Street, Jedburgh. Opening standard.
Adult: 25p, child: 12p, group rates. (AM)
Perhaps the most impressive of the four great
Border Abbeys founded by David I, dating from
c 1118. The noble remains are extensive, the
west front has a fine rose window, known as St
Catherine's Wheel, and there is a richly carved
Norman doorway.

Jim Clark Memorial Trophy Room:
see No 198.

Kay Park Museum: see No 133.

592 Keir Gardens
Map 12

Off B824, 6m NNW of Stirling. Apr-Oct,
Tue to Thu 1400-1800. Adult: 40p.
(Lt Col Wm Stirling of Keir)
Gardens of a mansion where Chopin was a guest
in 1848. Features include rhododendrons,
azaleas, a water garden, a yew tree house,
daffodils and herbaceous borders.

593 Keith Statue
Map 6

Peterhead town centre. All times. Free.
Statue of James Keith, Earl Marischal and brother of George Keith, founder of Peterhead (1593). James became a marshal in the army of Frederick the Great of Prussia. The statue was presented in 1868 by William I of Prussia.

594 Kelburn Country Centre
Map 11

Off A78 at Fairlie, 2m SE of Largs. May-Sep (incl) daily 1000-1800. Adult: 60p, child: 30p, group rates. (Viscount Kelburn)
Exhibitions, gardens, nature trails, pony trekking, adventure course, based in the 18th-century farm buildings which form a small village square. The Castle (12th century) is not open to the public.

595 Kellie Castle, Arbroath
Map 9

½m N of A92, 2m SW of Arbroath. Mar-23 Dec, daily exc Tues, 1100-1700. Adult: 50p, child: 25p. (A L Kerr-Boyle)
A fine tower which was extended by Sir William Irvine of Drum in 1614. Well restored a century ago and still lived in. The old library has been converted into a gallery where Scottish artists can display their work.

596 Kellie Castle and Gardens, Pittenweem
Map 9

Off A921, 10m S of St Andrews. (Castle) Good Friday-30 Sep, daily exc Fri 1400-1800. (Gardens) Good Friday-30 Sep, daily 1000-dusk. (Castle and Gardens) Adult: 85p, child: 40p. (Gardens) Adult: 30p, child: 15p. (NTS)
Fine domestic architecture of the 16th/17th centuries though the oldest part dates from c 1360. Owned by the Oliphants for over 250 years, then by the Earls of Mar and Kellie, it was restored nearly a century ago by Professor James Lorimer. His grandson, the sculptor Hew Lorimer, is resident custodian. Notable plaster work and painted panelling. 16 acres of gardens.

597 Kelso Abbey
Map 16

Bridge Street, Kelso. Opening standard. Free. (AM)
This was the largest of the Border abbeys. One of the earliest completed by David I, it was founded in 1128. When the Earl of Hertford entered Kelso in 1545 the abbey was garrisoned as a fortress and was taken only at the point of the sword; the garrison of 100 men, including 12 monks, was slaughtered, and the building was almost entirely razed. The tower is part of the original building.

598 Kempock Stone
Map 11

On the cliff side of Gourock. All reasonable times. Free.
Granny Kempock's Stone, of grey schist six feet high, was probably significant in prehistoric times. In past centuries it was used by fishermen in rites to ensure fair weather. Couples intending to get married used to encircle the stone to get Granny's blessing.

Kilberry

599 Kilberry Sculptured Stones
Map 10

*Off B8024, 20m SSW of Lochgilphead. All
reasonable times. Free. (AM)*
A fine collection of late mediaeval sculptured
stones.

600 Kilchurn Castle
Map 10

*N tip of Loch Awe, 21m E of Oban. Not open to
the public, but may be viewed from the outside.
(AM)*
The keep was built in 1440 by Sir Colin Campbell
of Glenorchy, founder of the Breadalbane family.
The north and south sides of the building were
erected in 1693 by Ian, Earl of Breadalbane,
whose arms and those of his wife are over the
gateway. Occupied by the Breadalbanes until
1740, in 1746 it was taken by Hanoverian troops.
A gale in 1879 toppled one of its towers.

601 Kildalton Crosses
Map 10

*7½m NE of Port Ellen, Isle of Islay. All
reasonable times. Free. (AM)*
Two of the finest Celtic crosses in Scotland, and
sculptured slabs, are in Kildalton churchyard.

602 Kildrummy Castle
Map 7

*A97, 10m W of Alford. All reasonable times.
Adult: 15p, child: 7p, group rates. (AM)*
The most extensive example in Scotland of a
13th-century castle. The four round towers, hall
and chapel remains belong in substance to the
original. The great gatehouse and other work is
later, to the 16th century. It was the seat of the
Earls of Mar, and played an important part in
Scottish history until 1715 when it was
dismantled.

603 Kildrummy Castle Gardens
Map 7

*A97, 10m W of Alford. Apr-Oct, daily 0900-1700.
Adult: 25p, group rates.
(Kildrummy Castle Garden Trust)*
The shrub and alpine garden in the ancient
quarry are known to botanists for their interest
and variety. A burn runs through the Den to the
water garden with a shrub bank above it.

Killiecrankie: see No 776.

604 Kilmartin Sculptured Stones
Map 10

*A816, 7½m N of Lochgilphead. All reasonable
times. Free. (AM)*
In this typical West Highland churchyard are
preserved a number of grave slabs and
fragments of at least two crosses, one showing
Christ crucified on the front and Christ in Majesty
on the back. The cross dates from the 16th
century.
The area north of the Crinan Canal to Kilmartin
has many reminders of both prehistoric and
mediaeval times. These include: 1. Bronze Age
cup-and-ring engravings at Ballygowan;
2. Bronze Age and earlier burial cairns at
Dunchraigaig, Nether Largie, Ri Cruin and
Kilmartin Glebe; 3. A Stone Circle, c 2000 BC at
Temple Wood.

605 Kilmory Knap Chapel
Map 10

Off road along E side of Loch Sween, 18m SW of Lochgilphead. All reasonable times. Free. (AM)
A typical small West Highland church with notable sculptured stones.

606 Kilmory Cairns
Map 10

At S end of Arran, off A841. All times. Free.
Cairn Baan, 3½m NE of Kilmory village, is a notable Neolithic long cairn. ½m SW of A841 at the Lagg Hotel is Torrylin Cairn, a Neolithic chambered cairn. There are many other cairns in this area.

607 Kilmuir Croft Museum
Map 4

Off A855, 20m NNW of Portree, Skye. Easter-Oct, 0900-1200. Adult: 20p, child: 10p, group rates.
Exhibits include a wall bed, farming and domestic implements.

608 Kilmun Arboretum
Map 11

By Forest Office on A880, 1m E of junction with A815. 5m N of Dunoon. All year. Daily, all day. Free. (FC)
A fascinating collection of tree species on a hillside to the northeast of Holy Loch within the Argyll Forest Park. (See also No 50.)

609 Kiloran Gardens
Map 10

Kiloran, Isle of Colonsay. Daily, all reasonable times.
An island garden noted for its rhododendrons and shrubs, including embothriums and magnolias.

610 Kilpheder Wheelhouse
Map 2

2m W of A865 by Kilpheder at S end of Isle of South Uist. All times. Free.
Slight remains of an ancient circular dwelling, c 200 AD, divided into 'stalls' like the spokes of a wheel.

611 Kilt Rock
Map 4

Off A855, 17m N of Portree, Skye. Seen from the road. Care should be taken not to go too near the edge of the cliff.
The top rock is composed of columnar basalt, the lower portion of horizontal beds, giving the impression of the pleats in a kilt. There is also a waterfall nearby.

612 Kiltmaking Display
Map 5

Hector Russell (Highland Industries) Ltd.
49 Huntley Street, Inverness. Jun-Sep, Mon-Fri
0900-1800. Free.
Display of military and civilian kiltmaking,
spinning wheels and looms, with special feature
of the Culloden Battlefield.

613 Kincorth
Map 3

From A96, 5m NW of Forres take unclassified
road N (signposted). Jun-Aug daily 0900-2100.
Adult: 10p. (Lt Col and Mrs A D Mackintosh)
Specimen trees, rose borders and herbaceous
borders, shrubbery and lawns.

614 Kingholm Quay
Map 18

Off B725 1m S of Dumfries.
One of two small quays on the banks of the Nith
which Burns visited regularly in his capacity as
Exciseman. (See also No 505.)

615 King's Cave
Map 10

On shore, 2m N of Blackwaterfoot on the west
coast of Arran. All times. Free.
A two-mile walk along the shore from the golf
course at Blackwaterfoot leads to a series of
caves, the largest being the King's Cave. Said to
have been occupied by Finn MacCoul and later
by Robert the Bruce, this is one of the possible
settings for the "Bruce and the spider" legend.
Carvings of figures are on the walls.

616 Kinkell Church
Map 6

On the E bank of the Don, 1m SSE of Inverurie,
off B993. All reasonable times. Free. (AM)
The ruins of an early 16th-century parish church
with some ornate details including a rich
sacrament house of unusual design, dated 1524.

Kinloch Castle

617 Kinloch Castle
Map 4

Isle of Rhum. By boat from Arisaig and Mallaig.
All year except 1st week May and 1st week Aug.
Extraordinary and magnificent residence built
at the turn of the century for Sir George Bullough
still containing many of its sumptuous fittings.
The island itself is a nature reserve.
(See also No 815.)

618 Kinmount Gardens
Map 18

Kinmount, 4m WNW of Annan. Easter-Nov, daily 1000-1700. Adult: 15p, child: 10p, group rates. (Hoddom and Kinmount Estates)
Fine gardens with signposted walks through woodland and around lakes. Particularly noted for azaleas and rhododendrons.

619 Kinneff Church
Map 7

Off unclassified road, E of A92, 2m N of Inverbervie. All reasonable times. Free.
It was here that the Scottish regalia (crown, sword and sceptre) were hidden in 1652, from Commonwealth troops besieging Dunnottar Castle. In the present church, which dates from 1738, are memorials to the parish minister, Rev James Grainger, who buried the regalia, and to the Governor of the castle, Sir George Ogilvy of Barras. (See also No 320.)

620 Kinneil House
Map 12

Off A904, 4m NW of Linlithgow. Opening standard. Adult: 15p, child: 7p, group rates. (AM)
In the grounds of this 16th/17th-century seat of the Dukes of Hamilton (which contains some of the finest contemporary wall paintings and decorated ceilings in Scotland) is the outhouse where James Watt developed his invention of the steam engine, the first being erected at a nearby colliery in 1765. (See also No 100.)

621 Kinross House Gardens
Map 8

½m SE of Kinross. May-Sep, daily 1400-1900. Adult: 50p, child: 10p. (Sir David Montgomery)
Formal gardens surrounding a 17th-century house.

622 Kinross Museum
Map 8

High Street. May-Sep, Tues-Sat 1300-1700. Free.
Items relating to local history, including archaeological finds, a display of local linen manufacturing, some examples of peat cutting, and local military exhibits.

623 Kintail
Map 4

N of A87 between Lochs Cluanie and Duich, E of Kyle of Lochalsh. (NTS)
Magnificent Highland scenery including the Five Sisters of Kintail, peaks rising to 3,500 feet. Red deer and wild goats. Visitor Centre at Morvich, with audio-visual display, open Good Friday-30 Sep.

624 Kippen Church
Map 11

Fore Road, Kippen, 10m W of Stirling.
0900-dusk. Free.
Beautifully renovated in 1925 under the direction of Sir D Y Cameron, RA, this modern church with rich interior furnishings is one of the most attractive of its kind in Scotland.

625 Kirk Yetholm
Map 16

Off B6352, 8m SE of Kelso.
Attractive village, with Town Yetholm, once famous as the home of the Scottish gypsies, now the northern end of the Pennine Way.

626 Kirkcaldy Burgh School Plaques
Map 13

On corner of Hill Street/Kirk Wynd. All times.
Free.
Plaques on the site of the former Burgh School, where Adam Smith (1723-1790) and Robert Adam (1728-1792) went to school. Thomas Carlyle was later schoolmaster there.

627 Kirkcaldy Industrial Museum
Map 13

Abbotshall Road, near railway station. 1 May-30
Sep, Mon-Sat 1400-1700. Free.
Permanent display relating to the linoleum industry, coal mining and other local industries. There is a collection of horse-drawn vehicles and a reconstructed Edwardian shop.

628 Kirkcaldy Museum and Art Gallery
Map 13

By railway station. All year, Mon-Sat 1100-1700,
Sun 1400-1700. Free.
A permanent display of the history of Kirkcaldy, the natural history of the area and the maritime history of the Firth of Forth. The paintings are Scottish from the 18th century to the present day, notably by William McTaggart, and there are frequent changing exhibitions.

Kirkcudbright Tolbooth and Mercat Cross:
see No 688.

629 Kirkmadrine Stones
Map 17

Off A716. 8m S of Stranraer. All reasonable
times. Free. (AM)
Three of the earliest Christian monuments in Britain, showing the Chi-Rho symbol and inscriptions dating from the 5th or early 6th century are to be seen outside a little church (closed).

Kirkwynd Cottages: see No 32.

630 Kisimul Castle
Map 2

On a tiny island in the bay by Castlebay, Isle of
Barra. May-Sep, Wed and Sat afternoons only.
Charge for boatman. (The Macneil of Barra)
For many generations Kisimul was the home and stronghold of the Macneils of Barra, widely noted for their lawlessness and piracy, and led by chiefs like Ruari the Turbulent, 35th chief, who did not fear to seize ships of subjects of Queen Elizabeth I. The main tower dates from about

1120. Restoration was commenced in 1938 by
the 45th clan chief, an American architect, and
completed in 1970.

631 Kitchener Memorial
Map 1

*At Marwick Head, SW of Birsay Bay, Orkney.
All times. Free.*
The cruiser *Hampshire*, taking Lord Kitchener to
Russia was sunk in 1916 off the coast, close by
this point.

632 Knap of Howar
Map 1

*W side of island of Papa Westray, 800 metres
W of Holland House, Orkney. All reasonable
times. Free. (AM)*
Only recently recognised as one of the oldest
sites in Europe, these two 5000-year-old
dwellings have also yielded many unusual
artefacts—whalebone mallets and a spatula and
unique stone borers and grinders.

633 Knock Castle
Map 4

*Off A851, 12m S of Broadford, Isle of Skye.
All reasonable times. Free.*
A ruined stronghold of the MacDonalds.

Knockan Cliff: see No 584.

Knocknagael Boar Stone: see No 97.

634 Lady Gifford's Well
Map 16

At West Linton, 17m SSW of Edinburgh.
The village of West Linton was well-known in
former days for its stonemasons. The figure on
'Lady Gifford's Well' was carved in 1666. There
are other carvings, probably by the same hand,
on a house opposite, dated 1660 and 1678.

635 Lady Kirk
Map 14

*On B6470 4m E of Swinton. All reasonable
times. Free.*
The church was built by James IV c 1500 as a
thanks-offering for his escape from drowning in
the River Tweed. It was built entirely of stone to
avoid the risk of fire.

636 Laggangairn Standing Stones
Map 17

*9m N of Glenluce on Barrhill road, then 3m walk.
All reasonable times. Free. (AM)*
At Laggangairn (*Hollow of the Cairns*) the
crosses on the two grey standing stones date
from the Dark Ages. A slab with a simple Latin
cross leans against a wall by the ruined
farmhouse.

637 Laidhay Caithness Croft
Map 3

*On A9, 1m N of Dunbeath. Easter-30 Sep, daily
0900-1700. Adult: 20p, child: 10p, group rates.*
An early 18th-century croft complex with stable,
dwelling house and byre under one thatched roof
with adjoining barn. Completely furnished in the
fashion of its time. The barn has a notable crux
roof.

638 William Lamb Studio
Map 7

*Market Street, Montrose. Apr-Sep, Sun
1400-1700, and by arrangement,
tel: Montrose 3232. Free.*
Studio of William Lamb, noted Montrose sculptor
and etcher, containing a selection of his works.

639 Land o' Burns Centre
Map 15

*Opposite Alloway Kirk, 2m S of Ayr. Spring and
autumn 1000-1800, summer 1000-2100, winter
1000-1700. Admission free; charge for audio-
visual display: Adult: 20p, child: 10p. (Kyle and
Carrick District Council)*
This visitor centre has an open-air agricultural
museum, an exhibition area, and an audio-visual
display on the life and times of Robert Burns.

640 Landmark Visitor Centre, Carrbridge
Map 5

*Carrbridge, 9m W of Grantown-on-Spey.
All year. Free. (Exhibition and auditorium): Adult:
40p, child: 20p, group rates.*
This 'Landmark' Visitor Centre was the first of its
kind in Europe. Ten thousand years of Highland
history are excitingly shown in the triple-screen
audio-visual theatre, and a dramatic exhibition
interprets the history of Strathspey. Craft and
book shop, restaurant, bar, nature trail and
woodland walk.

641 Landmark Visitor Centre, Stirling
Map 12

*On the Castle esplanade, Stirling. All year,
normally 0900-1700. (Exhibition and
auditorium): Adult: 40p, child: 20p, group rates.*
Set high above the town, Landmark brings alive
the history of Stirling in a multi-screen audio-
visual show. Craft and book shops, and tea
garden.

642 Lapidary Workshops
Map 7

*Garlogie School, Skene. All year, Mon-Sat
(except Fri) 0900-1230, 1400-1730. Free.*
Demonstrations of stone cutting and polishing.

643 Largs Museum
Map 11

*Manse Court, Largs. Jun-Sep, Mon-Sat 1430
1700. Donation box.
(Largs and District Historical Society)*
The museum holds a small collection of local
bygones, with a library of local history books and
numerous photographs.

Leadhills Library: see No 804.

644 Lecht Ski Tow
Map 7

*Off A939 7m SE of Tomintoul. During ski-ing
season only. (Lecht Ski Co Ltd)*
Ski tows operating to slopes on both sides of the
Lecht Road, famous for its snowfalls.

645 Leglen Wood
Map 15

2m S of A758, 4m E of Ayr. All times. Free.
An attractive wood above the River Ayr which
has associations with Burns' hero, William
Wallace. Burns often visited the spot now
marked by a cairn with inscription.

646 Leith Hall
Map 6

*B9002, 7m S of Huntly. (House) 1 May-
30 Sep, Mon-Sat 1100-1715, Sun 1400-1715.
(Garden) All year, daily 0930-dusk. (House)
Adult: 75p, child: 35p: Garden and grounds by
donation.*
For three centuries the home of the Leith and
Leith-Hay family. The earliest part of the building
is incorporated in the north wing and dates from
1650. Additions were made in the 18th and
19th centuries. The family tradition of military
service is reflected in the Exhibition Room, which
includes a writing case presented by Prince
Charles Edward Stuart on the eve of Culloden
(1746). A winding path with zig-zag herbaceous
border and rock garden are attractive features of
the gardens. Pond walk with observation hide,
picnic area and Soay sheep.

647 Lennoxlove House
Map 14

*On B6369, 1m S of Haddington. During
Edinburgh Festival, Wed and Sat 1400-1700;
any other times by arrangement to parties, tel:
Haddington 3720. Adult: £1, child: 50p.*
Originally named Lethington, it was the home of
the Maitland family (Maitland of Lethington was
Mary Queen of Scots' secretary). The house,
now a 17th-century mansion, was later named
Lennoxlove after 'La Belle' Stewart, Duchess
of Lennox, whose family acquired it in the
17th century.

Leuchars Norman Church

648 Leuchars Norman Church
Map 9

*A919, 5½m NW of St Andrews. All reasonable
times. Free.*
One of the best Norman churches in Scotland,
built by the De Quincie family. Original chancel
and apse.

649 Lewis Black House
Map 2

At Arnol, 15m NW of Stornoway, Isle of Lewis.
Opening standard except closed Sun.
Adult: 15p, child: 7p, group rates. (AM)
A good example of a traditional type of
Hebridean dwelling, built without mortar and
roofed with thatch on a timber framework and
without eaves. Characteristic features are the
central peat fire in the kitchen, the absence of
any chimney and the byre under the same roof.
The house retains many of its original
furnishings.

650 Lewis Castle Grounds
Map 2

W of Harbour, Stornoway, Isle of Lewis.
All reasonable times. Free. (Grounds only)
The modern castle, now a technical college (not
open to the public), stands in fine wooded
grounds given to the town by Lord Leverhulme.
Noted for their rhododendrons.

651 Leyden Obelisk and Tablet
Map 16

Denholm on A698 NE of Hawick. All times. Free.
The village was the birthplace of John Leyden
(1776-1811), poet and orientalist, friend of
Sir Walter Scott and also Sir James Murray, who
edited the Oxford English Dictionary. An obelisk
was set up in Leyden's memory in 1861 and a
tablet on a cottage records his birth in 1776.

652 Lincluden College
Map 18

Off A76, 1m N of Dumfries. Opening standard.
Adult: 15p, child: 7p, group rates. (AM)
A 15th-century Collegiate Church and Provost's
House remarkable for heraldic adornment and
for the tomb of Princess Margaret, daughter of
Robert III. There is a motte in the grounds.

653 Lindores Abbey
Map 9

Off A913, just E of Newburgh, 10m WNW of
Cupar. All reasonable times. Free.
Ruins of a great religious centre, founded in 1178
by the Benedictines. Here Sir William Wallace
celebrated his victory on Black Earnside.
Lindores' Abbot Lawrence became Grand
Inquisitor in Scotland and he tried many of the
men who were burned at the stake as heretics.

654 Linlithgow Palace
Map 12

S shore of loch, Linlithgow. Opening standard.
Adult: 25p, child: 12p, group rates. (AM)
The splendid ruined Palace overlooking the loch
is the successor to an older building which was
burned down in 1424. The Chapel and Great Hall
are late 15th-century and the fine quadrangle
has a richly-carved 16th-century fountain. In
1542 Mary Queen of Scots was born here while
her father, James V, lay dying at Falkland
Palace. In 1746 the palace was burned, probably
by accident, when occupied by General
Hawley's troops. George V held a court in the
Lyon Chamber here in 1914.

655 Lillie Art Gallery
Map 11

*Milngavie, off A81, 8m N of Glasgow. All year,
Tue-Fri 1100-1700, 1900-2100, Sat and Sun
1400-1700. Free.*
A modern purpose-built art gallery with a
permanent collection of 20th-century Scottish
paintings, sculpture and ceramics, and
temporary exhibitions of contemporary art.

656 Livingstone National Memorial
Map 11

*At Blantyre, A724, 3m NW of Hamilton. All year,
daily 1000-1800, Sun 1400-1800. Adult: 40p,
child: 20p: group rates.*
Shuttle Row is an 18th-century block of mill
tenements where David Livingstone, the famous
explorer/missionary was born in 1813, went to
school and worked while studying to become a
doctor. The National Memorial, containing very
many interesting relics of the Industrial
Revolution and of Africa, is in this building, now
surrounded by parkland. An Africa pavilion
illustrates modern Africa and a new social history
museum deals with agriculture, cotton spinning
and mining in Blantyre and district.

657 Loanhead Stone Circle
Map 6

*¼m NW of Daviot, 5m NNW of Inverurie, off
B9001. All reasonable times. Free. (AM)*
The best known example of a widespread group
of recumbent stone circles in east Scotland.

658 Loch Broom Highland Museum
Map 3

*Quay Street, Ullapool. May-Oct, Mon-Sat 0900-
1730. Admission by donation.*
A collection of items of both local and general
interest.

659 Loch Doon Castle
Map 17

*From A713, 2m S of Dalmellington, take road to
Loch Doon. All reasonable times. Free. (AM)*
This early 14th-century castle was devised to fit
the island on which it was originally built. When
the waters of the loch were raised in connection
with a hydro-electric scheme the castle was
dismantled and re-erected on the shores of the
loch. The walls of this massive building, once
known as Castle Balliol, vary from 7-9 feet thick
and stand about 26 feet high.

660 Loch Druidibeg National Nature Reserve
Map 2

*In the N part of South Uist, Outer Hebrides.
All year, daily. Free. (NCC)*
The most important surviving breeding ground of
the native greylag goose in Britain, in a typical
example of the Outer Hebrides environment,
machair, fresh and brackish lochs.

661 Loch Garten Nature Reserve
Map 5

Off B970, 8m NE of Aviemore. If Ospreys present, daily mid Apr-Aug 1000-2000 along signposted track to Observation Post. Other access into bird sanctuary strictly forbidden. Free. (RSPB)

Ospreys, extinct in Scotland for many years, returned here to breed in 1959. Their treetop eyrie may be viewed through fixed binoculars from the Observation Hut. The surrounding area, owned by the RSPB, includes extensive stretches of old Caledonian Pine forest with rich and varied wild life.

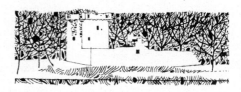

662 Loch Leven Castle
Map 8

On an island on Loch Leven, Kinross. Daily, May to first Mon in Oct 1000-1800, Sun 1400-1800. Access by ferry from lochside. Adult: 25p, child: 12p (inclusive of ferry). Group rates. (AM)

The tower is late 14th or early 15th-century. Mary Queen of Scots was imprisoned here in 1567 and from it escaped eleven months later.

Loch Leven Nature Reserve: see No 975.

Loch Lomond Bear Park: see No 147.

663 Loch of the Lowes
Map 8

Off A923, 2m NE of Dunkeld. (SWT)
Ospreys nest in the area and may be watched from the hide. The ecology of the area is demonstrated at the Visitor Centre.

664 Loch Morar
Map 4

SE of Mallaig.
Said to be the deepest loch in Scotland and the home of Morag, a monster with a strong resemblance to the Loch Ness Monster.

665 Loch Nan Uamh Cairn
Map 4

Off A830 S of Arisaig.
The loch is famous for its association with Bonnie Prince Charlie. The memorial cairn on the shore marks the spot from which Prince Charles Edward Stuart sailed for France on 20th September 1746 after having wandered round the Highlands as a fugitive with a price of £30,000 on his head.

666 Loch Ness
Map 5

SW of Inverness.
This striking 24-mile-long loch in the Great Glen forms part of the Caledonian Canal which links Inverness with Fort William. Cruisers sail from Inverness, notably to look for the Loch Ness Monster, said to live in the deep water.

667 Lochalsh Woodland Garden
Map 4

Off A87, 3m E of Kyle of Lochalsh. All year, daily. Adult: 20p, child: 10p. (NTS)
A wide variety of native trees and shrubs and more exotic plants from Tasmania, New Zealand, the Himalayas, Chile, Japan and China in the grounds of Lochalsh House (not open to the public). There are pleasant walks and an ecology display in the coach house.

668 Loch-an-Eilean Visitor Centre
Map 5

B970, 2½m S of Aviemore. May-Sep. Free. (NCC).
This exhibition in a cottage by the loch traces the history of the native Scots Pine forest from the Ice Age until today.

669 Lochindorb
Map 5

Unclassified road off A939, 10m NW of Grantown-on-Spey.
On an island on this lonely loch stands the 13th-century castle, once a seat of the Comyns. It was occupied in person by Edward I in 1303 and greatly strengthened. In 1336 Edward III raised the siege in which the Countess of Atholl was beleaguered by David II's troops. In 1372 the castle become the stronghold of the 'Wolf of Badenoch', the vicious Earl of Buchan who terrorized this area. It was dismantled c 1458.

670 Lochmaben Castle
Map 18

S shore of Castle Loch, by Lochmaben, 9m ENE of Dumfries. All reasonable times. Free.
This castle was captured and recaptured twelve times and also withstood six attacks and sieges. James IV was a frequent visitor, and Mary Queen of Scots was here in 1565. Now a ruin, this early 14th-century castle is on the site of a castle of the de Brus family, ancestors of Robert the Bruce. who is said to have been born here.

671 Lochranza Castle
Map 10

On N coast of Isle of Arran. Opening standard. Free. Apply custodian. (AM)
A picturesque ruin with two square towers, erected in the 13th/14th centuries and enlarged in the 16th. Robert the Bruce is said to have landed here on his return in 1307 from Rathlin in Ireland at the start of his campaign for Scottish Independence.

672 Lochty Private Railway
Map 9

*On B940 (Cupar/Crail road), 7m W of Crail.
11 Jun-3 Sep, Sun only 1400-1700. Train
fare: Adult: 50p. child: 25p, group rates.
(Lochty Private Railway Co)*
This private railway operates a steam-hauled
passenger train service over 1½ miles of track.
Locomotives, shunter and passenger coaches.

673 Logan Botanic Garden
Map 17

*Off B7065, 14m S of Stranraer. Daily Apr-Sep
1000-1700. 30p per car, group rates.*
Here a profusion of plants from the warm and
temperate regions of the world flourish in some of
the mildest conditions in Scotland. There are
cabbage palms, tree ferns and many other
Southern Hemisphere species.

674 Logan Fish Pond
Map 17

*Off B7065, 14m S of Stranraer. Easter-Sep,
Mon, Wed-Fri and Sun 1000-1200, 1400-1730.
Adult: 15p, child: 10p.
(Sir Ninian Buchan-Hepburn, Bt.)*
This tidal pool in the rocks, 30 feet deep and
53 feet round, was completed in 1800 as a fresh-
fish larder for Logan House. Damaged by a mine
in 1942, it was reopened in 1955. It holds some
30 fish, mainly cod, so tame that they come to be
fed by hand.

675 Loudon Hall
Map 15

*Boat Vennel, off Cross in Ayr town centre. Mid
Jul-end Oct, Mon-Sat 1100-1800 or by
arrangement, tel: Prestwick 79077. Free.
(Loudoun Hall Trustees)*
A late 15th-century/early 16th-century town
house built for a rich merchant. It is thought to be
the oldest surviving example of its type
in Scotland.

676 Luffness Castle
Map 14

*1m E of Aberlady on A198. By arrangement,
tel: Aberlady 218. Free. (Col and Mrs Hope)*
A 16th-century castle with a 13th-century keep
built on the site of a Norse camp. There are
extensive old fortifications and an old moat.

677 Lyte Plaque
Map 16

At Ednam on bridge. All times. Free.
The plaque to Henry Francis Lyte was fixed to the
bridge spanning the Eden Water in 1952. He was
a hymnologist and author of *Abide With Me*.

678 Lyth Arts Centre
Map 3

*Off A9, 10m NW of Wick. Early Jun-mid Sep,
daily 1000-1800. Adult: 25p. (Mr W Wilson)*
Travelling exhibitions and a variety of craftsmen
in residence throughout the summer.

679 McCaig's Tower
Map 10

Oban. All times. Free.
McCaig was a local banker who tried to curb unemployment by using local craftsmen to build the tower from 1897-1900 as a memorial to his family. Its walls are 2 feet thick and from 30-47 feet high. The courtyard within is landscaped and the tower is floodlit at night in summer.

MacCulloch's Fossil Tree: see No 123.

680 McDonald's Mill
Map 10

Off A816, ½m S of Oban. All year. Mon-Fri 0900-1930, Sat 0900-1700. Demonstration weekdays 0900-1730. Free.
Exhibition of the story of spinning and weaving, with demonstrations of hand spinning and hand weaving.

681 Flora Macdonald's Birthplace
Map 2

W of A865, 200 yds up farm track ½m N of Milton, Isle of South Uist. All times. Free.
A cairn on the top of a small hill marks the spot where Flora Macdonald was born in 1722.

682 Flora Macdonald Monument
Map 5

Inverness Castle. All times. Free.
Monument to Flora Macdonald (1722-1790) on the terracing of the Victorian Castle.

683 MacDonald Tower
Map 3

Mitchell Hill, Dingwall. All times. Free.
An impressive monument erected to the memory of General Sir Hector MacDonald, who was born near Dingwall. (See also No 263.)

684 McEwan Gallery
Map 7

On A939, 1m W of Ballater. All year, Mon-Sat 1000-1700, or by arrangement (esp winter), tel: Ballater 429. Free.
An unusual house built by the Swiss artist Rudolphe Christen in 1902, containing works of art, mainly of the Scottish School. Occasional special exhibitions are held.

685 Roderick Mackenzie Memorial
Map 5

1m E of Ceannacroc on A887, 13m W of Invermoriston. All times. Free.
A cairn on the south of the road commemorates Roderick Mackenzie, who, in 1746, feigned to be Prince Charles Edward Stuart and was killed by soldiers searching for the Prince after Culloden.

686 Maclaurin Art Gallery
Map 15

1½m S of Ayr, off road to Alloway. All year, Mon-Sat 1100-1300, 1400-1700. May-Sep, Sun 1400-1700. Free. (Trustees of the late Mrs Mary E Maclaurin)
The gallery consists of four rooms, formerly stables and servants' quarters, attached to Rozelle House. There are exhibitions of fine art, photography and local history, especially local military history, Ayrshire embroidery and civic relics. The gallery is set in extensive parkland with a nature trail.

687 McLean Museum and Art Gallery
Map 11

Greenock. All year, Mon-Sat 1000-1700 (closed Sat 1300-1400). Free.
(Inverclyde District Council)
A local museum with art collection, natural history, shipping exhibits and items relating to James Watt, who was born in Greenock.

MacLellan's Castle

688 MacLellan's Castle
Map 17

Off High Street, Kirkcudbright. Opening standard. Adult: 20p, child: 10p, group rates. (AM)
A handsome castellated mansion overlooking the harbour, dating from 1582. Elaborately planned with fine architectural details, it has been a ruin since 1752. In Kirkcudbright also see the 16th/17th-century Tolbooth, the Mercat Cross of 1610, the Stewartry Museum (No 909) and Broughton House (No 114).

689 Macpherson Monument
Map 5

On A9, 3m NE of Kingussie. All times. Free.
Obelisk to James 'Ossian' Macpherson (1736-1796), Scottish poet and 'translator' of the Ossianic poems.

690 MacRobert Arts Centre
Map 12

University of Stirling.
A five-hundred seat theatre, art gallery and recital room, providing all year theatre, opera, ballet, films, concerts and exhibitions.

691 Maes Howe
Map 1

Off A965, 10m W of Kirkwall, Orkney. Opening standard. Adult: 20p, child: 10p. (AM)
An enormous burial mound, 115 feet in diameter, dating back to c 1800 BC, and containing a burial chamber which is unsurpassed in Western Europe. In the 12th century Viking marauders broke into it in search of treasures and Norse crusaders sheltered from a storm in the Howe. They engraved a rich collection of Runic inscriptions upon the walls.

692 Magnum Leisure Centre
Map 15

Harbourside, Irvine. All year, daily 0900-2300. Adult: 10p, child: 5p (sports extra).
The centre, by the beach and in 150 acres of park, has two swimming pools, an ice rink, squash courts, theatre, cinema and many other facilities.

693 Maid of the Loch
Map 11

Balloch Pier, 5m N of Dumbarton. Mid May-mid Sep, Mon-Fri 1040 and 1440, Sat-Sun 1100 and 1440. Charge according to journey.
This fine white paddle steamer sails from the south to the north end of Loch Lomond, with opportunities to disembark and is one of the best ways of seeing Scotland's largest inland loch.

694 Maiden Stone
Map 6

Off A96, 6m WNW of Inverurie. All reasonable times. Free.
A notable early Christian monument with a Celtic Cross and Pictish symbols.

695 Maison Dieu
Map 7

Off Market Street, Brechin. Opening standard. Free. (AM)
An interesting fragment of mid-13th-century ecclesiastical architecture.

696 Malleny Gardens
Map 13

In Balerno, off A70, 7½m SW of Edinburgh. 1 May-30 Sep, daily 1000-dusk. Adult: 30p, child: 15p. (NTS)
Adjoining a 17th-century house (not open) is a garden with many interesting plants including a good collection of shrub roses.

697 Manderston
Map 14

Off A6105, 2m E of Duns. Mid May-Sept, Thurs & Sun 1400-1730. House and grounds: £1. Grounds only: 40p. (Mr A Palmer)
One of the finest Edwardian country houses in Scotland with extensive estate buildings and gardens particularly noted for their rhododendrons.

698 Marjoribanks Monument
Map 16

At E entrance to Coldstream. All times. Free.
Obelisk with a stone figure of Charles
Marjoribanks, elected the First Member of
Parliament for Berwickshire after the passing of
the Reform Act of 1832.

699 Mar's Wark
Map 12

*At the top of Castle Wynd, Stirling. All times.
Free. (AM)*
Mar's Wark is one of a number of fine old
buildings on the approach to Stirling Castle. Built
c 1570 by the first Earl of Mar, Regent of
Scotland, it was a residence of the Earls of Mar
until the 6th Earl had to flee the country after
leading the 1715 Jacobite Rebellion. It became a
barracks, then a workhouse (hence Mar's Wark
or Works) and then a ruin after a battering by
Jacobite forces in 1746.

David Marshall Lodge: see No 795.

700 Martello Tower
Map 1

*Hackness, Island of Hoy, Orkney. All times.
Can be viewed from the outside only. (AM)*
An impressive tower built during the Napoleonic
and American wars at the beginning of the
19th century. The tower was renovated in 1866
and used again in the First World War.

701 Martyrs' Monument
Map 17

*Near Wigtown, A714, 7m S of Newton Stewart.
All reasonable times. Free.*
A monument on the hill and a pillar on the shore
of Wigtown Bay where in 1685 two women, aged
18 and 63, were tied to stakes and drowned for
their religious beliefs.

702 Mary Queen of Scots House
Map 16

*Queen Street, Jedburgh. Mar-Oct, daily
1000-1730. Adult: 20p, child: 10p.
(Roxburgh District Council)*
A 16th-century bastle house in which Mary
Queen of Scots is reputed to have stayed in 1566
when attending the Court of Justice. Now a
museum containing several relics associated
with the Queen.

Mauchline Kirkyard: see No 129.

703 Maxwelton House
Map 18

*13m NW of Dumfries on B729, near Moniaive.
May-Sep, Wed and Thu afternoons and every
4th Sun, 1430-1700. Admission charge. Parties
by arrangement, tel: Moniaive 384.
(Mrs Hugh Stenhouse)*
The house dates back to the 14th/15th century.
Originally it was a stronghold of the Earls of
Glencairn, and later the birthplace of Annie
Laurie, to whom William Douglas of Fingland
wrote the famous poem. Museum of early
kitchen, dairy and small farming implements.

Meigle

704 Maybole Collegiate Church
Map 15

In Maybole, S of A77. Not open to the public—can be viewed from outside. Free. (AM)
The roofless ruin of a 15th-century church, built for a small college established in 1373 by the Kennedies of Dunure.

705 Meal and Flour Mill
Map 8

150 yards off A9 at Blair Atholl.
April-end Oct, Mon-Sat 1000-1800, Sun 1200-1800. Adult: 27p, child: 20p, group rates.
The 18th-century water mill still produces a small amount of oatmeal sold locally and flour which is mainly used in the small wholemeal bakery. Instruction in baking scones and oatcakes is available hourly in the bakery.

706 Meffan Institute
Map 7

Library, West High Street, Forfar. All year, Mon,Tue, Wed, Fri 0900-1900; Thur and Sat 0900-1700. Free. (Angus District Council)
Display of material relating to Forfar and district.

707 Megginch Castle Grounds
Map 9

A85, 10m E of Perth. Apr-Jun and Sep, Wed only 1400-1700, Jul and Aug, Mon-Fri 1400-1700. Adult: 50p, child: 25p.
(Capt and the Hon Mrs Drummond of Megginch)
The grounds around the 15th-century castle have daffodils, rhododendrons and 1,000-year-old yews.

Meigle Museum

708 Meigle Museum
Map 9

On A94, 12m WSW of Forfar. Opening standard but closed Sun. Adult: 15p, child: 7p, group rates. (AM)
This magnificent collection of 25 sculptured monuments of the Celtic Christian period, all found at or near the old churchyard, forms one of the most notable assemblages of Dark Age sculpture in Western Europe.

Meikleour Beech Hedge: see No 83.

709 Mellerstain House
Map 16

*Off A6089, 8m NW of Kelso. 1 May-end
Sep, daily except Sat, 1330-1730. Adult: 80p,
child: 40p, group rates. (Lord Binning)*
This is one of the most attractive mansions open
to the public in Scotland, with exceptionally
beautiful interior decoration and plaster work.
Begun about 1725 by William Adam, it was
completed between 1770 and 1778 by William's
son, Robert. There are attractive terraced
gardens and pleasant grounds with fine views.

710 Melrose Abbey
Map 16

*Main Square, Melrose. Opening standard.
Adult: 25p, child: 12p, group rates. (AM)*
This Cistercian Abbey, founded in 1136, is
notable for its fine traceried stonework. It
suffered the usual attacks of all the Border
abbeys during English invasions, but parts of the
nave and choir dating from a rebuilding of 1385
include some of the best and most elaborate
work of the period in Scotland. In addition to the
flamboyant stonework, note on the roof the figure
of a pig playing the bagpipes. There is an
interesting museum in the Commendator's
House, at the entrance.

711 Melville Monument
Map 8

*1m N of Comrie, 6m W of Crieff. Access by
footpath passing Comrie House.*
The obelisk in memory of Lord Melville
(1742-1811) stands on Dunmore, a hill of
837 feet, with delightful views of the surrounding
country.

712 Memsie Burial Cairn
Map 6

*Near village of Memsie, 3m SSW of
Fraserburgh. All reasonable times. Free. (AM)*
A fine example of a large stone-built cairn
probably dating to c 1500 BC.

Menstrie Castle

713 Menstrie Castle
Map 12

*In Menstrie, A91, 5m E of Stirling.
Exhibition Rooms, May-Sep, Wed, Sat and Sun
1430-1700, and by arrangement with caretaker
in flat in castle. Free.*
The 16th-century restored castle was the
birthplace of Sir William Alexander, James VI's
Lieutenant for the Plantation of Nova Scotia. A
Nova Scotia Exhibition Room (NTS) displays the
coats of arms of 107 Nova Scotian Baronetcies.

Monument

714 Merkland Cross
Map 18

Off A74, at Kirtlebridge, 7m NW of Gretna.
A fine 15th-century floriated wayside cross.

715 Midhowe Broch and Tombs
Map 1

On the W coast of the island of Rousay, Orkney.
All reasonable times. Free.
An Iron Age broch and walled enclosure situated
on a promontory cut off by a deep rock-cut ditch.
Also on the island is a rich collection of megalithic
chambered tombs.

716 Hugh Miller's Cottage
Map 3

Church Street, Cromarty, 16m NE of Dingwall.
1 May-30 Sep, Mon-Sat 1000-1200, 1300-1700
(Jun-Sep only, also Sun 1400-1700).
Adult: 40p, child: 20p.
The birthplace of Hugh Miller (1802-56),
geologist, naturalist, theologian and writer.
Collections of geological specimens, his writings
and his personal belongings.

Millport Marine Biological Station: see
No 972.

Millport Museum: see No 733.

717 Minard Castle
Map 10

Off A83, 14m S of Inveraray. May-Oct, Mon-Fri
1100-1600. By arrangement, tel: Minard 272.
Free.
The castle is originally 16th-century with
subsequent extensions and contains paintings of
the Franco-Scottish Royal House. There is an
annual piping contest.

718 Mingary Castle
Map 4

On B8007, 2m from Kilchoan on the
Ardnamurchan peninsula. W of Fort William. All
reasonable times. Free. Access by farm road.
A ruined late 13th-century castle with inner
buildings of the 15th century. Great care should
be taken.

Monreith Cross: see No 991.

719 Monument Hill
Map 10

2m SW of Dalmally, off the old road to Inveraray.
All times. Free.
Monument to Duncan Ban MacIntyre
(1724-1812) the ''Burns of the Highlands'', born
near Inveroran.

720 Morton Castle
Map 18

A702, 17m NNW of Dumfries. Closed to the public but may be viewed from the outside. (AM)
On a small loch, this castle was occupied by Randolph, first Earl of Moray, as Regent for David II. It afterwards passed to the Douglases and is now a well-preserved ruin.

721 Moss Farm Road Stone Circle
Map 10

South side of Moss Farm Road, 3 miles N of Blackwaterfoot, E of A841, Isle of Arran. All reasonable times. Free. (AM)
Remains of a Bronze Age cairn and stone circle. (See also No 904.)

722 Mote of Mark
Map 18

Off A710, 5m S of Dalbeattie. All reasonable times. Free.
An ancient hill fort on the estuary of the River Urr at Rockliffe, overlooking Rough Island, an NTS bird sanctuary.

723 Mote of Urr
Map 18

Off B794, 5m NE of Castle Douglas. All reasonable times. Free.
An almost circular mound surrounded by a deep trench. A good example of Norman 'motte-and-bailey' fortification.

724 Mousa Broch
Map 1

On an island off Sandwick, 7m S of Lerwick, Shetland. Daily bus service between Lerwick and Sandwick. Boat for hire; May-Sep afternoons; also Sat and Sun mornings. Opening standard. Free. (AM)
The best preserved example of the remarkable Iron Age broch towers peculiar to Scotland. The tower stands over 40 feet high.

Muchalls Castle

725 Muchalls Castle
Map 7

Off A92, 11m S of Aberdeen. May-Sep, Tue and Sun 1500-1700, and by arrangement, tel: Newtonhill 217. Adult: 30p, child: 20p. (Mr and Mrs A M Simpson)
Overlooking the sea this tiny 17th-century castle was built by the Burnetts of Leys in 1619. Ornate

plasterwork ceilings and fine fireplaces are features. There is a secret staircase.

726 Muck, Isle of
Map 4

Inner Hebrides. Ferry from Mallaig and Arisaig (no cars).
This tiny island lies to the southwest across the Sound of Eigg; fertile and unspoiled, it offers some visitor accommodation.

727 Muirshiel Country Park
Map 11

Off B786, N of Lochwinnoch, 9m SW of Paisley. (Renfrew District Council)
Picnic sites and an information centre are features in this attractive countryside. Castle Semple loch, a 200-acre water park, is 3 miles south east.

728 Mull and Iona Folklore Museum
Map 4

Tobermory, Isle of Mull. Jun-Sep, Mon-Sat 1100-1700. Adult: 20p.
Local folklore museum, with old island exhibits in an old Baptist church.

729 Mull Little Theatre
Map 4

Dervaig, Isle of Mull. Summer months only.
Officially the smallest professional theatre in the country, according to the Guinness Book of Records, providing a variety of performances in summer.

730 Muness Castle
Map 1

SE point of Isle of Unst, Shetland. Opening standard. Free. Apply key-keeper. (AM)
A late 16th-century building, rubble-built with fine architectural detail.

731 Murray Forest Centre
Map 17

Off A75, ½m E of Gatehouse of Fleet. Apr-Sep, daily 0900-1800. Free.
A log cabin with exhibits depicting broadleafed tree species of the Fleet Forest. There is also a forest walk.

732 Murray's Monument
Map 17

Above A712, 7½m NE of Newton Stewart. All reasonable times. Free.
Built to commemorate Dr Alexander Murray (1775-1813), a shepherd's son who rose to become Professor of Oriental Languages at Edinburgh University. At Talnotry, nearby, there is an extensive area of moor and hill containing wild goats.

733 Museum of the Cumbraes
Map 11

Garrison House, Millport, Isle of Cumbrae. Jun-Sep, Tue-Sat 1000-1630. Free. (Cunninghame District Council)
A new museum with a collection of photographs and objects illustrating the way of life of the island from the earliest times. There is a special feature on Victorian and Edwardian life, and cruising "Doon the Watter".

734 Museum of Flight
Map 14

Near East Fortune Airfield, off B1377,
4½m S of North Berwick. Daily Jul-Aug
1000-1600 and several open days. Free.
(Royal Scottish Museum)
Aircraft include a 1934 autogiro, a Spitfire,
several jet fighters and the Fairey Delta world
speed record holder of 1956. The rocket
collection is headed by the impressive Blue
Streak.

735 Museum of Islay Life
Map 10

200 yards N of road into Port Charlotte.
All year. May-Oct, Mon-Fri 1000-1700. Sun
1400-1700. Nov-Apr, Mon-Fri 1000-1230,
1330-1630. Closed Sat. Adult: 25p, child: free,
group rates.
A collection of historical and archaeological
material from the island, including an important
collection of carved stone dating from 6th-16th
century, in a United Free Church built in 1843.

736 Museum of the Scottish Lead Mining Industry
Map 16

Goldscaur Row, Wanlockhead, on B797,
8m ENE of Sanquhar. Apr-Jun, daily 1300-1700.
Jul-Sep, daily 1100-1700, and by arrangement.
Adult: 25p, child: 10p, group rates.
(Wanlockhead Museum Trust)
Cottage Museum with mining and social relics.
Open-air museum with lead mine beam engine,
smelt, butt-and-ben cottages. Library with books
and records of Reading Society founded in 1756.
Mineral collection.

737 Museum of Scottish Tartans
Map 8

Drummond Street, Comrie, 6m W of Crieff.
1 Nov-mid Mar, Mon-Fri 1000-1500, Sat 1000-
1300, Sun by arrangement, tel: Comrie 779. Mid
Mar-end Oct, Mon-Sat 0900-1700, Sun 1400-
1700. Adult: 40p, child 20p, group rates.
(Scottish Tartans Society)
The Scottish Tartans Society is the custodian of
the largest collection in existence of material
relating to tartans and Highland dress,
comprising a comprehensive library of books,
specimens, pictures, prints, maps, manuscripts
and a system that records details of every known
tartan. In an 18th-century Highland weaving
shed, the plucking of wool from Soay sheep, the
combing, dyeing and weaving of tartans as it was
done before 1745 is shown.

738 Musselburgh Bridge
Map 13

By A1 in Musselburgh. All times. Free.
An attractive 16th-century three-arched
footbridge across the River Esk.

739 Muthill Church and Tower
Map 8

At Muthill, A822, 3½m S of Crieff.
All reasonable times. Free. (AM)
Ruins of an important church of the 15th century.
Adjacent stands a Norman tower, 12th-century
or earlier.

740 Myreton Motor Museum
Map 14

*Off A198, 6m SW of North Berwick. May-Oct,
daily 1000-1800; winter Sat and Sun only, 1000-
1700. Adult: 40p, child: 10p. (Mr W Dale)*
A varied collection of cars, commercial vehicles,
motor cycles and cycles. Also horse-drawn and
historic military vehicles. Branch at Castle Park,
Dunbar.

741 Nairn Fishertown Museum
Map 5

*Laing Hall, King Street, May-Sep, Tue, Thu and
Sat 1430-1630; Mon, Wed and Fri 1830-2030;
and by arrangement, tel: Nairn 53331.
Adult: 15p, child: 5p, group rates.*
A collection of photographs and articles
connected with the Moray Firth and herring
fishing industries during the steam drifter era.
Exhibits on domestic life of the fishertown.

742 Nairn Literary Institute Museum
Map 5

*Viewfield House. 1 Jun-30 Sep, Sat 1400-1600
(and Wed in Jul). Free.*
The museum, founded in 1868, is housed in the
attics of Viewfield house (early 16th century) and
contains displays of local history, archaeology,
ethnology and relics of Culloden.

743 Neidpath Castle
Map 16

*A72, 1m W of Peebles. Thu before Easter
to second Sun in Oct, Mon-Sat 1000-1300,
1400-1800; Sun 1300-1800. Adult: 30p,
child: 10p. (Lord Wemyss' Trust)*
This early Fraser stronghold stands on the north
bank of the River Tweed, with panoramic view
from the top. It passed c 1310 to the Hays of
Tweeddale, whose family crest of a goat's head
surmounts the courtyard gateway, and was
garrisoned against Cromwell's troops in 1650.
The castle dates back to the early 14th century,
and some of its massive walls are 11 feet thick.

Neidpath Castle

744 Nelson Tower
Map 3

Cluny Hill, Forres. All reasonable times. Free.
The tower was built in 1806 and offers fine views over the surrounding countryside.

745 Neptune's Staircase
Map 4

3m NE of Fort William off A830 at Banavie.
A series of 8 locks, built between 1805 and 1822, which raises Telford's Caledonian Canal 64 feet. (See also No 144.)

746 Ness of Burgi
Map 1

On the coast at the tip of Scatness, about 1m SW of Jarlshof, S end of mainland Shetland. All reasonable times. Free. (AM)
A defensive stone-built structure of Iron Age date, which is related in certain features to the brochs.

747 Nether Largie Cairns
Map 10

½m SW of Kilmartin, Argyll. All reasonable times. Free.
Three cairns, North (c 1800-1600 BC), Mid (c 1800-1500 BC) and South (c third Millennium BC).

748 New Lanark
Map 16

1m S of Lanark.
The best example in Scotland of an industrial village, the product of the Industrial Revolution in the late 18th and early 19th centuries, now the subject of a major conservation programme. Founded in 1784 by David Dale and Richard Arkwright, it was the scene of early experiments in the paternalistic management and care for the workers, particularly by Robert Owen (1771-1858), Dale's son-in-law. Exhibition and heritage trail.

Newark Castle, Port Glasgow

749 Newark Castle, Port Glasgow
Map 11

Off A8, through shipyard at E side of Port Glasgow. Opening standard. Adult: 15p, child: 7p, group rates. (AM)
A large, fine-turreted mansion house of the Maxwells, overlooking the River Clyde, still almost entire and in a remarkably good state of preservation, with a 15th-century tower, a courtyard and hall, the latter dated 1597.

750 Newark Castle, near Selkirk
Map 16

Off A708, 4m W of Selkirk. Entry on application to Buccleuch Estates, Bowhill, Selkirk. Free. (Buccleuch Estates)
First mentioned in 1423, Newark or New Wark was so called to distinguish it from the older Auldwark Castle which stood nearby. This 5-storeyed oblong tower house, standing within a barmkin, was a royal hunting seat for the Forest of Ettrick; and Royal Arms of James I are on the west gable. In the courtyard 100 prisoners from the Battle of Philiphaugh (1645) were shot by Leslie. Care should be taken in the building.

751 Noltland Castle
Map 1

Isle of Westray, Orkney. Opening standard. Free. (AM)
Extensive ruins of a castle originally built in 1420 by Thomas de Tulloch, then the Governor. Later besieged by Sir William Sinclair of Warsetter, it fell into the hands of Gilbert Balfour of Westray, from whose time, around the mid 16th century, much of the building appears to date. It was partly destroyed in 1746. The stately hall, vaulted kitchen and fine winding staircase are impressive.

752 North Ayrshire Museum
Map 15

In Saltcoats, past railway station. All year. Mon, Tue, Thu, Fri, Sat 1000-1600. Adult: 3p, child: 2p.
A fine museum with both local and national exhibits in a mid 18th-century Scottish church.

753 North Berwick Law
Map 14

S of North Berwick, off B1347. All times, Free.
The 613-ft volcanic rock is a fine viewpoint and is crowned by a watch tower dating from Napoleonic times, and an archway made from the jawbone of a whale.

754 North Berwick Museum
Map 14

School Road. 6 Apr-3 Jun, Sat and Mon 1000-1300, 1400-1700. Fri and Sun 1400-1700. Jun-Sep, Mon-Sat 1000-1300, 1400-1700, Sun 1400-1700. Free. (East Lothian District Council)
A compact museum with galleries devoted to natural history, archaeology and the life of the North Berwick area, housed on the upper floor of a former school.

North Carr

755 North Carr Lightship
Map 9

*East Pier, Anstruther. Apr-Sep, daily 1000-1900
Adult: 20p, child: 10p. (North East Fife District
Council)*
The light ship, stationed off Fife Ness from
1938-1975, is now a floating museum and the
only one of its kind. All the interior fitments have
been refurbished to give a realistic impression of
life on board.

756 North Glen Gallery
Map 18

*Palnackie, 5m SE of Castle Douglas.
Daily, 1000-1800 and by arrangement, tel:
Palnackie 200. Adult: 25p, child: 5p.*
Studio demonstrating the blowing of glass,
assembly of sculpture, welding and cutting of
steel.

757 North Inch
Map 8

Perth.
A large park with modern sports facilities, where
in 1396 the notable clan combat between Clan
Chattan and Clan Kay took place. It was also a
famous Jacobite rallying place.

758 Noss Nature Reserve
Map 1

*Isle of Noss, 5m E of Lerwick, Shetland. Access
by warden's boat: see notice-board at Lerwick
harbour for full details. (NCC)*
Spectacular island with 450-feet cliffs and vast
colonies of breeding auks, gulls and gannets.

Nova Scotia Room: see No 713.

759 Old Baxter Shop
Map 6

*½m W of Fochabers on main
Aberdeen-Inverness road (A96). May-Sept,
tours Mon-Fri 1030, 1100, 1200, 1500. Free.
(W A Baxter and Sons Ltd)*
A replica of the original George Baxter and Sons
establishment in Spey Street, Fochabers, where
Baxters of Speyside were founded. Visitors'
Centre and restaurant.

760 Oatmeal Mill
Map 8

*McKerchar & MacNaughton Ltd, Mill Street,
Aberfeldy. All year, Mon-Fri 1000-1700.
Adult: 20p, child: 10p.*
Display of the complete process of milling from
raw grain to finished oatmeal. The mill is
powered by a water wheel.

761 Old Bridge House
Map 18

*Mill Road, Dumfries, at Devorgilla's Bridge. Apr-
Sep, Mon-Sat 1000-1300, 1400-1700 (closed
Tue); Sun 1400-1700. Free.*
The house, built in 1662, now has rooms
furnished in period style to illustrate life in
Dumfries over the centuries.
Devorgilla's Bridge was built in the 13th century
by Devorgilla Balliol, who endowed Balliol
College, Oxford.

762 Old Byre Folk Museum
Map 4

1m S of Dervaig off B8073 (Torloisk Road).
1 May-30 Sep, Mon-Fri 1030-1730. Sun 1400-
1730. Adult: 50p, child: 25p.
(Mrs G U D Richardson)
An attractive stone-built former byre, converted
to provide a museum of crofting life on Mull, using
lifelike figures and a sound commentary.

763 Old Inverlochy Castle
Map 4

On NE outskirts of Fort William. Not yet open to
the public—may be viewed from outside. (AM)
A ruined 13th-century square building, with
round corner towers. Nearby 19th-century
Inverlochy Castle is now a hotel.

764 Old Man of Hoy
Map 1

NW coast of Isle of Hoy, Orkney.
A 450-feet high isolated stack ('pillar') standing
off the magnificent cliffs of NW Hoy. Well seen
from the Scrabster-Stromness ferry.

765 Old Place of Mochrum
Map 17

Off B7005, 11m W of Wigtown. Not open to the
public; can be seen from the road.
Known also as Drumwall Castle, this is mainly
15th and 16th-century with two picturesque
towers.

Orchardton Tower

766 Orchardton Tower
Map 18

Off A711, 5½m SE of Castle Douglas. Opening
standard. Free. Apply custodian at nearby
cottage. (AM)
An example, unique in Scotland, of a circular
tower house, built by John Cairns about the
middle of the 15th century.

767 Orkney Chairs
Map 1

14 Palace Road, Kirkwall, Orkney. By
arrangement, tel: Kirkwall 2429. (Mrs R Eunson)
One of the few places where traditional Orkney
chairs are made.

768 Ormiston Market Cross
Map 14

*At Ormiston, B6371, 7½m WSW of Haddington.
(AM)*
A 15th-century cross in the main street.

769 Orphir Church
Map 1

*By A964, 6m SW of Kirkwall. All times. Free.
(AM)*
The remains of Scotland's only circular
mediaeval church, built in the first half of the 12th
century and dedicated to St Nicholas. Its design
was greatly influenced by the Crusades. Nearby
is the site of the Earl's Bu, a great hall of the Earls
of Orkney.

Ospreys: see Nos 661, 663.

770 Our Lady of the Isles
Map 2

*N of South Uist, Outer Hebrides. All reasonable
times. Free.*
On Reuval Hill—the Hill of Miracles—is the
statue of the Madonna and Child, erected in 1957
by the Catholic community with contributions
from all over the world. The work of Hew Lorimer,
it is 30 feet high.

771 Our Lady of Sorrows
Map 2

*Garrynamonie, South Uist, Western Isles. Daily
till 1900. Free.*
This modern church opened in 1964. There is a
mosaic on the front of the building depicting Our
Lady of Sorrows.

Paisley Abbey

772 Paisley Abbey
Map 11

*In Paisley, 8m W of Glasgow. Outwith the hours
of divine worship, open Jan-Dec, Mon-Sat
1000-1500. Free.*
A fine Cluniac Abbey Church founded in 1163
and almost completely destroyed by the English
in 1307. Much of the present building dates from
the mid 15th century. The west front and the
nave, which is used as the Parish Church, are
most noteworthy. Extensive restoration begun in
1897 was completed by Sir Robert Lorimer
between 1922 and 1928. The choir contains a
fine stone vaulted roof, stained glass and the
tombs of Princess Marjory Bruce and King
Robert III. See the St Mirin Chapel (1499) with
the St Mirin Carvings. Adjacent is the Place of
Paisley, mainly 15th-century, with a fine wooden
barrel-vaulted ceiling: visits by arrangement.

773 Paisley Art Gallery and Museum
Map 11

*High Street. Mon, Wed, Thu, Fri 1000-1700,
Tues 1000-2000, Sat 1000-1800. Free.*
Late 19th-century museum with modern
extension. The collection is varied and includes a
fine display of Paisley shawls. There is a fully
functioning observatory and weather station.

774 Palacerigg Country Park
Map 12

*Unclassified road, 2½m SE of Cumbernauld.
All year. (Park) dawn to dusk. (Nature Centre)
winter 1000-1630, summer 1000-2000.
No dogs. Donation box.
(Cumbernauld and Kilsyth District Council)*
Wildlife includes a wide selection of birds, deer,
fox, badger, stoat, weasel, etc; also many
species, including mink, wolves and wildcats, in
paddocks. Golf course. Museum being
developed.

775 Parallel Roads
Map 8

*Glen Roy, unclassified road off A86, 18m NE of
Fort William.*
These 'parallel roads' are hillside terraces
marking levels of lakes dammed by glaciers
during the Ice Age.

776 Pass of Killiecrankie
Map 8

*Off A9, 2½m N of Pitlochry. NTS Visitor
Centre: Good Friday-30 Jun and Sep, Mon-Sat
1000-1800. Jul-Aug, Mon-Sat 0930-1800, Sun
1300-1800.
Adult: 10p, child: free.*
A famous wooded gorge where in 1689 the
English troops were routed by Jacobite forces
led by 'Bonnie Dundee'. Soldier's Leap. NTS
centre features the battle, natural history and
ranger services.

777 Peel Ring of Lumphanan
Map 7

*A980, 11m NW of Banchory. All times. Free.
(AM)*
A major early mediaeval earthwork 120 feet in
diameter and 18 feet high. There are links with
Shakespeare's *Macbeth*.

778 Perth Art Gallery and Museum
Map 8

*George Street. All year, Mon-Sat 1000-1300,
1400-1700; Sun 1400-1600. Free.*
Collections of local history, fine and applied art,
natural history, archaeology and ethnography.
Changing programme of temporary exhibitions.

Perth Information Centre: see No 823.

779 Perth Repertory Theatre
Map 8

High Street.
An intimate Victorian theatre, built in 1900 in the
centre of Perth, offering a variety of plays in
season.

Phantassie Doocot: see No 791.

Picardy

780 Picardy Stone
Map 6

Unclassified road off A96, 8m SW of Huntly. All times. Free. (AM)
At Myreton, a whinstone monolith with ancient Celtic symbols. Other similar stones are in the Insch area.

781 Pierowall Church
Map 1

At Pierowall, Island of Westray, Orkney. All reasonable times. Free. (AM)
A ruin consisting of nave and chancel, the latter canted out of alignment. There are some finely lettered tombstones.

782 Pinkie House
Map 13

Off A1 at E end of Musselburgh. Mid Apr-mid Jul, mid Sep-mid Dec, Tue 1400-1700. Free. (Loretto School)
Early 17th-century building with many later additions. It is best known for its painted gallery (c 1630) and plaster ceilings.

783 Pitcaple Castle
Map 6

Beside A96, 4m NW of Inverurie. Apr-Sep 1100-1800 (if convenient). Adult: 50p, child: 25p. (Capt and Mrs Burges-Lumsden)
A fine example of the 15th-century Z-plan castle, still a family home. Three sovereigns have been entertained here, and the Marquis of Montrose was lodged here on his way to execution in Edinburgh. Family museum.

784 Pitlochry Festival Theatre
Map 8

Pitlochry.
Scotland's "Theatre in the Hills", now undergoing a major programme of expansion. The performances are especially geared to holidaymakers, with a different programme each night.

785 Pitlochry Power Station and Dam
Map 8

Off A9 at Pitlochry. Easter-end Sep daily 0900-2000. Free. (Exhibition: Adult: 15p, unaccompanied child: 5p, accompanied: free.) (North of Scotland Hydro-Electric Board)
One of nine hydro stations in the Tummel Valley. The dam created Loch Faskally where boating and fishing are available. Salmon can be seen through windows in a fish ladder. Exhibition inside power station.

786 Pitmedden Garden
Map 6

Outskirts of Pitmedden village. B999 off A920, 14m N of Aberdeen. All year. Daily 0930-dusk. Adult: 40p, child: 20p.
The 17th-century Great Garden originally laid out by Sir Alexander Seton, with elaborate floral designs, pavilions, fountains and sundials. The 'thunder houses' at either end of the west belvedere are rare in Scotland. A display the depicts the evolution of the formal garden. Highland cattle, woodland walk.

787 Pittencrieff House Museum
Map 13

*Pittencrieff Park, Dunfermline. May-Sep,
daily except Tues 1100-1700.*
The house, standing in a fine park, was built in
1610 for the Lairds of Pittencrieff, and was
bought by Andrew Carnegie in 1902. There are
displays of local history, costumes, and an art
gallery.

Place of Paisley: see No 772.

788 Pluscarden Abbey
Map 5

*From B9010 at Elgin take unclassified road to
Pluscarden, 6m SW. All year daily 0500-2030.
Free.*
Originally a Valliscaulian house, the monastery
was founded in 1230. In 1390 the Church was
burned, probably by the Wolf of Badenoch who
burned Elgin about the same time. It became a
dependent priory of the Benedictines' Abbey of
Dunfermline in 1454 until the suppression of
monastic life in Scotland in 1560. Thereafter the
buildings fell into ruins until 1948 when a group of
Benedictine monks from Prinknash Abbey,
Gloucestershire, returned to restore it.

789 Poosie Nansie's
Map 15

Mauchline. Normal public house hours.
Ale-house in Burns' time which inspired part of
his cantata *The Jolly Beggars*, and is still in use
today.

790 Powrie Castle
Map 9

*Off A929, 3m N of Dundee. By arrangement,
tel: Dundee 456743. Adult: 70p child: free. (Mr P
Clarke)*
A 16th-century tower house with a 17th-century
domestic building presently being restored.

Poosie Nansie's

Preston

791 Preston Mill
Map 14

Off A1 at East Linton, 6m W of Dunbar.
1 Apr-30 Sep, Mon-Sat 1000-1230, 1400-1930,
Sun 1400-1930. 1 Oct-31 Mar, closes 1630.
Adult: 40p, child: 20p. (NTS)
A picturesque water-mill, possibly the only one of
its kind still in working condition in Scotland.
Nearby is Phantassie Doocot, an excellent
example of a traditional Scottish doocot
(dovecote).

792 Prestongrange Mining Museum and Historic Site
Map 13

At Morrisons' Haven, on B1348,
8m E of Edinburgh. All year, Mon-Fri 0830-1600,
1st Sun of month, Apr-Oct 1030-1530, Sat by
arrangement,
tel: 031-661 2718. Free.
(East Lothian District Council)
A former colliery site with 800 years of recorded
running history. The centre piece is an 1874
Cornish Beam Pumping Engine and its 5-floor
Engine House. The former Power House is now
an exhibition hall with many mining artefacts,
plans, photographs and documents. There are
also two steam locomotives, a hundred-year-old
steam navvy and a colliery winding engine on
site.

793 Prestonpans Battle Cairn
Map 14

E of Prestonpans on A198. All times. Free.
The cairn commemorates the victory of Prince
Charles Edward over General Cope at the Battle
of Prestonpans in 1745.

794 Priorwood Gardens
Map 16

In Melrose, by Abbey. Easter-mid Oct, Mon-Sat
1000-1800, Sun 1330-1730; mid Oct-24 Dec,
Mon 1400-1730, Tue-Sat 1000-1730. Free.
(NTS)
A new garden which specialises in flowers
suitable for drying. There is an NTS Visitor
Centre.

795 Queen Elizabeth Forest Park
Map 11

Between the E shore of Loch Lomond and the
Trossachs. (FC)
In this 45,000 acres of forest, moor and
mountainside there are many walks. On A821 is
the David Marshall Lodge, a picnic pavilion and
information centre. 'Duke's Road' from Aberfoyle
to the Trossachs has fine views.

796 Queensberry Aisle
Map 18

Durisdeer, unclassified road off A702, 6m N of
Thornhill. All reasonable times. Free.
This striking little church dates from 1699, and is
noted for the elaborate monument, by Van Nost,
to the second Duke of Queensberry (died 1711)
and his duchess (died 1709).

Ramsay

797 Queen's Own Highlanders Museum
Map 5

Fort George, near Ardersier. Apr-Sep, Mon-Sat 1000-1800, Sun 1400-1800. Oct-Mar, Mon-Sat 1000-1600.
Regimental museum with collections of medals, uniforms and other items showing the history of the Queen's Own Highlanders.

798 Queen's View, Loch Lomond
Map 11

Off A809, 12m NNW of Glasgow.
From the west side of the road a path leads to a viewpoint where in 1879, Queen Victoria had her first view of Loch Lomond.

799 Queen's View, Loch Tummel
Map 8

On B8019, off A9, 8m NW of Pitlochry.
A magnificent viewpoint along Loch Tummel to the peak of Schiehallion, 3,547 feet. Queen Victoria visited it in 1866.

800 Quiraing
Map 4

Off A855 at Digg, 19m N of Portree, Isle of Skye.
An extraordinary mass of towers and pinnacles into which cattle were driven during forays. A rough track zigzags up to the 'Needle', an imposing obelisk 120 feet high, beyond which, in a large amphitheatre, stands the 'Table', a huge grass-covered rock-mass. Impressive views.

801 Quoyness Chambered Tomb
Map 1

E side of Els Ness, S coast of island of Sanday, Orkney. All reasonable times. Free. (AM)
A spectacular tomb with a main chamber standing to a height of about 13 feet. Analysis suggests that the tomb was in use about 2900 BC.

802 Raiders' Road
Map 17

From A712 near Clatteringshaws Dam, or A762 at Bennan near Mossdale. June-Sep daily 0900-2100. 50p per car. (FC).
A 10-mile forest drive through the fine scenery of the Galloway Forest Park. (See also No 452.)

803 Rammerscales
Map 18

On B7020, 2½m S of Lochmaben. 5 Jun-16 Sep, Tue and Thu 1400-1700, and 2 Suns per month. Adult: 40p, child: 20p. (Mr A M Bell Macdonald)
A Georgian manor house begun in 1760 for Dr James Mounsey, personal physician to the Tsarina Elizabeth of Russia. Gardens and woodland walks.

804 Allan Ramsay Library
Map 16

On B797 at Leadhills—enquire at Post Office.
Lead miners' subscription library, founded in 1741, with rare books, detailed 18th-century mining documents and local records.

805 Randolph's Leap
Map 5

Off B9007, 12m SE of Nairn.
The River Findhorn winds through a deep gorge in the sandstone, and from a path above are impressive views of the clear brown water swirling over rocks or in still dark pools. Randolph's Leap is the most striking part of this valley.

806 Ravenscraig Castle
Map 13

On a rocky promontory between Dysart and Kirkcaldy. Opening standard. Adult: 15p, child: 7p, group rates. (AM)
Imposing ruin of a castle founded by James II in 1460. Later it passed into the hands of the Sinclair Earls of Orkney. It is perhaps the first British castle to be symmetrically designed for defence by firearms.

807 Red Castle
Map 7

Off A92, 7m S of Montrose. All times. Free.
This red stone tower on a steep mound beside the sandhills of Lunan Bay probably dates from the 15th century when it replaced an earlier fort built for William the Lion by Walter de Berkely to counter raids by Danish pirates. Robert the Bruce gave it to his son-in-law, Hugh, 6th Earl of Ross, in 1328.

808 Reedie Hill Farm
Map 9

Off A983, N of Auchtermuchty. Fork left on Mournipea Road, then 2-3 miles. All year. Mon-Fri 0900-1800. Adult: 50p. (Dr T J Fletcher)
The first commercial red deer farm in Britain in which the deer are fully domesticated and approachable.

809 Reindeer on the Range
Map 5

Reindeer House, Loch Morlich. A951 from Aviemore; signposted from Loch Morlich Campsite. All year, daily (subject to weather), 1100 departure. Adult: 50p, child: 30p.
Visitors may accompany the herdsman on his daily check of Britain's only herd of reindeer.

810 Rennibister Earth House
Map 1

About 4½m WNW of Kirkwall on the Finstown road (A965), Orkney. All reasonable times. Free. (AM)
An excellent example of the Orkney type of Iron Age souterrain or earth-house, consisting of a passage and underground chamber with supporting roof-pillars.

811 Rennie's Bridge
Map 16

Kelso. All times. Free.
A fine 5-arched bridge built over the River Tweed in 1803 by Rennie to replace one destroyed by the floods of 1797. On the bridge are two lamp posts from the demolished Old Waterloo Bridge in London, which Rennie built in 1811. There is also a fine view to Floors Castle (No 439).

812 Rennie Memorial
Map 14

By A1 on East Linton by-pass. All times. Free.
The memorial is to the engineer and architect
John Rennie (1761-1821) who was born at the
mansion of Phantassie nearby.

813 Renwick Monument
Map 18

*Above Moniaive village on A702 NW of
Dumfries. All times. Free.*
James Renwick (1662-1688) was the last of the
Covenanter martyrs, who was executed in
Edinburgh, aged 26.

814 Restenneth Priory
Map 7

*Off B9113, 1½m ENE of Forfar. All reasonable
times. Free. (AM)*
A house of Augustinian canons, probably
founded by David I, in an attractive setting. There
are remains of the chapel built in Saxon style by
King Nechtan of the Picts in AD 710. A feature of
the ruins is the tall square tower, with its shapely
broach spire.

815 Rhum, Isle of
Map 4

*Inner Hebrides. Ferry from Mallaig and Arisaig
(no cars).*
A mountainous island where the Nature
Conservancy Council have for some years
conducted experiments in deer and forestry
management. Kinloch Castle (see
No 617) is a Victorian and Edwardian
extravaganza. Accommodation is limited.

816 Ring of Brodgar
Map 1

*Between Loch of Harray and Loch of Stenness,
5m NE of Stromness, Mainland, Orkney.
All times. Free. (AM)*
Magnificent stone circle of 36 stones (originally
60) surrounded by a deep ditch cut into solid
bedrock. Nearby are large mounds and other
standing stones, notably the Comet Stone.
(See also No 905.)

817 Rob Roy's Grave
Map 8

Balquhidder Churchyard, off A84, 14m NNW of Callander. All reasonable times. Free.
Three flat gravestones enclosed by railings are the graves of Rob Roy, his wife and two of his sons. The church itself contains St Angus' Stone (8th-century), a 17th-century bell from the old church and old Gaelic Bibles.

818 Rob Roy's Statue
Map 7

Peterculter by A93. All times. Free.
Statue of Rob Roy standing above the Leuchar Burn can be seen from the bridge on the main road.

Rodel Church: see No 840.

819 Rossdhu
Map 11

25m N of Glasgow on A82, 2m S of Luss. Easter Sun to end Sep, daily (except Sat) 1030-1700. Adult: 60p, child: 30p, group rates.
Historic home of the chiefs of Clan Colquhoun. A charming Georgian house of modest size, Rossdhu overlooks Loch Lomond and its islands.

Rosslyn Chapel

820 Rosslyn Chapel
Map 13

At Roslin, off A703, 7½m S of Edinburgh. Apr to end Oct, 1000-1300, 1400-1700, closed Sun. Adult: 30p, child: 10p.
The 15th-century chapel is one of Scotland's loveliest and most historic churches, renowned for its magnificent sculpture and Prentice Pillar.

821 Rothesay Castle
Map 10

*At Rothesay, Isle of Bute. Opening standard.
Adult: 20p, child: 10p, group rates. (AM)*
One of the most important mediaeval castles in
Scotland, Rothesay was stormed by Norsemen
in 1240; their breach can still be detected. The
walls, heightened and provided with four round
towers in the late 13th century, enclose a circular
courtyard unique in Scotland.

822 Rough Castle
Map 12

*Off B816, 6m W of Falkirk. All reasonable times.
Free. (AM)*
The best-preserved of the forts of the Antonine
Wall, with wall and ditches easily seen.

Rough Island: see No 722.

823 The Round House
Map 8

*Marshall Place, Perth. Jun-Sep, Mon-Sat
0900-2000, Sun 1400-1800; Oct-May, Mon-Fri
0900-1300, 1400-1715, Sat 0900-1300. Free.
(Perth and Kinross District Council/
Perth Tourist Association)*
The first Perth City waterworks, built in 1832 to a
design by Dr Adam Anderson, Professor of
Natural Philosophy at St Andrews University and
Rector of Perth Academy, and restored in 1974
by Perth Town Council. It is now in use as the
Tourist Information Centre, and its special
feature is a 360^0 slide programme showing
Perthshire in sound and vision.

824 Rovie Lodge Gardens
Map 3

*Off A839, 8½m E of Lairg. Mid Jul-end Sep,
1400-1800. Free. (Mrs George Rawstorne)*
Sloping lawns, herbaceous borders, heaths.
water garden.

825 Rowallan Castle
Map 15

*In the Rowallan Estate, off B751, 3m N of
Kilmarnock. Not yet open to the public; may be
viewed from outside. (AM)*
This house is a fine specimen of a superior
Scottish mansion of the 16th and 17th centuries.

826 Royal Caledonian Curling Club Museum
Map 8

*Perth Ice Rink, Dunkeld Road, Perth.
Oct-Apr, daily 1000-2300, May-Sep, Mon-Fri
1000-1200, 1400-1700. Free.*
A collection of paintings, stones and other items
illustrating the history of curling.

827 Roxburghe Castle
Map 16

Off A699, 1m SW of Kelso. All times. Free.
The earth works are all that remain of the
once mighty castle, destroyed by the Scots in the
15th century, and the walled Royal Burgh which
gave its name to the county. The present village
dates from a later period.

Ruthven

828 Ruthven Barracks
Map 5

On B970, ½m S of Kingussie. All reasonable times. Free. (AM)
Considerable ruins, on a site once occupied by a fortress of the Wolf of Badenoch, of barracks built 1716-18 to keep the Highlanders in check, and added to by General Wade in 1734. After the disaster of Culloden, 1746, Prince Charles' Highlanders assembled at Ruthven hoping he might take the field again. When they realised the cause was hopeless, they blew up the barracks.

Ruthven Castle: see No 567.

829 Ruthwell Cross
Map 18

In Ruthwell Church, B724, 6½m W of Annan. All reasonable times. Free. (AM)
This preaching cross, which is 18 feet high, is carved with Runic characters. It dates back to the 8th century and is a major monument of Dark Age Europe.

830 Saddell Abbey
Map 10

B842, 9m NNW of Campbeltown. All reasonable times. Free.
The abbey was built in the 12th century by Somerled, Lord of the Isles, or his son Reginald. Only the walls of the original building are left, with sculptured carved tombstones.

Safari Park: *see No 870.*

831 St Abbs Head
Map 14

1m N of St. Abbs.
Rocky cliffs, home to a wide variety of seabirds. Coldingham Bay nearby is particularly noted for its coloured pebbles.

832 St Andrews Castle
Map 9

Shore at St Andrews. Opening standard. Adult: 25p, child: 12p, group rates. (AM)
The ruined castle, overlooking the sea, was founded in 1200 and rebuilt in the late 14th century. Here Cardinal Beaton was murdered in 1546, and the first round of the Reformation struggle was fought out in the siege that followed.

833 St Andrews Cathedral
Map 9

Beside the castle at St Andrews.
Opening standard. Free. Charge for Museum
and St Rule's (Regulus') Tower: Adult: 20p,
child: 10p, group rates. (AM)
The cathedral was once the largest church in the
country. The remains include parts of the east
and west gables, the south wall of the nave, and
portions of the choir and south transept, mostly
built in the 12th and 13th centuries.

834 St Andrews Preservation Trust
Map 9

12 North Street. Jul-Sep, Thu and Fri 1430-
1800, Sun 1430-1630. Free.
A mid 18th-century detached cottage in the old
quarter of St Andrews has been restored. There
is a small museum and annual exhibition.

835 St Andrews University
Map 9

The oldest university in Scotland, founded
in 1412. See the 15th-century Church of
St Salvator, now the chapel for the united
colleges of St Salvator (1455) and St Leonard
(1512); St Mary's College (1537) with its
quadrangle; and the 16th-century St Leonard's
Chapel. Also in the town are St Mary's House
built in 1523 and now St Leonard's School
Library, and Holy Trinity Church with a
16th-century tower and interesting interior
features.

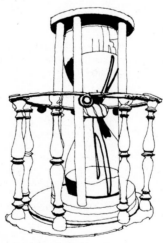

St Andrews University
(in St Salvator's)

836 St Bean's Church
Map 8

At Fowlis Wester, off A85, 5m NE of Crieff.
An attractive 13th-century church, restored in
1927, and containing a finely-carved Pictish
stone cross.

837 St Blane's Chapel
Map 10

8½m S of Rothesay, Isle of Bute. All reasonable
times. May be seen from the outside only. Free.
(AM)
Ruins of a chapel built c 1700. Nearby are the
foundations of a monastery founded by St Blane
in the 6th century.

St Bride's

838 St Bride's Church
Map 16

Douglas, 12m SSW of Lanark. Opening standard. Free. Apply key-keeper.
The restored chancel of this ancient church contains the tomb of the 'Bell the Cat' Earl of Angus (died 1514). The nearby tower (1618) has a clock of 1565 said to have been gifted by Mary Queen of Scots.

839 St Bridget's Church
Map 13

Dalgety, off A92, 3m E of N approach to Forth Road Bridge. All reasonable times. Free.
Ruins of an ancient church dedicated to St Bridget in 1244.

840 St Clement's Church
Map 2

At Rodel, S end of Harris, Western Isles. All reasonable times. Free; apply key-keeper. (AM)
A cruciform church of c 1500 with rich decoration and sculptured slabs.

841 St Columba's Cave
Map 10

1m N of Ellary on W shore of Loch Killisport (Caolisport), 10m SW of Ardrishaig. All times. Free.
Traditionally associated with St Columba's arrival in Scotland, the cave contains a rock-shelf with an altar, above which are carved crosses. A large basin, perhaps a Stone Age mortar, may have been used as a font. The cave was occupied from the Middle Stone Age. In front are traces of houses and the ruins of a chapel (possibly 13th-century), and another cave is nearby.

842 St Cormac's Chapel
Map 10

Isle of Eilean Mor, E of Jura. All reasonable times. Free. (AM) Access: private launch to Eilean Mor (tel: Ormsary 239 evenings, Mr Rodgers).
This mediaeval chapel is 15 feet by 8 feet with an upper chamber only accessible by ladder. It contains a sculpture of a priest.

843 St Duthus Chapel and Church
Map 3

Tain. Chapel: All reasonable times. Free. Church: Open daily, enquire locally. Free.
The chapel was built between 1065 and 1256. St Duthus died in 1065 and was buried in Ireland, but 200 years later his remains were transferred to Tain. The chapel was destroyed by fire in 1427. St Duthus Church was built c 1360 by William, Earl and Bishop of Ross, in Decorated style, and became a notable place of pilgrimage.

844 St Fillan's Cave
Map 9

Cove Wynd, Pittenweem (near harbour), 9m SSE of St Andrews. All year, 1000-1230, 1400-2000. Adult: 10p, child: free, group rates. (St John's Episcopal Church)
St Fillan's Cave gave Pittenweem (Pictish for *The Place of the Cave*) its name. In the 12th century, Augustinian monks from the Isle of May

established the Priory, the Great House and the Prior's Lodging above the cave, cutting through the rock from the garden to the holy cave-shrine below. Restored and rededicated in 1935.

St Fillan's Parish Church: see no 17.

845 St John's Kirk
Map 8

St John's Street, Perth.
A fine cruciform church largely dating from the 15th century, and restored 1923-28 as a war memorial. Here John Knox in 1559 preached his momentous sermon urging the 'purging of the churches from idolatry'.

846 St Kilda
Map 2

110m W of Scottish mainland.
Access difficult: NTS organises expeditions.
(NTS leased to NCC)
This remote and spectacular group of islands were evacuated in 1930. The cliffs at Conachair, 1397 feet, are the highest in Britain. The wild life, some of which (eg Soay sheep, St Kilda mouse and wren) is unique, includes the world's biggest gannetry and myriads of fulmars and puffins. Considerable remains of the primitive dwellings; working parties to maintain these visit in summer.

847 St Magnus Cathedral
Map 1

Kirkwall, Orkney. Mon-Sat 0900-1300, 1400-1700. Closed Sun (except for services). Free.
Founded by Earl Rognvald in 1137 and dedicated to his uncle St Magnus. The remains of both men are in the massive central piers. The original building dates from 1137 to 1200, but additional work went on for a further 300 years. It is still in regular use as the Parish Church, and contains some of the finest examples of Norman architecture in Scotland, with small additions in transitional styles and very early Gothic.

848 St Magnus Church
Map 1

Isle of Egilsay, Orkney. All times. Free. (AM)
An impressive church, probably 12th-century, with a remarkable round tower of the Irish type, which still stands to a height of nearly 50 feet.

849 St Mary's Chapel, Bute
Map 10

A845, ½m S of Rothesay. Opening standard, on application to custodian at Rothesay Castle. Free. (AM)
The remains of the late mediaeval Abbey Church of St Mary, including two fine recessed and canopied tombs containing effigies of a knight in full armour, and a lady and child.

850 St Mary's Chapel, Crosskirk
Map 3

Off A836, 6½m WNW of Thurso. All reasonable times. Free. (AM)
A rudely-constructed chapel with very low doors narrowing at the top in Irish style. Probably 12th century.

St Mary's Church

St Mary's Chapel, Wyre: see No 204.

851 St Mary's Church, Auchindoir
Map 6

Off A97, 11m SSW of Huntly. All reasonable times. Free. (AM)
Ruins of one of the finest mediaeval parish churches remaining in Scotland.

852 St Mary's Church, Grandtully
Map 8

At Pitcairn Farm, 2m ENE of Aberfeldy, off A827. All times. Free. (AM)
A 16th-century church, with a remarkable painted wooden ceiling of heraldic and symbolic subjects.

853 St Mary's Loch
Map 16

Off A708, 14m ESE of Selkirk.
Beautifully set among smooth green hills, this three-mile-long loch is now also used for sailing. On the neck of land separating it from Loch of the Lowes at the south end stands Tibbie Shiel's Inn, long kept by Tibbie Shiel (Elizabeth Richardson, 1783-1878) from 1823, and a meeting-place for many 19th-century literati. Beside the road towards the north end of the loch is a seated statue of James Hogg, the 'Ettrick Shepherd', author of the *Confessions of a Justified Sinner* and a friend of Scott's, who farmed in this district.

854 St Mary's Pleasance
Map 14

Sidegate, Haddington. Open at all reasonable times. Free. (Haddington Garden Trust)
These gardens of Haddington House have been restored as a 17th-century garden, with rose and herb, meadow, cottage and sunken gardens. The Pleached Alley leads to St Mary's Gate and the restored mediaeval church of St Mary's.

855 St Michael's Parish Church
Map 12

Beside Linlithgow Palace, on S shore of the loch, Linlithgow. Oct-May, daily except Thur, 1000-1200, 1400-1600. Jun-Sep, daily 1000-1200, 1400-1600, and by arrangement, tel: Linlithgow 2195. Free.
One of the finest examples of a mediaeval parish church in Scotland. Contemporary 'golden' crown by Geoffrey Clarke replaced the mediaeval crown which collapsed in 1820.

St Monans Church: see No 189.

856 St Ninian's Cave
Map 17

3½m SW of Whithorn. From A747 take unclassified road to Kidsdale, then ¾m footpath to coast. All reasonable times. Free. (AM)
A cave on the seashore said to be the retreat of St Ninian (see also No 991). Early Christian crosses are carved on to the rock.

857 St Ninian's Chapel
Map 17

At Isle of Whithorn, 3m SE of Whithorn. All times. Free. (AM)
Ruins of a 13th-century chapel on a site traditionally associated with St Ninian.

858 St Ninian's Isle
Map 1

By B9122 off W coast of Mainland, Shetland. All times. Free.
Holy Well, foundations of chapel circa 12th century and pre-Norse church where a hoard of Celtic silver was discovered (now in the National Museum of Antiquities in Edinburgh).
(See No 371.)

859 St Orland's Stone
Map 9

1½m NE of Glamis railway station and 3½m W of Forfar, in a field near the farmhouse of Cossans. All reasonable times. Free. (AM)
An upstanding sculptured slab of the Early Christian period.

860 St Peter's Church
Map 3

Near the harbour at Thurso. All reasonable times. Free.
Ruins situated in the attractively restored old part of Thurso. Of mediaeval or earlier origin; much of the present church dates from the 17th century.

861 St Vigean's Museum
Map 9

Off A92, 1½m N of Arbroath. Opening standard, except closed Sun. Adult: 15p, child: 7p, group rates. (AM)
A cottage museum containing Pictish gravestones which are among the most important groups of early Christian sculpture in Scotland.

862 Saltcoats Harbour and Maritime Museum
Map 15

Saltcoats. Summer only. Adult: 3p, child: 2p.
The museum contains relics recalling the era when coal was exported to Ireland and when the area was famous for the manufacture of salt.

863 Sanquhar Museum
Map 15

N end of High Street, Sanquhar.
By arrangement, 42 High Street, tel: Sanquhar 303.
(Mr T A Johnstone). Free.
(Nithsdale District Council)
Items of local interest, displayed in one room of the old Tolbooth, a building designed by William Adam, dated 1735 and featuring a clock tower.

864 Sanquhar Post Office
Map 15

Main Street, Sanquhar.
Britain's oldest post office, functioning in 1783, a year before the introduction of the mail coach service, and still in use today.

865 Santa Claus Land
Map 5

By Aviemore Centre. All year, daily, 1000-1800. Adult: 80p, child: 50p, group rates.
A landscaped park with a wide variety of activities for children. (See also No 61.)

Savings Bank Museum: see No 293.

Scalloway

866 Scalloway Castle
Map 1

6m W of Lerwick, Shetland. Opening standard. Free. (AM)
Built in 1600 by Earl Patrick Stewart, in mediaeval style. When the Earl, a notoriously cruel character, was executed in 1615, the castle fell into disuse.

867 Scapa Distillery
Map 1

Off A964 2m S of Kirkwall, Orkney. (Taylor & Ferguson Ltd). Free. Feb-Jun, Aug-Nov, Wed and Thu 1400-1500. By arrangement, tel: Kirkwall 2071.
Brewing and distillation of malt whisky.

868 Scapa Flow
Map 1

Sea area, enclosed by the mainland of Orkney and the islands of Birsay, South Ronaldsay, Flotta and Hoy.
It was a major naval anchorage in both wars and the scene of the surrender of the German Fleet in 1918. Today Scapa Flow is again a centre of marine activity as Flotta has been developed as a pipeline landfall and tanker terminal for North Sea Oil. (See also No 922.)

869 Scone Palace
Map 8

Off A93 (Braemar road), 2m N of Perth. May-Sep, Mon-Sat 1000-1730, Sun 1400-1730. (House, grounds and pinetum) Adult: 80p, child: 40p, group rates. (Earl of Mansfield)
The present castellated palace, enlarged and embellished in 1803, incorporates the 16th-century and earlier palaces. It has notable grounds and a pinetum, and is still a family home. The Mote Hill at Scone, known in the 8th century and earlier, was the site of the famous coronation Stone of Scone, brought there in the 9th century by Kenneth MacAlpine, King of Scots. In 1296 the Stone was seized and taken to Westminster Abbey. The ancient Abbey of Scone was destroyed in 1559 by followers of John Knox. Magnificent collection of porcelain, furniture, ivories, 18th-century clocks and 16th-century needlework.

Scottish Horse

870 Scotland's Safari Park
Map 11

At Blair Drummond on A84 between Stirling and Doune (exit off M9). Mid Mar-end Oct, daily from 1000. Car and occupants: £2.50. Safari bus available for visitors without own transport: Adult: 90p, child and OAP: 60p.
The collection includes lions, elephants, zebras, camels, monkey jungle, giraffes, Siberian tigers, antelope, buffalo, Ankole cattle and Pere David deer. There is a pets corner and play area. Summer only: performing dolphins, boat safari round chimp island and hippo pool.

871 Scots Dyke
Map 18

Off A7, 7m S of Langholm. All reasonable times. Free.
The remains of a wall made of clods of earth and stones, which marked part of the border between England and Scotland.

872 Scotstarvit Tower
Map 9

Off A916, 3m S of Cupar. Opening standard. Free. (AM)
A fine tower known to have been in existence in 1579.

873 Captain Scott and Dr Wilson Fountain
Map 7

In Glen Prosen on unclassified road NW of Dykehead. All times. Free.
The fountain was erected in memory of the Antarctic explorers, Captain Scott and Dr Wilson; who reached the South Pole in 1912.

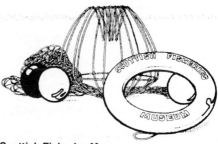

Scottish Fisheries Museum

874 Scottish Fisheries Museum
Map 9

At Anstruther harbour, 10m SSE of St Andrews. Apr-Oct, 1000-1230, 1400-1800; Sun 1400-1700; Nov-Mar, Wed to Mon 1430-1630. Closed Tue. Adult: 40p, child: 20p, group rates.
In St Ayles Land (with a charter dated 1318), a collection of items illustrating aspects of the Scottish fisherman's life both at home and at sea, historical and modern. The museum also contains a marine aquarium and is restoring a 70-foot sailing 'Fifie' in the harbour.

875 The Scottish Horse Museum
Map 8

The Cross, Dunkeld. Easter to mid Oct, daily, 1030-1230, 1400-1700. Adult: 10p. (Scottish Horse Trust)
Exhibits, uniforms, photographs, maps and rolls of all those who served in this Yeomanry Regiment.

Scottish Museum

876 Scottish Museum of Wool Textiles
Map 16

On main road (A72) at Walkerburn, 9m ESE of Peebles. All year. Mon-Fri 1000-1700. Easter-end Sep, Sat 1100-1600, Sun 1400-1600. Adult: 20p, child: 10p. (Henry Ballantyne and Sons Ltd)
This display features the growth of the Scottish textile trade, with many interesting exhibits. Demonstrations of hand spinning.

877 Scottish Railway Preservation Society
Map 12

Wallace Street off Grahams Road, Falkirk. All year, Sat and Sun 1100-1700. Adult: 15p, child: 10p, family: 50p.
Museum and workshop for the restoration of railway vehicles. There is a comprehensive collection, some of which are used on excursions.

Scottish Rifles: see No 148.

878 Scottish White Heather Farm
Map 10

At Toward, 5m SW of Dunoon. 0900-1800 (Sun by arrangement, tel: Dunoon 237). Free.
Extensive gardens on the Clyde with demonstrations of the make up of white heather sprays and horse shoes.

879 Scott's View
Map 16

B6356, 7 m ESE of Galashiels.
A view over the Tweed to the Eildon Hills, beloved by Scott; here the horses taking his remains to Dryburgh for burial stopped as they had so often before for Sir Walter to enjoy this panorama.

880 Duns Scotus Statue
Map 14

At Duns, in public park. All times. Free.
Duns was the birthplace of John Duns Scotus (1265-1308), a Franciscan who became a leading divine and one of the greatest mediaeval philosophers. (See also No 962.)

881 Seton Collegiate Church
Map 14

Off A198, 13m E of Edinburgh. Opening standard. Adult:15p, child:7p, group rates.(AM)
An important ecclesiastical monument of the late 14th century, with a fine vaulted chancel and apse.

882 Shawbost Folk Museum
Map 2

A858, 19m NW of Stornoway, Isle of Lewis. Apr-Nov, Mon-Sat, 1000-1800. Donation box.
Created under the Highland Village Competition 1970, the museum illustrates the old way of life in Lewis. A Norse watermill has been restored; directions at the museum.

883 Shetland Museum
Map 1

Lower Hillhead, Lerwick. All year, Mon,Wed & Fri 1000-1300, 1430-1700, 1800-2000. Tue & Sat 1030-1300, 1430-1700. Thu 1000-1300. Free. (Shetland Islands Council)
The collection in this museum is entirely local in

Skara

character. The theme is the history of man in Shetland from pre-history to the present day. Four contiguous galleries are devoted to archaeology, art and textiles, folk life and shipping.

884 Shetland Workshop Gallery
Map 1

4-6 Burns Lane, Lerwick. All year, daily (except Wed) 0930-1300, 1415-1700. Free. (R and H Hughson)
Two old dwelling houses in one of Lerwick's oldest lanes have been combined to provide a gallery for local artists and craftsmen.

885 Signal Tower
Map 9

Ladyloan, Arbroath. All year, Mon-Sat 0930-1300, 1400-1700. Free. (Angus District Council)
The museum collection relates to the history of Arbroath, including fishing, the sea, flax industry, Shanks lawnmowers, the Bell Rock lighthouse (for which the Signal Tower was once the shore base) and folk life.

886 SS 'Sir Walter Scott'
Map 8

From Trossachs Pier, E end of Loch Katrine, 9m W of Callander. Mid May-end Sep. Adult: 70p, child: 35p, group rates. (Strathclyde Water Board)
Regular sailings in summer from the pier to Stronachlachar in this fine old steamer. Views include Ben Lomond.

887 Sir Walter Scott's Courtroom
Map 16

Market Square, Selkirk. By application to: Ettrick & Lauderdale District Council, Paton St, Galashiels, Selkirkshire, tel: Galashiels 4751. Free.
The bench and chair from which Sir Walter Scott, as Sheriff of Selkirk, administered justice for 30 years, are on display, with relics of James Hogg, Mungo Park and Robert Burns, and ancient charters.

888 Skara Brae
Map 1

7½m N of Stromness, Mainland, Orkney. Opening standard. Adult: 20p, child: 10p, group rates. (AM)
A Neolithic village with about 10 one-roomed houses, containing stone beds, fireplaces and cupboards. There are also covered passages from one house to another and a paved open court where communal problems were discussed. The village was probably hastily evacuated in a sandstorm, and it remained under the sand dunes for many centuries, until uncovered by a storm in 1850.

Skara Brae

889 Skelmorlie Aisle
Map 11

Bellman's Close, off main street, Largs. Opening standard, Apr-Sep. Adult: 15p, child: 7p, group rates. (AM)
A splendid mausoleum of 1636, with painted roof, interesting tombs and monuments.

890 Skipness Castle and Chapel
Map 10

Skipness, B8001, 10m S of Tarbert, Loch Fyne. Closed to the public but may be viewed from outside. (AM)
The remains of the ancient chapel and the large 13th-century castle overlook the bay.

891 Skye Water Mill and Black House
Map 4

B884, 8m W of Dunvegan, Isle of Skye. Easter-end Sep, Mon-Sat 1000-1900. (Black House open Sun 1000-1900). Water Mill, adult: 25p, child: 10p Black House, adult: 30p, child: 10p.
A crofter's cottage whose contents include a replica of a whisky still. A watermill which used to grind corn is 2 miles down the road.

892 Slains Castle
Map 6

Off A975, 7m SSW of Peterhead. All reasonable times. Free.
Extensive ruins of a castle of 1664 to replace an earlier Slains Castle, 4 miles south, extended and rebuilt later by the 9th Earl of Errol.
Dr Johnson and James Boswell visited here in 1773.

893 Smailholm Tower
Map 16

Off B6404, 7m W of Kelso. Opening standard. Free. (AM)
An outstanding example of a 16th-century Border peel tower built to give surveillance over a wide expanse of country. It is 57 feet high, in a good state of preservation. At nearby Sandyknowe farm Walter Scott spent some childhood years.

894 Adam Smith Centre
Map 13

Bennochy Road, Kirkcaldy.
Theatre, exhibition and general arts centre with performances all year, named after Adam Smith, the economist who was born in Kirkcaldy.

895 Smith Art Gallery and Museum
Map 12

Albert Place, Stirling, 1/4m W from centre of town. All year, daily 1400-1700. Free.
Room within a Victorian building used for temporary displays.

896 Smithies
Map 18

Gretna Green, just off A74 at English border. Free. Museum: 10p. (Gretna Museum Co)
The little River Sark is the border between Scotland and England, and Gretna Green was the haven for runaway couples seeking to take advantage of Scotland's then-laxer marriage

laws. Couples could be married by a declaration before witnesses. A residential qualification was required for at least one of the couple from 1856, and marriage by declaration was made illegal in 1940. Among the places where marriages took place were the Sark Toll Bar (now bypassed by A74) and the well-known Smithy at Gretna Green where curios are preserved.

897 Smollett Monument
Map 11

On A82 N of Dumbarton at Renton. All times. Free.
A monument to Tobias Smollett (1721-1771), novelist and surgeon. Dr Johnson wrote the Latin epitaph to him in 1773.

Smoo Cave

898 Smoo Cave
Map 3

A838, 1½m E of Durness. All reasonable times. Free.
Three vast caves at the end of a deep cleft in the limestone cliffs. The entrance to the first resembles a Gothic arch. The second cavern, access difficult, has a waterfall. The third is inaccessible.

899 Souter Johnnie's House
Map 15

At Kirkoswald, on A77, 7m WSW of Maybole. 1 Apr-30 Sep, daily (except Fri) 1200-1700; other times by arrangement, tel: Kirkoswald 243. Adult: 30p, child: 15p. (NTS)
This thatched cottage was the home of the village cobbler (Souter) John Davidson at the end of the 18th century. Davidson and his friend Douglas Graham of Shanter Farm, known to Robert Burns in his youth in Kirkoswald, were later immortalised in *Tam o' Shanter*. The cottage contains Burnsiana and contemporary tools of the cobbler's craft.

900 South Queensferry Museum
Map 13

Burgh Chambers, Main Street. All year, Mon-Fri, admission by application to Burgh Chambers. Free.
A small collection of items relating to local history and particularly to the building of the Forth Railway Bridge.

901 South Uist Folk Museum
Map 2

*Off Uist main road, ½ mile along Eochar
road, beyond new school. By arrangement,
tel: Carnan 225. Free.
(South Uist Antiquarian Society)*
Traditional thatched house with relics of local
social history.

902 Spynie Palace
Map 6

*Off A941, 2m N of Elgin. Can be viewed from the
outside. (AM)*
Ruins of an impressive stone tower of c 1470,
formerly the Castle of the Bishops of Moray.

Staffa: see No 435.

903 Standing Stones of Callanish
Map 2

*Callanish, off A858, 16m W of Stornoway, Isle of
Lewis. All times. Free. (AM)*
A cruciform setting of megaliths unique in
Scotland and second in importance in the UK
only to Stonehenge. It was probably carried out
in a series of additions between 2000 and
1500 BC. An avenue of 19 monoliths leads to a
circle of 13 stones, with rows of more stones
fanning out.

904 Standing Stones of Machrie Moor
Map 10

*1½m E of A841, along Moss Farm Road, south
of Machrie on W coast of Arran. All reasonable
times. Free. (AM)*
These 15 feet high standing stones are the
remains of six Bronze Age stone circles. Some
have now fallen. (See also No 721.)

905 Standing Stones of Stenness
Map 1

*Between Loch of Harray and Loch of Stenness,
5m NE of Stromness, Mainland, Orkney. All
times. Free. (AM)*
Four large upright stones are the dramatic
remains of a stone circle, c 3000 BC, encircled by
a ditch and bank. The area around Stenness is
particularly rich in such remains. See also Ring of
Brodgar, No 816.

906 Staneydale Temple
Map 1

*2¾m ENE of Walls, Shetland. All reasonable
times. Free. (AM)*
Second millennium BC structure, heel-shaped
externally, and containing an oval chamber.

907 Steinacleit Cairn and Stone Circle
Map 2

*At the south end of Loch an Duin, Shader, 12m N
of Stornoway, off A857, Isle of Lewis. All times.
Free. (AM)*
The fragmentary remains of a chambered cairn
of Neolithic date (c 2000 BC).

908 James Stewart Tablet
Map 4

2m SW of Ballachulish on the shores of Loch Linnhe beside the ruined Kirk of Veil. All times, Free.

James Stewart was tried and unjustly hanged for the Appin murder committed in 1752 and made famous in Stevenson's *Kidnapped*.

909 Stewartry Museum
Map 17

St Mary Street, Kirkcudbright. Easter-Oct, Mon-Sat 1000-1200, 1300-1700. Adult: 20p, child: 10p. (Stewartry Museum Association)

A museum depicting the life of the area with prehistoric articles, relics of domestic life and crafts of earlier days. Works of local artists are featured, especially Jessie M King (1875-1949). John Paul Jones, a founder of the American Navy who was born in the Stewartry and had varied associations with Kirkcudbright, is also the subject of a special display.

910 Stirling Bridge
Map 12

By A9 N of Stirling town centre. All times, Free.

The Old Bridge built c 1400, was for centuries of great strategic importance as the 'gateway to the north' and the lowest building point of the River Forth.

911 Stirling Castle
Map 12

At Stirling. Apr, May and Sep, 0930-1815, Sun 1100-1800; Jun-Aug 0930-2000, Sun 1100-1900; Oct-Mar 0930-1600, Sun 1300-1600. Adult: 30p (1 Apr-30 Sep); 25p (1 Oct-31 Mar); child: 15p (1 Apr-30 Sep); 12p (1 Oct–31 Mar). Group rates. (AM)

Stirling Castle on its 250-feet great rock has dominated much of Scotland's vivid history. Wallace recaptured it from the English in 1297; Edward I retook it in 1304, until Bruce won at nearby Bannockburn in 1314. Later it was a favourite Royal residence; James II was born here in 1430 and Mary, Queen of Scots and James VI both spent some years here. General Monk took it in 1651. Long used as a barracks, and frequently rebuilt, the old towers built by James III remain. as do the fine 15th-century hall, the splendid Renaissance palace of James V, the Parliament Hall, the Chapel Royal of 1594, and other buildings.

Stone of Mannan: see No 192.

912 Stonehaven Tolbooth Museum
Map 7

At quay at Stonehaven. Jun-Sep, daily (except Tue) 1400-1700, Sat 1000-1200. Free. (Kincardine & Deeside District Council)

This 16th-century former storehouse of the Earls Marischal was later used as a prison. In 1748-49, Episcopal ministers lodged inside and baptised children through the windows. The museum displays local history, archaeology and particularly fishing.

913 Storr
Map 4

2m walk from A855, 8m N of Portree, Isle of Skye
A series of pinnacles and crags whose
2,360-feet summit (3-4 hours) gives fine views of
the Outer Hebrides and Ross-shire mountains.
The Old Man of Storr, at the east end of the
mountain, is a black obelisk, 160 feet high, first
climbed in 1955.

914 Strathallan Air Museum
Map 8

From Auchterarder take B8062 (Crieff road),
then follow airfield signs. All year, 1000-1700.
Adult: 80p, child: 30p, group rates.
(Sir William D Roberts)
A collection of historic aircraft, predominantly
World War II era, dating back to 1930. There are
flying displays in summer.

915 Strathaven Castle
Map 15

Kirk Street/Stonehouse Road, Strathaven,
14m W of Lanark. All reasonable times. Free.
Also known as Avondale Castle, this ruin dates
from the 15th century.

916 Strathclyde Country Park
Map 11

On both sides of M74 between Hamilton and
Bothwell interchanges (A723 and A725). All
year. Free (charges for facilities).
A countryside park with man-made loch, nature
reserve (permit only), sandy beach and a wide
variety of sporting activities. (See also No 542.)

917 Strathisla Distillery
Map 6

Keith. Mid Jun-mid Sep, Mon-Fri 0900,
1200, 1400-1600. Free. (Chivas Bros Ltd)
A typical small old-fashioned distillery, the oldest
established in Scotland, dating from 1786.

918 Strathnaver Museum
Map 3

Off A836, at Farr, near Bettyhill. Summer,
Mon-Wed and Sat, 1400-1700. Donations.
(J and R McKay)
The former Farr Church (18th-century) now
houses this museum of local history. This is
historic Clan MacKay country and is associated
with the Sutherland Clearances.

919 Strathspey Railway
Map 5

Aviemore to Boat of Garten (off A95, 6½m NNE).
No access at Aviemore until new station built.
Easter weekend, weekends May-Sep, and daily
(except Mon and Fri) Jul-Aug, 0930-1800, Sat
1200-1800. May-Jun and Sep, Sat 1300-1800,
Sun 1200-1800. Fares: Adult: £1 return trip, 50p
single; child: 50p and 25p.
(Strathspey Railway Company Ltd)
The line is part of the former Highland Railway
(Aviemore/Forres section), closed in 1965.
Since 1972 volunteers have been restoring the
line and station at Boat of Garten and now offer a
limited steam service. Some of the rolling stock is
on display, and smaller relics can be seen in the
museum at the station.

Study

920 Strathyre Forest Information Centre
Map 8

A84 at S end of Strathyre Village. Daily, May-30 Sep, 0900-1900. Free. (FC)
An attractive display illustrating a working forest and also many forms of recreation and leisure to be enjoyed in Scotland's forests.

921 Strome Castle
Map 4

Unclassified road off A890, NW shore of Loch Carron. All reasonable times. Free. (NTS)
Scant ruins of an ancient castle, destroyed in 1602 after a long siege.

922 Stromness Museum
Map 1

Stromness, Orkney. All year, Mon-Sat 1100-1230, 1330-1700 (Thurs 1100-1300). Jul-Aug 1030-1230, 1330-1700. Adult: 10p. (Orkney Natural History Society)
A fine collection of preserved birds, eggs and Orkney shells. The maritime collection includes a selection of ship models and a permanent feature on the First World War German Fleet scuttled on Scapa Flow. (See also No 868.)

923 Strone Gardens
Map 8

*A815, 12m E of Inveraray. Apr-Sep, daily 0900-2100. Adult: 30p.
(Rt Hon Lord Glenkinglas)*
Daffodils, primulas, exotic shrubs and rhododendrons. The Pinetum contains the tallest tree in Scotland.

924 The Study
Map 12

In Culross. Oct-Apr, Sat 0930-1230, 1400-1600, Sun 1400-1600, or by arrangement, tel: Newmills 880359. Sat 0930-1230, 1400-1600, Sun 1400-1600. Admission by donation. (NTS)
Built in 1633, the tower contains a turnpike stair and a large room on the first floor houses a museum. Fine views of the Forth.

925 John McDouall Stuart Museum
Map 13

Rectory Lane, Dysart, 2m N of Kirkcaldy.
May-Sep, daily 1400-1700. Free.
A 17th-century building restored by NTS.
Birthplace of the explorer John McDouall Stuart
(1815-1866) who crossed Australia in 1862-63.
Permanent display relating to the explorer and
also temporary exhibitions.

926 Sueno's Stone
Map 3

Beside B9011, 1m NE of Forres. All times. Free.
(AM)
One of the most remarkable early sculptured
monuments in Scotland, 20 feet high with
elaborate carving.

927 Summer Isles
Map 3

Off Achiltibuie, NW of Ullapool.
An attractive group of islands, the largest of
which is Tanera More. Cruises can be arranged
from Ullapool and Achiltibuie.

928 Suntrap
Map 13

At Gogarburn, between A8 and A71, 6m W of
Edinburgh. Garden all year, daily 0900-dusk.
Advice Centre all year, Mon-Fri 0900-1700
(1 Mar-31 Oct also Sat and Sun 1430-1700).
Adult: 30p child: 15p (NTS)
A gardening advice centre, of particular interest
to owners of small gardens, offering courses of
instruction.

Sweetheart Abbey

929 Sweetheart Abbey
Map 18

At New Abbey, A710, 7½m S of Dumfries.
Opening standard. Adult: 20p, child: 10p, group
rates. (AM)
Founded in 1273 by Devorgilla in memory of her
husband John Balliol (she also founded Balliol
College, Oxford). this beautiful ruin has a
precinct wall built of enormous boulders. (See
also No 761.)

930 Symington Church
Map 15

Off A77 at Symington. All reasonable times.
Free.
The small restored church has a trio of
round-headed Norman windows, dating from the
12th century, and also an ancient roof of open
timber.

Talnotry: See No 453.

931 Tamdhu Distillery
Map 5

Off B9102 8m W of Craigellachie at Knockando.
May-Sep 1000-1600. Free.
(The Highland Distilleries Co)
Guided tour with large graphic display and views
of distilling plant from viewing gallery.

932 Tam o'Shanter Museum
Map 15

High Street, Ayr. Apr-Sep, Mon-Sat 0930-1730;
(Jun-Aug, Sun 1430-1600). Oct-Mar, Mon-Sat
1200-1600. Adult: 20p, child: 10p, group rates.
A brewhouse in Burns' time to which Douglas
Graham of Shanter supplied malted grain and
who was immortalised by Burns as
Tam o'Shanter. Now a Burns Museum.

933 Tankerness House
Map 1

Broad Street, Kirkwall, Orkney. All year, Mon-
Sat 1030-1300, 1400-1700. Free.
(Orkney Islands Council)
Dating from 1574, this is a fine example of an
Orkney merchant-laird's mansion, with
courtyard and gardens. Now a museum of life in
Orkney through 4,000 years, with additional
special exhibitions.

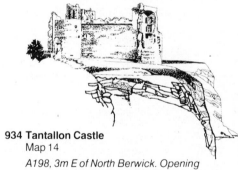

Tantallon Castle

934 Tantallon Castle
Map 14

A198, 3m E of North Berwick. Opening
standard. Adult: 25p, child: 12p, group rates.
(AM)
Extensive red ruins of a 14th-century stronghold
of the Douglases, in magnificent clifftop setting.
Although the castle withstood a regular siege by
James V in 1528, it was eventually destroyed by
General Monk in 1651.

935 Tarves Mediaeval Tomb
Map 6

4m NE of Oldmeldrum, in the kirkyard of Tarves.
All reasonable times. Free. (AM)
A fine altar-tomb of William Forbes, the laird who
enlarged Tolquhon Castle. It shows an
interesting mixture of Gothic and Renaissance
styles. (See also No 947.)

936 Tay Bridges
Map 9

The railway bridge, built between 1883 and 1888, carries the main railway line from Edinburgh to Aberdeen and is successor to the earlier structure which was blown down by a gale in 1879 while a train was crossing.

The road bridge, opened to traffic in 1966, spans the Tay from Newport to Dundee for 1½ miles. It is constructed on box girders on 42 pairs of pillars erected on 42 piers.

937 Tealing Earth House and Dovecot
Map 9

Off A929, 5m N of Dundee, ½m on unclassified road to Tealing and Auchterhouse. All reasonable times. Free. (AM)
A well-preserved example of an Iron Age souterrain or earth-house comprising a passage and long curved gallery and small inner chambers. Nearby is a fine dovecote built in 1595.

938 Telford Memorial
Map 18

At Westerkirk, B709, 6m NW of Langholm. All times. Free.
Memorial to Thomas Telford (1757-1834), the engineer who was born in the valley of the Meggat Water near Westerkirk. There are several reminders of him nearby at Langholm.

939 Tentsmuir Point National Nature Reserve
Map 9

S and W of Tayport between estuaries of rivers Tay and Eden. A919, B945 from St Andrews or Tayport. (NCC)
An area of foreshore (Abertay Sands) and inland area of dunes, trees and marsh. Large population of migrant birds.

940 James Thomson Obelisk
Map 16

At Ferniehill, 2m NE of Kelso, off A698. All times. Free.
James Thomson (1700-1748), born at Ednam, is best known for writing the words of *'Rule Britannia'*.

941 Joseph Thomson Memorial
Map 18

Thornhill, 13m NNW of Dumfries. All times. Free.
Bust of Joseph Thomson (1858-1895), African explorer born at Penpont, who went to school in Thornhill.

942 Threave Castle
Map 17

N of A75, 1½m W of Castle Douglas. Opening standard. Adult: 20p, child: 10p (inclusive of ferry), group rates. (AM)
Early stronghold of the Black Douglases, on an island in the Dee. The four-storeyed tower was built between 1639 and 1690 by Archibald the Grim, Lord of Galloway. In 1455 it was the last Douglas stronghold to surrender to James II, who employed Mons Meg (the famous cannon now in Edinburgh Castle) in its subjection.

Tomintoul

943 Threave House and Gardens and Wildfowl Refuge
Map 17

S of A75, 2m W of Castle Douglas. Gardens: All year, daily 0900-sunset. Walled garden and glasshouses: All year 0900-1700. Visitor Centre: 1 Apr-31 Oct. Wildfowl refuge: access Nov-Mar. Adult: 75p, child: 35p. (NTS)
The gardens of this Victorian mansion display acres of naturalised daffodils in April and May. There are peat, rock and water gardens and a visitor centre. The house (not open to the public) is a school of Practical Gardening. Threave Wildfowl Refuge nearby is a roosting and feeding place for many species of wild geese and ducks on and near the River Dee; access during November to March, to selected points only to avoid disturbance.

944 Thurso Folk Museum
Map 3

Town Hall. Jun-Sep, Mon-Sat 1000-1300, 1400-1700, 1900-2100. Adult: 10p, child: 5p.
Exhibition of agricultural and domestic life, local trades and crafts with a room of an old Caithness cottage.

945 Tingwall Valley Agricultural Museum
Map 1

At Veensgarth off A971, 5m NW of Lerwick, Shetland. May-Sep, Mon-Fri 1000-1300, 1400-1700, Sat and Sun 1300-1700. Adult: 30p, child: 20p. (Mrs P Sanderson)
A private collection of tools and equipment used by the Shetland crofter: housed in a mid 18th-century granary, stables and bothy.

946 Tinnis Castle
Map 16

Off B712, 9m SW of Peebles. All reasonable times. Free. (Tod Holdings Ltd)
A sheepwalk leads to the ruin of Tinnis, built at the beginning of the 16th century. It was the home of the head of the clan Tweedies.

947 Tolquhon Castle
Map 6

Off B999, 7m ENE of Oldmeldrum. Opening standard. Adult: 15p, child: 7p, group rates. (AM)
Once a seat of the Forbes family, an early 15th-century rectangular tower, with a large quadrangular mansion of 1584-89. Two round towers, a fine carved panel over the door, and the courtyard are features. (See also No 935.)

948 Tomatin Distillery
Map 5

On A9 16m S of Inverness at Tomatin. Jun-Sep, Mon-Fri 1500. By arrangement, tel: Tomatin 234. Free.
Demonstration of the process of whisky distilling.

949 Tomintoul Museum
Map 5

The Square. Daily, May, 1000-1230, 1330-1730. Jun-Sep, 1000-1230, 1330-1800. Jul-Aug 1000-1230, 1330-1900. Free.
A display relating to local history, including turn-of-the-century photographs, old tools and harness, and a reconstructed farm kitchen.

950 Tomnaverie Stone Circle
Map 7

4m NW of Aboyne. All times. Free. (AM)
The remains of a recumbent stone circle
probably 1800-1600 BC. Unexcavated.

951 Tongland Power Station
Map 17

*By A711, 2m N of Kirkcudbright. Jul-Sep, Mon-
Sat 0900-1700. (South of Scotland Electricity
Board).*
Hydro-electric power station and dam.

952 Torhouse Stone Circle
Map 17

*Off B733, 3½m W of Wigtown. All reasonable
times. Free. (AM)*
A circle of 19 boulders standing on the edge of a
low mound. Probably Bronze Age.

953 Torosay Castle
Map 4

*A849, 1½m SSE of Craignure, Isle of Mull.
May-mid Oct, Mon-Fri (also Sun in Jul/Aug)
1000-1800. Adult: 50p, child: 25p.*
The gardens and part of the house are open to
the public. The Victorian castle is of Scottish
Baronial architecture in a magnificent setting; its
features include reception rooms and a variety of
exhibition rooms. The 11 acres of Italian terraced
gardens by Lorimer contain a statue walk and
water garden.

954 Torphichen Church
Map 12

B792, 5m SSW of Linlithgow. All times. Free.
The present 16th-century church was built over
the former nave of the original Norman church of
the Knights Templar. The chancel arch and the
foundations of the choir remain and seats are
marked for the Order of the Knights of St John.

955 Torphichen Preceptory
Map 12

*B792, 5m SSW of Linlithgow. Opening
standard. Adult: 15p, child: 7p, group rates. (AM)*
Once the principal Scottish seat of the Knights
Hospitallers of St John, it shows the martial style
of ecclesiastical architecture prevalent in Scotland in the 15th century. An exhibition depicts the
history of the Knights in Scotland and overseas.

956 Torridon
Map 4

*Off A896, 8m WSW of Kinlochewe.
Deer Museum and audio-visual display, 1 Jun-
30 Sep, Mon-Sat 1000-1800, Sun 1300-1800.
Deer Museum: Adult: 20p, child: 10p. Audio-
visual: Adult: 20p, child: 10p. (NTS)*
Over 14,000 acres of some of Scotland's finest
mountain scenery whose peaks rise over
3,000 feet. Of major interest also to geologists:
Liathach (3,456 feet) and Beinn Eighe (3,309
feet) are of red sandstone, some 750 million
years old and are topped by white quartzite some
600 million years old. The NTS Visitor Centre at
the junction of A896 and Diabaig road has audio-
visual presentations of wild life. At the Mains
nearby is a static display of the life of the red
deer. (See also No 84.)

Torrylin Cairn: see No 606.

957 Towie Barclay Castle
Map 6

Off A947, 3m N of Fyvie. By arrangement.
Adult: 60p, child: 30p.
An ancient stronghold of the Barclays dating
from 1136 and recently restored. The grounds
contain a formal walled garden.

958 Town House
Map 12

Sandhaven, Culross. Apr-Oct, or by
arrangement, tel: Newmills 880359. Mon-Sat
0930-1230, 1400-1730, Sun 1400-1730. Audio-
visual presentation: Adult: 20p, child: 10p. Town
House, by donation and by arrangement, tel:
Newmills 359.
Built in 1526, with a double stair on the outside, it
has a prison (criminals on the ground floor,
witches in the attic) and a meeting place for the
Town Council.

959 Town Mill
Map 15

Strathaven.
Attractively restored grain mill with arts centre.

960 Traprain Law
Map 14

Off A1, 5m W of Dunbar. All times. Free.
734 feet high whale-backed hill, with Iron Age
fortified site, probably continuing in use as a
defended Celtic township until 11th century. A
treasure of 4th-century Christian and pagan
silver excavated here in 1919 is now in the
Edinburgh National Museum of Antiquities. (See
No 371.)

961 Traquair House
Map 16

B709, off A72, 8m ESE of Peebles. Easter, Jul-
Aug, 1030-1700. May-Oct, daily 1330-1730.
Admission charge, please check, tel:
Innerleithen 830323. (P Maxwell Stuart)
Dating back to the 10th century, this is said to be
the oldest continuously-inhabited house in
Scotland. Twenty-seven Scottish and English
monarchs have visited it, including Mary Queen
of Scots, of whom there are relics. It was once the
home of William the Lion who held court here in
1209. The well-known Bear Gates were closed in
1746, not to be re-opened until the Stuarts
should ascend the throne. Ale is still produced at
the 18th-century brewhouse, and there are
woodland walks and craft workshops.

962 Trinity Temple (Teampull Na Trionaid)
Map 2

Off A865, 8m SW of Lochmaddy, Isle of North
Uist. All times. Free.
Ruins of a mediaeval college and monastery said
to have been founded by Beathag, daughter of
Somerled in the early 13th century, where Duns
Scotus studied. (See No 880.) Beside it is
Teampull Clann A'Phiocair, the chapel of the
MacVicars, teachers at the college; several
ancient cup and ring marks; and the Field of
Blood, site of a clan battle.

963 The Trushel Stone
Map 2

½m N of A857 at Ballantrushel, Isle of Lewis. All times. Free.
An impressive monolith 20 feet high, probably the tallest in Scotland. Other large stones nearby suggest it was part of a group. (See also No 907.)

964 Tullibardine Chapel
Map 8

Off A823, 8m SE of Crieff. All reasonable times. Free. Apply adjacent farmhouse. (AM)
Founded in 1446, this is one of the few Collegiate churches in Scotland which was entirely finished and still remains unaltered.

965 Tummel Forest Centre
Map 8

On B8019, 5½m NW of Pitlochry. Easter-end Sep, weekdays 0930-1830, Sun 1000-1830. Free. (FC)
Audio-visual slide show and presentation of various aspects of local history and industries. Forest walks, reconstructed Highland clachan and partly excavated ring fort.

966 Turnberry Castle
Map 15

Off A719, 6m N of Girvan. All reasonable times. Free.
The scant remains of the castle where Robert the Bruce was probably born in 1274.

967 Tweed Bridge
Map 16

A697 at Coldstream, 9m ENE of Kelso.
The 300 feet long bridge was built in 1776 by Smeaton and in the past was a crossing into Scotland for eloping couples taking advantage of Scotland's then-easier marriage laws.

968 Tyninghame House Gardens
Map 14

1m N of A1 between Dunbar and East Linton. 1 May-30 Sep, Mon-Fri 1030-1630. Admission charge. (The Earl of Haddington)
Colourful herbaceous border, walled garden, terraced gardens and lovely 'secret' garden. Ruins of St Baldred's Church (Norman).

969 Ui Church
Map 2

At Aignish, off A866, 2m E of Stornoway, Isle of Lewis. All reasonable times. Free.
Ruined church (pron. 'eye') containing some finely carved ancient tombs of the Macleods of Lewis.

970 Union Canal
Map 13

The canal was opened in 1822. It originally ran from Lothian Road, Edinburgh to lock sixteen on the Forth and Clyde Canal and was about 13½ miles long. The canal runs through some attractive country and excursions by canal boat are available at Ratho and Linlithgow. (See also Nos 151, 976.)

971 Union Suspension Bridge
Map 14

Across River Tweed, 2m S of Paxton on
unclassified road. This suspension bridge, the
first of its type in Britain, was built by Samuel
Brown in 1820 and links England and Scotland.

972 University Marine Biological Station
Map 11

*Great Cumbrae Island; ferry from Largs to
Millport or Cumbrae Slip. All year, Mon-Fri
0930-1230, 1400-1700. Easter, Jun-Sep, Sat
0930-1230, 1400-1700. Apr-May, Sat 0930-
1200. Adult: 10p, child: 5p, group rates.
(Universities of Glasgow and London)*
This marine biological station at Keppel Pier near
Millport includes aquaria.

973 Unstan Chambered Tomb
Map 1

*2m NE of Stromness, by A965, Orkney. Opening
standard. Free. (AM)*
A cairn containing a chambered tomb (over 6 feet
high) divided by large stone slabs. The type of
pottery discovered in the tomb is now known as
Unstan Ware.

Urquhart Castle

974 Urquhart Castle
Map 5

*2m SE of Drumnadrochit, on W shore of Loch
Ness. Opening standard. Adult: 25p, child: 12p,
group rates. (AM)*
Once one of the largest castles in Scotland, the
castle is situated on a promontory on the banks
of Loch Ness, from where sitings of the 'monster'
are most frequently reported. The extensive
ruins are on the site of a vitrified fort, rebuilt with
stone in the 14th century. The castle was gifted
by James IV, in 1509, to John Grant of Freuchie,
whose family built much of the existing fabric and
held the site for four centuries. The castle was
blown up in 1692 to prevent its being occupied by
Jacobites.

975 Vane Farm Nature Reserve
Map 13

*On the S shore of Loch Leven, on B9097, off
M90 and B996, 4½m S of Kinross. Apr-Oct,
daily except Fri, 1000-1700, Nov-Mar, Sat and
Sun 1000-1630. Adult: 10p, child: 10p. (RSPB)*
The Nature Centre is a converted farm building
equipped with displays designed to interpret the
surrounding countryside and the loch. Between
the last week of September and April, the area is
a favourite feeding and resting place for vast
numbers of wild geese and duck, and binoculars
are provided for observation.

Victoria

976 'Victoria'
Map 12

Manse Road Basin, Linlithgow. Easter-Sep, Sat and Sun, 1400-1700. Also evening charters by arrangement, tel: Linlithgow 2452 (Mr Aitken).
Replica of a Victorian steam packet boat offering half-hour pleasure cruises on the Union Canal. (See also Nos 151 and 970.)

977 Victoria Falls
Map 4

Off A832, 12m NW of Kinlochewe, near Slattadale: All times. Free.
Waterfall named after Queen Victoria who visited Loch Maree and area in 1877.

978 Wade's Bridge
Map 8

On B846, north of Aberfeldy. All times. Free.
The bridge across the River Tay was begun in 1733 by General Wade with William Adam as architect. It is considered to be the finest of all Wade's bridges.

979 Wallace Memorial
Map 11

On A737, 2m W of Paisley at Elderslie. All times. Free.
The town is the traditional birthplace of William Wallace. A modern memorial has been erected near an old house, perhaps on the site of the patriot's former home.

980 Wallace Monument
Map 12

Off A997 (Hillfoots Road), 1½m NNE of Stirling.
Daily, Nov-Jan 1000-1600; Feb and Oct
1000-1700; Mar and Sep 1000-1800; Apr and
Aug 1000-1900; May-Jul 1000-2000.
Adult: 15p, child: 10p, group rates.
(Stirling District Council)
Commemorates William Wallace, who defeated
the English at the Battle of Stirling Bridge in 1297.
Built in 1870, with a statue of Wallace on the side
of the tower. There is also an audio visual
display.

981 Wallace Tower
Map 15

High Street, Ayr. All times. Free.
The 113 feet high Wallace Tower, built in 1828,
has a statue of Sir William Wallace by a local
self-taught sculptor.

Wanlockhead Museum: see No 736.

982 Waterloo Monument
Map 16

Off B6400, 5m N of Jedburgh.
This prominent landmark on the summit of
Penielheugh Hill (741 feet) was built in 1815 by
the Marquess of Lothian and his tenants.

983 PS 'Waverley'
Map 11

Historically one of the most interesting vessels
still in operation in the British Isles, the *Waverley*
is the last paddle steamer to be built for service
on the Clyde, and now the last sea-going paddle
steamer in the world. A variety of cruises from
Glasgow and Ayr along the Clyde Coast, with
entertainments on board, meals, bar and light
refreshments available.
Rates and full details of departure points and
times from the Waverley Steam Navigation Co
Ltd, Waverley Terminal, 54 Stobcross Quay,
Glasgow G3; tel: 041-221 8152.

Weaver's Cottage

984 Weaver's Cottage
Map 11

Kilbarchan, off A761, 5m W of Paisley.
1 May-31 Oct, Tue, Thu, Sat and Sun 1400-
1700. Adult: 40p, child: 20p. (NTS)
In the 18th century Kilbarchan was a thriving
centre of handloom weaving. The cottage is
preserved as a typical weaver's home of the
period.

Well

985 Well of Seven Heads
Map 5

Off A82 on the W shore of Loch Oich. All times. Free.
A curious monument inscribed in English, Gaelic, French and Latin and surmounted by seven men's heads, stands above a spring and recalls the grim story of the execution of seven brothers for the murder of the two sons of a 17th century chief of Keppoch.

986 West Highland Museum
Map 4

Cameron Square, Fort William. All year, Mon-Sat 0930-1300, 1400-1700 (mid Jun-mid Sep 0930-2100). Adult: 20p, child: 10p.
Historical, natural history and folk exhibits, local relics and a tartan section. Jacobite relics including a secret portrait of Prince Charles Edward Stuart.

987 Westside Church
Map 1

Bay of Tuquoy, south coast of island of Westray, Orkney. All reasonable times. Free. (AM)
A 12th-century church, with nave and chancel, the former lengthened in the latter Middle Ages.

988 White Corries Chairlift
Map 8

Off A82 by Kingshouse. Jan-Apr & Easter holidays, daily 0900-1730. Jul-mid Sep, daily 1000-1700. Adult: £1.20 child: 60p.
Chairlift to 2,100 feet offers magnificent views of the areas around Glencoe and Rannoch Moor.

989 Whitekirk
Map 14

On A198, 5m SE of North Berwick. All reasonable times. Free.
The 15th-century church whose massive tower has a wooden spire, has the unusual distinction of having been damaged in 1914 by suffragettes. The damage has been repaired. The nearby two storeyed barn, part 16th-century, was once used by the monks of Holyrood to store grain.

990 Whiten Head
Map 3

5m N of A838 and 6m E of Durness. No road access; boat trips from Durness in summer.
A splendid perpendicular cliff with a fine series of caves.

991 Whithorn Priory and Museum
Map 17

Main Street, Whithorn, 10m S of Wigtown. Opening standard. Adult: 15p, child: 7p, group rates. (AM)
Here St Ninian founded the first Christian Church in Scotland in 397. The present priory ruins date from the 12th century. Early Christian crosses, some carved in the rock, others now displayed in the museum attached to the priory, are notable.

Wool

992 Wick Heritage Centre
Map 3

Bank Row. Opening 1980.
(Wick Society)
Exhibition of domestic and farming life in the area
and the herring fishing industry.

993 Wideford Hill Cairn
Map 1

2½m W of Kirkwall on W slope of Wideford Hill,
Orkney. All reasonable times. Free. (AM)
A conspicuous megalithic chambered cairn with
three concentric walls.

994 Wigtown District Museum
Map 17

London Road, Stranraer. All year, Mon-Fri
0930-1330, 1400-1700, Sat 0930-1300. Free.
(Wigtown District Council)
A local history museum with special exhibits of
dairy farming; and material related to Sir John
Ross, the Arctic explorer.

Wilton Lodge Park: see No 548.

995 Winton House
Map 14

B6355, 6m SW of Haddington. Open by prior
arrangement, to parties only or people very
specially interested. Tel: Pencaitland 340222.
Adult: 50p, child: 35p.
(Sir David and Lady Ogilvy)
A gem of Scottish Renaissance architecture
dating from 1620. Associations with Charles I
and Sir Walter Scott. Beautiful plaster ceilings,
unique carved stone chimneys, fine pictures and
furniture. Personally conducted tours.

996 Woodside Studio Gallery
Map 18

William Street, Dalbeattie. All year, daily,
0930-2100. Adult: 5p.
Exhibition of original paintings, mostly of local
subjects.

997 Wool Stone
Map 14

In Stenton, B6370, 5m SW of Dunbar. All
reasonable times. Free.
The mediaeval Wool Stone, used formerly for the
weighing of wool at Stenton Fair, stands on the
green. See also the 14th-century Rood Well,
topped by a cardinal's hat, and the old doocot.

Wren's

998 Wren's Egg Stone Circle
Map 17

2m SE of Port William near farmhouse of Blairbuie. All reasonable times. Free. (AM)
The remains of a standing stone circle, originally a double concentric ring.

999 Yarrow Kirk
Map 16

A708, W from Selkirk.
A lovely valley praised by many writers including Scott, Wordsworth and Hogg, who lived in this area. Little Yarrow Kirk dates back to 1640. Scott's great-great-grandfather was minister there. The nearby Deuchar Bridge (not now in use) was built in 1653. On the hills around Yarrow are the remains of ancient Border keeps.

1000 'Paraffin' Young Heritage Trail
Map 12

The 40-mile-long trail can be followed at all times and starts at the BP Information Centre, Grangemouth. Open Apr-30 Sep, Mon-Fri 0900-1700. Free.
A car trail tracing the life of James 'Paraffin' Young and the development of the shale oil industry, which he founded. Places to visit include Pumpherston, West Calder, Winchburgh, Broxburn and Bathgate. Roadside signs describe notable features along the trail.

1001 Younger Botanic Garden
Map 10

A815, 7m NNW of Dunoon. Apr-Oct daily 1000-1800. Adult: 10p, child: 5p, group rates.
Extensive woodland gardens featuring rhododendrons, azaleas, many other shrubs and a magnificent avenue of sequoias.

Council of Europe: Nature and Tourism Year

Scotland has unique attractions for the visitor in the richness and variety of countryside and wild life. These are well recognised and their enjoyment is encouraged wherever possible. Throughout Scotland there are reserves and conservation areas which give the visitor access to unspoilt scenic beauty and wild life in its natural surroundings.

As a contribution to a Council of Europe campaign on Conservation of Wildlife and Natural Habitats, 1980 will be Tourism and Conservation Year in Scotland, and you will find many of the sites that will be promoted during that year in this book.

Further information on sites of particular interest during Nature and Tourism Year are available from the Scottish Tourist Board.

Index

Index

Index

Index

Index

Index

Index